Key Issues

HERBERT SPENCER AND THE LIMITS OF THE STATE

To J. B. with love

Key Issues

HERBERT SPENCER AND THE LIMITS OF THE STATE

The Late Nineteenth-century Debate
between Individualism and Collectivism

Edited and Introduced by
MICHAEL TAYLOR
London Guildhall University

Series Editor
ANDREW PYLE
University of Bristol

THOEMMES PRESS

© Thoemmes Press 1996

Published in 1996 by
Thoemmes Press
11 Great George Street
Bristol BS1 5RR, England

US office: Distribution and Marketing
22883 Quicksilver Drive
Dulles, Virginia 20166, USA

ISBN
Paper : 1 85506 452 9
Cloth : 1 85506 453 7

Herbert Spencer and the Limits of the State
Key Issues No. 13

British Library Cataloguing-in-Publication Data

A catalogue record of this title is available
from the British Library

Printed in Great Britain by Antony Rowe Ltd., Chippenham

CONTENTS

INTRODUCTION

The Political Context

Between the beginning of the 1880s and the outbreak of the
First World War British politicians abandoned the ideal of a
minimalist, nightwatchman state and accepted the need for
the public authority to assume a positive role in promoting
social welfare. This change was the outcome of an extended
debate about the legitimate role and limits of the state, in
which many fundamental issues of principle were raised and
discussed. Thus the episode is of more than historical interest,
since it not only laid the theoretical foundations of the mixed
economy and welfare state of the twentieth century, but also
caused a number of perennial issues in political thought to be
thoroughly examined. The debate gave extensive consideration to the grounds on which individual liberty may be
curtailed in the common interest; the tension between individualism and community; and the effects of an extended sphere
of state action on individual moral character. These problems
remain with us still, and one of the most striking features of
this debate is simply the extent to which our current concerns
echo those of a century ago. The purpose of this volume is
to present a cross-section of the theories and opinions
presented during this important period in British political
thought.

The focal point for many of the theoretical contributions to
this late Victorian debate was Herbert Spencer's 1884 polemic
The Man Versus the State, a work which has earned the
status of a kind of living fossil as the only part of his extensive
oeuvre, including the monumental *System of Synthetic
Philosophy*, to be widely read today. This state of affairs
would have appalled Spencer himself, who considered the
work as no more than an exercise in pamphleteering, a

response to a set of immediate political events, and not an enduring contribution to the stock of human ideas. His four articles which initially appeared in the *Contemporary Review* in the first half of 1884 were merely an attempt to apply his principles to the political debate which raged throughout the first half of the 1880s as a direct consequence of the activist policies promoted by the second Gladstone administration.

Shortly after Gladstone's return to office in April 1880 it became evident that his government was striking out in a direction which many of its supporters believed to be inconsistent with the traditions of Liberalism. To Liberal traditionalists the party's true role was to promote a further reduction in the state's powers, an extension of freedom of contract, and the defence of the rights of the individual to 'do what he will with his own'. Seen from this perspective, the Gladstone administration appeared to be pursuing a legislative programme which amounted to a betrayal of principle of the first order.[1] The Ground Game Act, the Employers Liability Act, and especially the 1881 Irish Land Act, had as a common feature interference with freedom of contract and the rights of property. For example, the Irish Land Act established a Land Court with extensive powers to interfere with contracts between Irish landlords and their crofter tenants in order to meet the demands of the Land League for the 'three Fs' of fixity of tenure, free sale, and fair rents. Legislation with this character convinced many Liberals that their party had abandoned its historical principles. G. J. Goschen, who was to break with the party over Irish Home Rule and later served as Salisbury's Chancellor of the Exchequer, remarked in 1885 that 'we seem almost to have arrived at this formula – little freedom in making contracts, much freedom in breaking them'.[2] As another writer of the period observed, the traditional Liberal view of the function of the state as being to 'protect people in their liberty and property...so long as they do not interfere with or injure

---

[1] For a discussion of the opponents of Gladstone's activist policies, see M. W. Taylor, *Men Versus the State: Herbert Spencer and Late Victorian Individualism* (Oxford, 1992), pp. 8ff.

[2] G. J. Goschen, 'Since 1880', *Nineteenth Century*, vol. 17 (1885), pp. 723–4.

other people' was being supplanted by the view that it was 'a great machine which is to endeavour...to grind out...a greater amount of material enjoyment and happiness for the bulk of the people'.[3]

This new view of the functions of the state was enthusiastically endorsed by the devotees of 'advanced' Radicalism, chief among whom were two of Gladstone's Cabinet colleagues, Joseph Chamberlain and Sir Charles Dilke. The Chamberlainite 'Radical Programme' which appeared in the pages of the *Fortnightly Review* from the summer of 1883 to that of 1885 argued for free primary education, land reform and powers of compulsory purchase for local authorities for the creation of smallholdings, a moderate graduated income tax, and a levy on the 'unearned' increment in land values.[4] These practical politicians were supported by a growing chorus of political writers and pamphleteers, especially those associated with the newly-established Fabian Society, who endeavoured to sway public opinion in favour of an ever more extensive sphere of activity for the state.

Spencer saw himself as the defender of traditional liberal principles against the statist perversion of them which was rapidly gaining ground from the beginning of the 1880s. However the immediate provocation for him entering the lists was an article by Lord Salisbury, then Conservative leader of the opposition, which advocated government loans to build working-class housing.[5] To Spencer this was merely evidence that the spectre of socialism was stalking both major political parties. Thus he felt duty bound to rush into print in an attempt (as he saw it) to return the Liberals to their senses, and the Liberal party to its historic mission. This *The Man Versus the State* sought to achieve.

---

[3] E. Pleydell-Bouverie, *The Province of Government* (London, 1884), p. 10.

[4] *The Radical Programme* (London, 1885).

[5] R. Cecil, third Marquis of Salisbury, 'Labourers' and Artisans' Dwellings', *National Review*, vol. 2 (1883), pp. 301–16.

Individualism and Collectivism

Although it was once believed that *The Man Versus the State* was simply the isolated protest of a thinker whose leading ideas were already discredited, recent scholarship has demonstrated both that Spencer's reputation as Savant General to the Victorian reading public was at its zenith in the early 1880s, and that there were many other Liberals and Liberal-sympathizers who shared his concerns.[6] Thus rather than being a voice crying in the wilderness, Spencer was instead the leading representative of a powerful current within Victorian political opinion. The views he expressed are best seen as the conventional wisdom of the late Victorian era, a pattern of belief with which all the theories favouring an extended role for the state inevitably had to contend.

The many thinkers, writers and pamphleteers who took their lead from Spencer generally referred to themselves as 'Individualists'. Theirs was a defensive, conservative creed which aimed to resist any further extension of the state's activities and, if possible, to curtail them still further. At the core of Individualism was Spencer's law of equal freedom, namely that 'every man may claim the fullest liberty to exercise his faculties compatible with the possession of like liberty by every other man'.[7] On the basis of this principle, Donisthorpe argued, Individualists disapproved of 'all meddlesome legislation. They would restrict the functions of the State to the administration of justice, the maintenance of order, the defence of the country against foreign antagonism, and the collection and management of revenue for these purposes; and leave other matters to take care of themselves.'[8] However, he was also at pains to stress that this position was not equivalent to anarchism: not only did the state possess a legitimate, albeit limited, role in upholding the individual's rights to liberty and property, but there were a variety of self-regulating mechanisms within society which could be relied

---

[6] On this point see Taylor, *Men Versus the State, passim.*

[7] Herbert Spencer, *Social Statics* (London, 1851), p. 94.

[8] W. Donisthorpe, *Liberty or Law*, p. 26 of this volume.

upon to generate social order.

It has become usual to portray the late Victorian era as one in which the Individualists were confronted by a similarly coherent political perspective, characterized either as Socialism or, more frequently, as 'Collectivism'. The dichotomy seems to have its origin in A. V. Dicey's lectures on the relationship of law and public opinion in the nineteenth century, in which he famously contrasted the period of 'Benthamism or individualism' which had dominated policy making in the middle of the century with the 'sentiment' of 'collectivism' which had come to dominate state policy during its closing decades.[9] Dicey's conceptual framework has been subsequently taken up and developed by a number of leading historians of ideas. Thus, for example, Stephan Collini has suggested that the late Victorian 'disagreement over the role of the state was conceptualized in terms of the opposition between Individualism and Collectivism', while W. H. Greenleaf's monumental study of British political thought and practice, *The British Political Tradition*, has this same dichotomy built into its very foundations.[10]

However, as James Meadowcroft has argued in his detailed study of the concept of the state in the period between 1880 and 1914, the terms 'Individualism' and 'Collectivism' had shifting meanings, an observation which renders otiose the attempt to reduce the point at issue between them to a simple formula of less versus more state activity. As Meadowcroft notes, the term 'Individualism' could refer to the doctrines of the proponents of a 'nightwatchman' state, but it could also be used by their critics as a rebuke to an allegedly atomistic notion of the social constitution – essentially the proposition, to be made famous by a late twentieth-century Prime Minister, that there is 'no such thing as society'. The imprecision of meaning was at its greatest, however, on the

[9] A. V. Dicey, *Lectures on the Relation of Law and Public Opinion in England during the Nineteenth Century* (London, 1905), esp. pp. 63ff.

[10] Collini, *Liberalism and Sociology: L. T. Hobhouse and Political Argument in England 1880–1914* (Cambridge, 1978), pp. 14–15; Greenleaf, *The British Political Tradition*, vol. 2: *The Ideological Heritage* (London, 1983), p. 15.

Collectivist side of the supposed dichotomy. Among the senses noted by Meadowcroft are 'support for the complete abolition of private ownership of the means of production; a tendency to favour increased governmental regulation of social or economic affairs; an ethical creed which emphasized that "co-operation not competition is the basis of social life."'[11] Thus, he argues, these senses could, when combined in different ways, denote different kinds of cleavage, and the attempt to force all late Victorian political argument into a single framework of pro versus anti-state interventionism – what might be called the 'Westminster Model' of political argument – is destined to fail.

The range of responses available to late Victorian political thinkers is well illustrated by the selections contained in the present volume. On the Individualist side the clearest cleavage was between a group of radically anti-statist political ideologues who derived direct inspiration from Spencer's writings – men like Wordsworth Donisthorpe, Auberon Herbert and Thomas Mackay – and centrist, establishment figures who articulated a conservative and moderate individualism which broadly accepted the boundaries of the mid-Victorian state. The leading theoretician of moderate Individualism was the Cambridge philosopher Henry Sidgwick, but it was a point of view also expressed by practical politicians of a conservative tendency, represented in the present collection by Goschen and Lord Pembroke. Although the latter eschewed the 'Individualist' label, they shared in common with the Spencerians a nostalgia for the lost paradise of liberalism of the 1860s, and a desire to resist any extension of the state's powers beyond those established circa 1870. Spencer and the Spencerians might have been more rigorous and uncompromising in the pursuit of their principles than were the practical politicians, but the extent to which they found it possible to make common cause is exemplified by an organization like the Liberty and Property Defence League, a loose association of landed and manufacturing interests actively opposed to all instances of 'socialistic' legislation, with which Donisthorpe, Herbert, and Pembroke

---

[11] J. Meadowcroft, *Conceptualizing the State* (Oxford, 1995), p. 231.

were all associated.[12]

The Collectivist side of the supposed dichotomy was even more fragmented. For instance, 'Collectivism' as it was used by a writer like Bosanquet clearly belongs to the third sense identified by Meadowcroft – the notion that there is a higher ethical life than that represented by crude competition. And yet his reluctance to develop this insight into a case for an extensive sphere of state action lead to him being branded an 'Individualist' by other thinkers who held Collectivist views of a different character, an example being that of the New Liberal thinker J. A. Hobson. Even within the 'Collectivist' camp there were substantial differences of opinion about the legitimate functions of the state, and the distance between the 'moral' socialism represented by Ritchie and the positivistic views of Sidney Webb was not inconsiderable. Thus rather than conceptualizing the distinction between the Individualists and their critics as a conflict between two great armies, it would be more accurate to regard Individualism as the entrenched position, which was under assault from a variety of loosely associated guerrilla bands who were as often as not in conflict with each other.

The debate between the Individualists and their critics thus took place at many different levels, ranging from metaphysical disputes about whether the individual has reality when abstracted from the social context, to economic arguments about the range of activities the state must necessarily perform in a maturing industrial economy. This is clearly illustrated by the range of territory on which the writers represented in the third section attempted to combat Individualist positions. On the other hand, this diversity should not altogether obscure the deep and genuine differences of opinion which existed between the Individualists and their critics, a point which is brought out especially forcefully by the exchange – never previously reprinted in its entirety – between Auberon Herbert and J. A. Hobson in section four. Within this brief exchange some of the most fundamental differences between the Individualists and their critics were uniquely distilled into

[12] For a discussion of the different strands within Individualism see Taylor, *Men Versus the State*, pp. 17–18.

their bare essentials. An especially difficult issue for the Individualists concerned the legitimacy of private ownership of the land, since Spencer had embraced the proposal with enthusiasm in his *Social Statics* of 1851.[13] Under the influence of the strongly anti-aristocratic radicalism of his youth, he had argued that private possession of the earth was tantamount to the denial of the 'equal liberties' of the landless, and had advocated public ownership of the land with the right to use it being leased to the highest bidders. By the 1880s he was at pains to distance himself from all socialistic schemes, and claimed that land nationalization was only valid in a distant ideal state. Nonetheless, the fact that their mentor had once supported land nationalization as a logical corollary of his equal liberties principle was an embarrassment for his followers, and, as Hobson's contribution indicates, it was exploited to the full by their critics.

Three Theoretical Contrasts

The remainder of this introduction will concentrate on just three broad issues which constituted significant fault-lines between the Individualists and their opponents. These three issues concern (i) the divergent interpretations which were placed on the notion that there are substantive analogies between society and a biological organism; (ii) their differing conceptions of social progress and of the direction of history; and (iii) the conception of character, with particular reference to the role of the state in fostering or hindering the development of the desired qualities.

(i) The Social Organism

Spencer's late nineteenth-century fame as one of the founders of sociology rested mainly on his conception of the 'social organism', the notion that there are certain basic similarities of structure and function between societies and biological organisms. Among the parallels identified by Spencer in

---

[13] For a discussion of Spencer's early views on land nationalization and subsequent change of mind see Michael Taylor, 'Introduction' to *Social Statics*, volume 3 of *Herbert Spencer: Collected Writings* (London, 1996).

works like the *Principles of Sociology* were that both societies and organisms are aggregates which can exist for much longer than their component parts, and that they undergo a process of growth in the course of which their structures develop through a multiplication and differentiation of parts.[14] The latter process also reflects the progressive differentiation of function among the constituent parts. However, the most important of these parallels was the social division of labour, since it was that 'which in the society, as in the animal, makes it a living whole. Scarcely can I emphasize sufficiently the truth that in respect of this fundamental trait, a social organism and an individual organism are entirely alike.'[15]

Thus the 'social organism' conception was not a vague analogy; in Spencer's view society was literally an organism in most important respects, except that – unlike a biological organism – it did not possess consciousness distinct from that of its component parts, and therefore could not have interests which were distinct from theirs.

Although Spencer presented his theory as a value-neutral account of the nature of social aggregates, he nonetheless readily drew political conclusions from it. The key element was the idea that as organisms became more highly evolved, the more did each of their organs perform progressively more specialized tasks. When translated to the political sphere the principle of specialization suggested that the state – as an organ of the social organism – ought to concentrate on those limited activities which were its unique function. Spencer also had no doubt about the precise nature of this function: it was to uphold justice in the sense of ensuring that no one individual's exercise of freedom infringed the equal liberty of any other individual. Any activity beyond this on the part of the state would constitute an injustice, and would be contrary to a social theory which emphasized the necessity of political practice conforming to scientifically established laws of social development.

On the other hand, even within the terms of the naturalistic

[14] These points of analogy are examined in Taylor, *Men Versus the State*, pp. 138f.

[15] Spencer, *Principles of Sociology*, vol. 1 (London, 1876), p. 470.

version of the analogy developed by Spencer, there were many who claimed to find support for a radically different political position to that which he defended. Organicism in this naturalistic, scientific sense was invoked by Sidney Webb as providing support for socialism on the grounds that it demonstrated the necessity of substituting 'consciously regulated co-ordination among the units of each organism for their internecine competition'.[16] Even a moderate Individualist, like Pembroke, could find in the social organism analogy support for a more extensive sphere of state action than that countenanced by Spencer: although many functions of the social organism were self-regulating, others (like sanitation and public education) were not, and required the active intervention of the state.

Although Spencer's formulation of the social organism analogy undoubtedly exercised considerable influence, he did not possess a monopoly on an idea which was 'in the air' during the 1880s and 1890s. An almost equally influential usage of the organicist imagery was invoked by political thinkers influenced by philosophical idealism to emphasize 'the psychical interrelation of minds, and society was spoken of as a "spiritual" or "moral" organism'.[17] Whereas Spencer had insisted that there was a fundamental difference between a biological organism and a social organism, to the extent that the latter could not have interests or purposes which were distinct from those of its constituent individuals, the 'philosophical' sense of the organic metaphor lent itself precisely to this conclusion. Thinkers who invoked the concept in this sense, for example D. G. Ritchie or Bernard Bosanquet, were thus able to claim that there was a common good which was distinct from that which would emerge from the mere free play of individual interests. Although the thinkers who invoked this conception of organicism varied considerably in terms of their practical prescriptions, all used it to support a degree of state action which went beyond the nightwatchman minimum. In the most extreme cases (represented by Hobson), philosophical organicism was said to require

[16] Webb, *The Difficulties of Individualism*, p. 148 of this volume.

[17] Meadowcroft, *Conceptualizing the State*, p. 60.

substantial modification of the existing regime of property, inheritance and taxation. The debate about the proper scope and limits of the state thus took place within the frame of reference provided by the image of society as in some sense an organic unity: the issue concerned the nature of the parallel and the practical conclusions which could be drawn from it.

(ii) Social Evolution

Evolutionary language was as important in late nineteenth-century political debate as was the image of society as an organism. Indeed, the two conceptions were intimately linked since, if society was an organism, then it could be expected to undergo a process of evolutionary growth. Spencer's socio-logical theory envisaged a progression from 'militancy', a custom-bound, aggressive, hierarchical type of social organization based on relations of command and obedience, to 'industrialism', the open, free, progressive and democratic society of classical liberalism with its voluntarily assumed contractual social relations.[18]

The militant social type was created by the need for mutual protection in a world of unsocialized and warlike individuals. At the dawn of history individual human beings lack the psychological traits which make for peaceful social co-operation, and hence the formation of a social order must necessarily be the product of force and coercion. Since each militant society is surrounded by similar social types which are bent on aggression and conquest, each must be constantly prepared and organized for war. At the militant stage of development, Spencer observed, the 'society is the quiescent army and the army the mobilized society...'.[19] But its social organization is fundamentally very simple: the only clear distinction is between rulers and ruled, between those who give orders and those who are obliged to obey them, if necessary by force. The state dominates every aspect of the individual's existence, including the forms of religious worship

[18] See Taylor, *Men Versus the State*, pp. 173ff.

[19] Spencer, 'From Freedom to Bondage', p. 9 of the present volume, echoing a similar passage in *The Man Versus the State*.

which may be practised. The rights of the individual are not recognized, the economic system is under the direction of the ruling elite, and property is held in common by the community.

The industrial social type is made possible by an improvement in individual moral character which is the work of many generations. As individuals become more socialized, and develop 'higher' moral sentiments, like a love of liberty and a respect for the rights of others, so the social order comes to be produced spontaneously by their voluntary contractual agreements. In contrast to the simple, homogeneous social structure typical of militancy, industrial society is complex, reflecting the greater heterogeneity and diversity permitted by 'spontaneous' social co-operation. Moreover, individual rights, including the right to private property, are widely recognized, and the government merely acts to protect the individual in the enjoyment of those rights, leaving vast areas of social life to be self-regulating. Indeed, some of Spencer's followers believed that the end-state would be one of pure anarchy, since individual moral development would reach a point at which everyone spontaneously acted so as to respect the rights of others without the need for coercive force. Spencer himself had entertained such thoughts in his youth, but in the period with which we are concerned he instead promoted a vision of a society in which the state performed only 'nightwatchman' functions, leaving the field free to voluntary social co-operation across a wide range of activities, ranging from commerce to religion.

The idea that social evolution exhibits a development from militancy to industrialism was at the heart of Spencer's analysis in *The Man Versus the State*, and is repeated in the essay reprinted in the present volume. According to this account of social evolution the increased role which the state had assumed during the closing decades of the nineteenth century was nothing short of a regression to a more primitive stage of society. Socialism, quite literally, belonged to the past.

Spencer's critics did not doubt that history was progressive or that it developed according to certain defined stages; their only dispute with him concerned the nature of the society towards which it was progressing. One response, exemplified by Ritchie, was derived from Hegel. This contrasted the 'merely natural' processes of social evolution described by Spencer with a 'higher' process in which humanity achieved consciousness of these processes and was able to shape them for its own ends. Social evolution thus became a conscious process which required the active intervention of the state.[20] An alternative view was put by Sidney Webb, who took over Spencer's sense of the inevitability of the processes of social evolution, but turned it on its head. According to Webb, the evolution of society (including the growing complexity of social relations predicted by Spencer's theory) positively enjoined the need for a more extensive sphere of state activity. The very complexity which Spencer identified with the higher stages of evolution was incompatible with reliance on the forces of 'spontaneous' social organization, and a deliberate, planned approach to society, using the powers of the state, was essential to the health of society.

(iii) Character

The Victorian notion of character contained both a descriptive and a normative element. The descriptive element referred to an individual's settled dispositions, a sense in which the word continues to be used. In the normative sense, character referred not simply to strongly developed dispositions, but to habits of action of certain desirable kinds. This evaluative sense of character was constituted by a basic core of qualities which included self-restraint, perseverance, strenuous effort, courage, self-reliance, thrift, and a sense of personal responsibility and duty. It was a conception which enjoyed such an extraordinary status and centrality in Victorian thought that it transcended all the conventional political categories. Indeed, as Stefan Collini has remarked, by the end of the nineteenth century there was a 'swelling chorus of politicians of all parties who professed to stand in the same relation to any scheme which might be said to weaken character as the

[20] Ritchie, *The Moral Function of the State*, p. 172 of this volume.

preacher did to sin'.[21]

It was not only practical politicians who joined this chorus; political theorists sang from the same hymn sheet with gusto. Take, for example, Spencer's booming baritone from *The Principles of Ethics*:

> The end which the statesman should keep in view as higher than all other ends, is the formation of character. And if there is entertained a right conception of the character which should be formed, and of the means by which it may be formed, the exclusion of multiplied state-agencies is necessarily excluded.[22]

On Spencer's view the moral qualities which formed 'character' were similar to physical powers to the extent that each required exercise to reach their full development. If individuals were permitted the freedom to exercise these qualities, as well as to experience the consequences of their conduct, then their moral powers would be strengthened and passed on from generation to generation according to the Lamarckian mechanism of the inheritance of acquired characteristics. With each generation the moral powers would grow, until eventually they would become 'organic' in the race, and behaving morally would become (quite literally) second nature.[23] Thus his objection to 'state interference' – for example in the form of the Poor Law – was that by absolving individuals of their personal responsibility, either for self or others, it weakened the moral qualities, thereby undermining character and indefinitely postponing the promised future time when every individual would spontaneously act in a moral way. His theory thus provided pseudo-scientific validation for the common Victorian view that state provided assistance to the poor, whether in the form of poor relief, old age pensions or other 'eleemosynary' provision, was destructive of the virtues of thrift, providence, and self-

---

[21] S. Collini, 'The Idea of "Character" in Victorian Political Thought', *Transactions of the Royal Historical Society*, vol. 35 (1985), p. 31.

[22] Spencer, *The Principles of Ethics*, vol. 2 (London, 1893), p. 251.

[23] Spencer's pseudo-scientific account of character development is examined in detail in Taylor, *Men Versus the State*, chap. 3.

help which were key qualities of character.

It was the nature of the means to the formation of character, rather than the bundle of qualities which went to make up 'character', which was the point of contention between Spencer and his critics. Indeed, some social reformers acknowledged that the threat which state action posed to character was the strongest of all the arguments against their proposals.[24] However, while Individualists could oppose state action on the grounds that it was antithetical to the development of desirable moral qualities, those who supported state action in areas like housing, education and health-care could contend that it would foster the development of these same qualities. The crucial premise of the reformers' case was the individual's 'dependence on his environment in the widest sense of the term – human and non-human. Moral improvement became thus a question of reforming the framework within which the individual functioned.'[25] In other words, whereas Spencer thought that all that was necessary to promote character was to allow individuals the freedom to experience the consequences of their conduct, social reformers contended that this was to ignore the extent to which an individual's conduct reflected general environmental factors, and that high moral conduct could not be expected in conditions of poverty, poor housing, and ill-health. It was for this reason that Ritchie argued that it was the state's duty to 'provide all its members so far as possible with such an environment as will enable them to live as good lives as possible – good in every sense of the term'.[26]

Conclusion: an Enduring Debate

The three areas of debate examined in this introduction proceeded against the background of assumptions which subsequent generations have abandoned. Organic ideas and

[24] See for example Walter Blease, *A Short History of English Liberalism* (London, 1913), p. 337.

[25] Michael Freeden, *The New Liberalism* (Oxford, 1978), pp. 170–71.

[26] Ritchie, *The Moral Function of the State*, p. 174 of the present volume.

analogies no longer occupy a central place in our social and political thought. We no longer believe that history exhibits a particular direction, and the very idea of progress has lost credibility as the twentieth century has unfolded. Finally, we no longer think of 'character' in anything other than a descriptive sense, and a pervasive relativism has undermined the moral certainties of the Victorian age.

On the other hand, it is important not to lose sight of the continuities as well as the contrasts between the late Victorian debate and contemporary concerns. These continuities exist at two different levels. First, there are similarities between the kinds of arguments used by the writers in this volume and those encountered in contemporary debate. The idea that 'character' denotes a set of moral qualities may have been lost, but the suggestion that the welfare state may give rise to a 'dependency culture' is the direct descendant of the arguments once conducted around this concept. The notion that socialism is in some sense a regression to an atavistic form of society is to be found in Hayek as well as in Spencer. The claim that theorists of the minimal state ignore the social nature of the individual and fail to acknowledge the legitimate claims of the community can be found in the writings of David Ritchie or Bernard Bosanquet as well as in those of Michael Sandel or Amitai Etzioni.

The similarities in argument between two debates over a century apart also serve to illustrate that the issues which concerned the Victorians remain with us still. To what extent should the state interfere with freely contracted bargains between individuals? To what extent is it justified in curtailing property rights to promote a conception of the social good? In what circumstances should the state seek to realize goals which its citizens themselves cannot bring about by their free action? While we might believe that we are the first generation to have become concerned by the corrosive effects of a rampant individualism, or are the first to have acknowledged the essential role of 'community' in preserving a healthy body politic, similar arguments were put forward – often in remarkably similar terms – by the Victorian thinkers whose work is reprinted here. The eighteenth-century radical Joseph Priestley once wrote that 'new books in defence of any principles whatever, will be read by many persons, who will not look into old books, for the proper answers to them'. If being ignorant of history means we are destined to repeat it, then a neglect of intellectual history seems to give rise to the same result.

Michael W. Taylor
London Guildhall University, 1996

NOTES ON CONTRIBUTORS

HERBERT SPENCER (1820–1903) was widely regarded by many Victorians as the leading philosopher of the age. His ten-volume *System of Synthetic Philosophy* (1862–93) attempted to locate the truths of each of the special sciences within the intellectual architecture of the principle of evolution, which Spencer saw to be at work from the nebulae to the moral sentiments.

WORDSWORTH DONISTHORPE (1847–1914) read Moral Sciences at Trinity College, Cambridge. A barrister and a founder member of the Liberty and Property Defence League, he was also the author of several books, most notably *Individualism: A System of Politics* (1889).

THOMAS MACKAY (1849–1912) made a substantial fortune from his wine-merchant partnership with Charles Kinloch, and retired to write on social questions and to concentrate on his work for the Charity Organisation Society.

GEORGE JOACHIM GOSCHEN (1831–1907) served as MP for the City of London from 1863, holding office in Gladstone's first and second administrations, but becoming increasingly disenchanted with the direction of the latter. He finally broke with the Liberal party over Home Rule, later serving as Chancellor of the Exchequer under Salisbury (1887–92).

GEORGE HERBERT, thirteenth Earl of Pembroke (1850–95), was a Whig turned Conservative. Ill-health dogged his career, preventing him from attending university and cutting short his tenure as Under Secretary for War in Disraeli's ministry. He was a leading light in the Liberty and Property Defence League.

HENRY SIDGWICK (1838–1900) was Knightbridge Professor of Moral Philosophy at Cambridge, and is best remembered for his *Methods of Ethics* (1874), a classic of utilitarian philosophy. Sidgwick also wrote widely on politics and economics, although he seemed unable to express an opinion without immediately qualifying it. A Liberal who migrated to Liberal Unionism, he was married to the sister of Arthur Balfour, a former student and future Conservative Prime Minister.

SIDNEY WEBB (1859–1947) was instrumental in the foundation of the Fabian Society and the London School of Economics. He became a Labour MP in 1922, and held several administrative posts in the early Labour governments, subsequently being created Baron Passfield.

D. G. RITCHIE (1856–1903) was Fellow and Tutor at Jesus College, Oxford, and subsequently Professor of Logic and Metaphysics at St Andrews University. He was an early member of the Fabian Society.

BERNARD BOSANQUET (1840–1923) entered Balliol College in 1867. He was Fellow and Tutor, University College, Oxford (1871–81), Professor of Moral Philosophy at St Andrews (1903–08), and an active member of the Charity Organisation Society. His best known work is *The Philosophical Theory of State* (1899).

JOSEPH CHAMBERLAIN (1836–1914) was responsible for many measures of 'municipal socialism' as a reforming Mayor of Birmingham. He entered the Cabinet in 1880 as President of the Board of Trade. After breaking with Gladstone over Irish Home Rule, he took office under Salisbury in 1895 as Secretary of the Colonies. Even as a Unionist he continued to push the case for state intervention, and his advocacy of Tariff Reform was intended to provide the revenues for a programme of domestic social reform.

AUBERON HERBERT (1838–1906) was the third and youngest son of the Earl of Carnarvon. He served briefly as an MP, but his main activities were as a publicist and pamphleteer. His extreme version of Individualism, which he called 'Voluntaryism', is difficult to distinguish from anarchism, but his advocacy of a scheme of voluntary taxation appears less implausible in this time of the National Lottery.

J. A. HOBSON (1858–1940) was educated at Lincoln College, Oxford. After working briefly as a schoolmaster, his interests shifted to social and economic subjects and he became a leading spokesman for the New Liberalism, as well as a prolific author of over forty books.

Section 1

Spencer and the Spencerians

FROM FREEDOM TO BONDAGE
Herbert Spencer

OF the many ways in which common-sense inferences about social affairs are flatly contradicted by events (as when measures taken to suppress a book cause increased circulation of it, or as when attempts to prevent usurious rates of interest make the terms harder for the borrower, or as when there is greater difficulty in getting things at the places of production than elsewhere) one of the most curious is the way in which the more things improve the louder become the exclamations about their badness.

In days when the people were without any political power, their subjection was rarely complained of; but after free institutions had so far advanced in England that our political arrangements were envied by continental peoples, the denunciations of aristocratic rule grew gradually stronger, until there came a great widening of the franchise, soon followed by complaints that things were going wrong for want of still further widening. If we trace up the treatment of women from the days of savagedom, when they bore all the burdens and after the men had eaten received such food as remained, up through the middle ages when they served the men at their meals, to our own day when throughout our social arrangements the claims of women are always put first, we see that along with the worst treatment there went the least apparent consciousness that the treatment was bad; while now that they are better treated than ever before, the proclaiming of their grievances daily strengthens: the loudest outcries coming from "the paradise of women," America. A century ago, when scarcely a man could be found who was not occasionally intoxicated, and when inability to take one or two bottles of wine brought contempt, no agitation arose against the vice of drunkenness; but now that, in the course of fifty years, the voluntary efforts of temperance societies, joined with more general causes, have produced comparative sobriety, there are vociferous demands for laws to prevent the ruinous effects of the liquor traffic. Similarly again with education. A few generations back, ability to read and write was practically limited to the upper and middle classes, and the suggestion that the rudiments of culture should be given to labourers was never made, or, if made, ridiculed; but when, in the days of our grandfathers, the Sunday-school system, initiated by a few philanthropists, began to spread and was followed by the establishment of day-schools, with the result that among the masses those who could read and write were no longer the exceptions, and the demand for cheap literature rapidly increased, there began the cry that the people were perishing for lack of knowledge, and that the State must not simply educate them but must force education upon them.

And so is it, too, with the general state of the population in respect of food, clothing, shelter, and the appliances of life. Leaving out of the comparison early barbaric states, there has been a conspicuous progress from the time when most rustics lived on barley bread, rye bread, and oatmeal, down to our own time when the consumption of white wheaten bread is universal – from the days when coarse jackets reaching to the knees left the legs bare, down to the present day when labouring people, like their employers, have the whole body covered, by two or more layers of clothing – from the old era of single-roomed huts without chimneys, or from the 15th century when even an ordinary gentleman's house was commonly without wainscot or plaster on its walls, down to the present century when every cottage has more rooms than one and the houses of artizans usually have several, while all have fire-places, chimneys, and glazed windows, accompanied mostly by paper-hangings and painted doors; there has been, I say, a conspicuous progress in the condition of the people. And this progress has been still more marked within our own time. Any one who can look back 60 years, when the amount of pauperism was far greater than now and beggars abundant, is struck by the comparative size and finish of the new houses occupied by operatives – by the better dress of workmen, who wear broad-cloth on Sundays, and that of servant girls, who vie with their mistresses – by the higher standard of living which leads to a great demand for the best qualities of food by working people: all results of the double change to higher wages and cheaper commodities, and a distribution of taxes which has relieved the lower classes at the expense of the upper classes. He is struck, too, by the contrast between the small space which popular welfare then occupied in public attention, and the large space it now occupies, with the result that outside and inside Parliament, plans to benefit the millions form the leading topics, and everyone, having means is expected to join in some philanthropic effort. Yet while elevation, mental and physical, of the masses is going on far more rapidly than ever before – while the lowering of the death-rate proves that the average life is less trying, there swells louder and louder the cry that the evils are so great that nothing short of a social revolution can cure them. In presence of obvious improvements, joined with that increase of longevity which even alone yields conclusive proof of general amelioration, it is proclaimed, with increasing vehemence, that things are so bad that society must be pulled to pieces and re-organized on another plan. In this case, then, as in the previous cases instanced, in proportion as the evil decreases the denunciation of it increases; and as fast as natural causes are shown to be powerful there grows up the belief that they are powerless.

Not that the evils to be remedied are small. Let no one suppose that, by emphasizing the above paradox, I wish to make light of the sufferings which most men have to bear. The fates of the great majority have ever been, and doubtless still are, so sad that it is painful to think of them. Unquestionably the existing type of social organization is one which none who care for their kind can contemplate with satisfaction; and unquestionably men's activities accompanying this type are far from being admirable. The strong divisions of rank and the immense inequalities of means, are at variance with that ideal of human relations on which the sympathetic imagination likes to dwell; and the average conduct, under the pressure and excitement of social life as at present carried on, is in sundry respects repulsive. Though the many who revile competition strangely ignore the enormous benefits resulting from it – though they forget that most of the appliances and products distinguishing civilization from savagery, and making possible the maintenance of a large population on a small area, have been developed by the struggle for existence – though they disregard the fact that while every man, as producer, suffers from the under-bidding of competitors, yet, as consumer, he is immensely advantaged by the cheapening of all he has to buy – though they persist in dwelling on the evils of competition and saying nothing of its benefits; yet it is not to be denied that the evils are great, and form a large set-off from the benefits. The system under which we at present live fosters dishonesty and lying. It prompts adulterations of countless kinds; it is answerable for the cheap imitations which eventually in many cases thrust the genuine articles out of the market; it leads to the use of short weights and false measures; it introduces bribery, which vitiates most trading relations, from those of the manufacturer and buyer down to those of the shopkeeper and servant; it encourages deception to such an extent that an assistant who cannot tell a falsehood with a good face is blamed; and often it gives the conscientious trader the choice between adopting the malpractices of his competitors, or greatly injuring his creditors by bankruptcy. Moreover, the extensive frauds, common throughout the commercial world and daily exposed in law-courts and newspapers, are largely due to the pressure under which competition places the higher industrial classes; and are otherwise due to that lavish expenditure which, as implying success in the commercial struggle, brings honour. With these minor evils must be joined the major one, that the distribution achieved by the system, gives to those who regulate and superintend, a share of the total produce which bears too large a ratio to the share it gives to the actual workers. Let it not be thought, then, that in saying what I have said above, I under-estimate those vices of our competitive system which, 30 years ago, I described and denounced.[1] But it is not a question of absolute evils; it is a question of relative evils – whether the evils at present suffered are or are not less than the evils which would be suffered under another system – whether efforts for mitigation along the lines thus far followed are not more likely to succeed than efforts along utterly different lines.

This is the question here to be considered. I must be excused for first of all setting forth sundry truths which are, to some at any rate, tolerably familiar, before proceeding to draw inferences which are not so familiar.

Speaking broadly, every man works that he may avoid suffering. Here, remembrance of the pangs of hunger

[1] See essay on "The Morals of Trade."

prompts him; and there, he is prompted by the sight of the slave-driver's lash. His immediate dread may be the punishment which physical circumstances will inflict, or may be punishment inflicted by human agency. He must have a master; but the master may be Nature or may be a fellow man. When he is under the impersonal coercion of Nature, we say that he is free; and when he is under the personal coercion of some one above him, we call him, according to the degree of his dependence, a slave, a serf, or a vassal. Of course I omit the small minority who inherit means: an incidental, and not a necessary, social element. I speak only of the vast majority, both cultured and uncultured, who maintain themselves by labour, bodily or mental, and must either exert themselves of their own unconstrained wills, prompted only by thoughts of naturally-resulting evils or benefits, or must exert themselves with constrained wills, prompted by thoughts of evils and benefits artificially resulting.

Men may work together in a society under either of these two forms of control: forms which, though in many cases mingled, are essentially contrasted. Using the word coöperation in its wide sense, and not in that restricted sense now commonly given to it, we may say that social life must be carried on by either voluntary coöperation or compulsory coöperation; or, to use Sir Henry Maine's words, the system must be that of *contract* or that of *status* – that in which the individual is left to do the best he can by his spontaneous efforts and get success or failure according to his efficiency, and that in which he has his appointed place, works under coercive rule, and has his apportioned share of food, clothing, and shelter.

The system of voluntary coöperation is that by which, in civilized societies, industry is now everywhere carried on. Under a simple form we have it on every farm, where the labourers, paid by the farmer himself and taking orders directly from him, are free to stay or go as they please. And of its more complex form an example is yielded by every manufacturing concern, in which, under partners, come managers and clerks, and under these, time-keepers and overlookers, and under these operatives of different grades. In each of these cases there is an obvious working together, or coöperation, of employer and employed, to obtain in the one case a crop and in the other case a manufactured stock. And then, at the same time, there is a far more extensive, though unconscious, coöperation with other workers of all grades throughout the society. For while these particular employers and employed are severally occupied with their special kinds of work, other employers and employed are making other things needed for the carrying on of their lives as well as the lives of all others. This voluntary coöperation, from its simplest to its most complex forms, has the common trait that those concerned work together by consent. There is no one to force terms or to force acceptance. It is perfectly true that in many cases an employer may give, or an *employé* may accept, with reluctance: circumstances he says compel him. But what are the circumstances? In the one case there are goods ordered, or a contract entered into, which he cannot supply or execute without yielding; and in the other case he submits to a wage less than he likes because otherwise he will have no money wherewith to procure food and warmth. The general formula is not – "Do this, or I will make you;" but it is – "Do this, or leave your place and take the consequences."

On the other hand compulsory coöperation is exemplified by an army – not so much by our own army, the service in which is under agreement for a specified period, but in a continental army, raised by conscription. Here, in time of peace, the daily duties – cleaning, parade, drill, sentry work, and the rest – and in time of war the various actions of the camp and the battle-field, are done under command, without room for any exercise of choice. Up from the private soldier through the non-commissioned officers and the half-dozen or more grades of commissioned officers, the universal law is absolute obedience from the grade below to the grade above. The sphere of individual will is such only as is allowed by the will of the superior. Breaches of subordination are, according to their gravity, dealt with by deprivation of leave, extra drill, imprisonment, flogging, and, in the last resort, shooting. Instead of the understanding that there must be obedience in respect of specified duties under pain of dismissal; the understanding now is – "Obey in everything ordered under penalty of inflicted suffering and perhaps death."

This form of coöperation, still exemplified in an army, has in days gone by been the form of coöperation throughout the civil population. Everywhere, and at all times, chronic war generates a militant type of structure, not in the body of soldiers only but throughout the community at large. Practically, while the conflict between societies is actively going on, and fighting is regarded as the only manly occupation, the society is the quiescent army and the army the mobilized society: that part which does not take part in battle, composed of slaves, serfs, women, &c., constituting the commissariat. Naturally, therefore, throughout the mass of inferior individuals constituting the commissariat, there is maintained a system of discipline identical in nature if less elaborate. The fighting body being, under such conditions, the ruling body, and the rest of the community being incapable of resistance, those who control the fighting body will, of course, impose their control upon the non-fighting body; and the *régime* of coercion will be applied to it with such modifications only as the different circumstances involve. Prisoners of war become slaves. Those who were free cultivators before the conquest of their country, become serfs attached to the soil. Petty chiefs become subject to superior chiefs; these smaller lords become vassals to over-lords; and so on up to the highest: the social ranks and powers being of like essential nature with the ranks and powers throughout the military organization. And while for the slaves compulsory coöperation is the unqualified system, a coöperation which is in part compulsory is the system that pervades all grades above. Each man's oath of fealty to his suzerain takes the form – "I am your man."

Throughout Europe, and especially in our own country, this system of compulsory coöperation gradually relaxed in rigour, while the system of voluntary coöperation step by step replaced it. As fast as war ceased to be the business of life, the social structure produced by war and appropriate to it, slowly became qualified by the social structure produced by industrial life and appropriate to it. In proportion as a decreasing part of the community was devoted to offensive and defensive activities, an increasing part became devoted to production and distribution. Growing more numerous, more powerful, and taking refuge in towns where it was less under the power of the militant class, this industrial population carried on its life under the system of voluntary coöperation. Though municipal governments and guild-regulations, partially pervaded by ideas and usages derived from the militant type of society, were in some degree coercive; yet production and distribution were in the main carried on under agreement – alike between buyers and sellers, and between masters and workmen. As fast as these social relations and forms of activity became dominant in urban populations, they influenced the whole community: compulsory coöperation lapsed more and more, through money commutation for services, military and civil; while divisions of rank became less rigid and class-power diminished. Until at length, restraints exercised by incorporated trades having fallen into desuetude, as well as the rule of rank over rank, voluntary coöperation became the universal principle. Purchase and sale became the law for all kinds of services as well as for all kinds of commodities.

The restlessness generated by pressure against the conditions of existence, perpetually prompts the desire to try a new position. Everyone knows how long-continued rest in one attitude becomes wearisome – everyone has found how even the best easy chair, at first rejoiced in, becomes after many hours intolerable; and change to a hard seat, previously occupied and rejected, seems for a time to be a great relief. It is the same with incorporated humanity. Having by long struggles emancipated itself from the hard discipline of the ancient *régime*, and having discovered that the new *régime* into which it has grown, though relatively easy, is not without stresses and pains, its impatience with these prompts the wish to try another system: which other system is, in principle if not in appearance, the same as that which during past generations was escaped from with much rejoicing.

For as fast as the *régime* of contract is discarded the *régime* of status is of necessity adopted. As fast as voluntary coöperation is abandoned compulsory coöperation must be substituted. Some kind of organization labour must have; and if it is not that which arises by agreement under free competition, it must be that which is imposed by authority. Unlike in appearance and names as it may be to the old order of slaves and serfs, working under masters, who were coerced by barons, who were themselves vassals of dukes or kings, the new order wished for, constituted by workers under foremen of small groups, overlooked by superintendents, who are subject to higher local managers, who are controlled by superiors of districts, themselves under a central government, must be essentially the same in principle. In the one case, as in the other, there must be established grades, and enforced subordination of each grade to the grades above. This is a truth which the communist or the socialist does not dwell upon. Angry with the existing system under which each of us takes care of himself, while all of us see that each has fair play, he thinks how much better it would be for all of us to take care of each of us; and he refrains from thinking of the machinery by which this is to be done. Inevitably, if each is to be cared for by all, then the embodied all must get the means – the necessaries of life. What it gives to each must be taken from the accumulated contributions; and it must therefore require from each his proportion – must tell him how much he has to give to the general stock in the shape of production, that he may have so much in the shape of sustentation. Hence, before he can be provided for, he must put himself under orders, and obey those who say what he shall do, and at what hours, and where; and who give him his share of food, clothing, and shelter. If competition is excluded, and with it buying and selling, there can be no voluntary exchange of so much labour for so much produce; but there must be apportionment of the one to the other by appointed officers. This apportionment must be enforced. Without alternative the work must be done, and without alternative the benefit, whatever it may be, must be accepted. For the worker may not leave his place at will and offer himself elsewhere. Under such a system he cannot be accepted elsewhere, save by order of the authorities. And it is manifest that a standing order would forbid employment in one place of an insubordinate member from another place: the system could not be worked if the workers were severally allowed to go or come as they pleased. With corporals and sergeants under them, the captains of industry must carry out the orders of their colonels, and these of their generals, up to the council of the commander-in-chief; and obedience must be required throughout the industrial army as throughout a fighting army. "Do your prescribed duties, and take your apportioned rations," must be the rule of the one as of the other.

"Well, be it so;" replies the socialist. "The workers will appoint their own officers, and these will always be subject to criticisms of the mass they regulate. Being thus in fear of public opinion, they will be sure to act judiciously and fairly; or when they do not, will be deposed by the popular vote, local or general. Where will be the grievance of being under superiors, when the superiors themselves are under democratic control?" And in this attractive vision the socialist has full belief.

Iron and brass are simpler things than flesh and blood, and dead wood than living nerve; and a machine constructed of the one works in more definite ways than an organism constructed of the others – especially when the machine is worked by the inorganic forces of steam or water, while the organism is worked by the forces of living nerve-centres. Manifestly, then, the ways in which the machine will work are much more readily calculable than the ways in which the organism will work. Yet in how few cases does the inventor foresee rightly the actions of his new apparatus! Read the patent-list, and it will be found that not more than one device in fifty turns out to be of any service. Plausible as his scheme seemed to the inventor, one or other hitch prevents the intended operation, and brings out a widely different result from that which he wished.

What, then, shall we say of these schemes which have to do not with dead matters and forces, but with complex living organisms working in ways less readily foreseen, and which involve the coöperation of multitudes of such organisms? Even the units out of which this re-arranged body politic is to be formed are often incomprehensible. Everyone is from time to time surprised by others' behaviour, and even by the deeds of relatives who are best known to him. Seeing, then, how uncertainly anyone can foresee the actions of an individual, how can he with any certainty foresee the operation of a social structure? He proceeds on the assumption that all concerned will judge rightly and act fairly – will think as they ought to think, and act as they ought to act; and he assumes this regardless of the daily experiences which show him that men do neither the one nor the other, and forgetting that the complaints he makes against the existing system show his belief to be that men have neither the wisdom nor the rectitude which his plan requires them to have.

Paper constitutions raise smiles on the faces of those who

have observed their results; and paper social systems similarly affect those who have contemplated the available evidence. How little the men who wrought the French revolution and were chiefly concerned in setting up the new governmental apparatus, dreamt that one of the early actions of this apparatus would be to behead them all! How little the men who drew up the American Declaration of Independence and framed the republic, anticipated that after some generations the legislature would lapse into the hands of wire-pullers; that its doings would turn upon the contests of office-seekers; that political action would be everywhere vitiated by the intrusion of a foreign element holding the balance between parties; that electors, instead of judging for themselves, would habitually be led to the polls in thousands by their "bosses;" and that respectable men would be driven out of public life by the insults and slanders of professional politicians. Nor were there better previsions in those who gave constitutions to the various other states of the New World, in which unnumbered revolutions have shown with wonderful persistence the contrasts between the expected results of political systems and the achieved results. It has been no less thus with proposed systems of social re-organization, so far as they have been tried. Save where celibacy has been insisted on, their history has been everywhere one of disaster; ending with the history of Cabet's Icarian colony lately given by one of its members, Madame Fleury Robinson, in *The Open Court* – a history of splittings, re-splittings and re-re-splittings, accompanied by numerous individual secessions and final dissolution. And for the failure of such social schemes, as for the failure of the political schemes, there has been one general cause.

Metamorphosis is the universal law, exemplified throughout the Heavens and on the Earth: especially throughout the organic world; and above all in the animal division of it. No creature, save the simplest and most minute, commences its existence in a form like that which it eventually assumes; and in most cases the unlikeness is great – so great that kinship between the first and the last forms would be incredible were it not daily demonstrated in every poultry-yard and every garden. More than this is true. The changes of form are often several: each of them being an apparently complete transformation – egg, larva, pupa, imago, for example. And this universal metamorphosis, displayed alike in the development of a planet and of every seed which germinates on its surface, holds also of societies, whether taken as wholes or in their separate institutions. No one of them ends as it begins; and the difference between its original structure and its ultimate structure is such that, at the outset, change of the one into the other would have seemed incredible. In the rudest tribe the chief, obeyed as leader in war, loses his distinctive position when the fighting is over; and even where continued warfare has produced permanent chieftainship, the chief, building his own hut, getting his own food, making his own implements, differs from others only by his predominant influence. There is no sign that in course of time, by conquests and unions of tribes, and consolidations of clusters so formed with other such clusters, until a nation has been produced, there will originate from the primitive chief, one who, as czar or emperor, surrounded with pomp and ceremony, has despotic power over scores of millions, exercised through hundreds of thousands of soldiers and hundreds of thousands of officials. When the early Christian missionaries, having humble externals and passing self-denying lives, spread over pagan Europe, preaching forgiveness of injuries and the returning of good for evil, no one dreamt that in course of time their representatives would form a vast hierarchy, possessing everywhere a large part of the land, distinguished by the haughtiness of its members grade above grade, ruled by military bishops who led their retainers to battle, and headed by a pope exercising supreme power over kings. So, too, has it been with that very industrial system which many are now so eager to replace. In its original form there was no prophecy of the factory-system or kindred organizations of workers. Differing from them only as being the head of his house, the master worked along with his apprentices and a journeyman or two, sharing with them his table and accommodation, and himself selling their joint produce. Only with industrial growth did there come employment of a larger number of assistants, and a relinquishment, on the part of the master, of all other business than that of superintendence. And only in the course of recent times did there evolve the organizations under which the labours of hundreds and thousands of men receiving wages, are regulated by various orders of paid officials under a single or multiple head. These originally small, semi-socialistic, groups of producers, like the compound families or house-communities of early ages, slowly dissolved because they could not hold their ground: the larger establishments, with better sub-division of labour, succeeded because they ministered to the wants of society more effectually. But we need not go back through the centuries to trace transformations sufficiently great and unexpected. On the day when £30,000 a year in aid of education was voted as an experiment, the name of idiot would have been given to an opponent who prophesied that in 50 years the sum spent through imperial taxes and local rates would amount to £10,000,000 or who said that the aid to education would be followed by aids to feeding and clothing, or who said that parents and children, alike deprived of all option, would, even if starving, be compelled by fine or imprisonment to conform, and receive that which, with papal assumption, the State calls education. No one, I say, would have dreamt that out of so innocent-looking a germ would have so quickly evolved this tyrannical system, tamely submitted to by people who fancy themselves free.

Thus in social arrangements, as in all other things, change is inevitable. It is foolish to suppose that new institutions set up, will long retain the character given them by those who set them up. Rapidly or slowly they will be transformed into institutions unlike those intended – so unlike as even to be unrecognizable by their devisers. And what, in the case before us, will be the metamorphosis? The answer pointed to by instances above given, and warranted by various analogies, is manifest.

A cardinal trait in all advancing organization is the development of the regulative apparatus. If the parts of a whole are to act together, there must be appliances by which their actions are directed; and in proportion as the whole is large and complex, and has many requirements to be met by many agencies, the directive apparatus must be extensive, elaborate, and powerful. That it is thus with individual organisms needs no saying; and that it must be thus with social organisms is obvious. Beyond the regulative apparatus such as in our own society is required for carrying on national defence and maintaining public order and personal safety, there must, under the *régime* of socialism, be a regulative apparatus everywhere controlling all kinds of production and distribution, and everywhere apportioning the shares of products of each kind required for each locality, each working establishment, each individual. Under our existing voluntary cooperation, with its free contracts and its competition, production and distribution need no official oversight. Demand and supply, and the desire of each man to gain a living by supplying the needs of his fellows, spontaneously evolve that wonderful system whereby a great city has its food daily brought round to all doors or stored at adjacent shops; has clothing for its citizens everywhere at hand in multitudinous varieties; has its houses and furniture and fuel ready made or stocked in each locality; and has mental pabulum from halfpenny papers hourly hawked round, to weekly shoals of novels, and less abundant books of instruction, furnished without stint for small payments. And throughout the kingdom, production as well as distribution is similarly carried on with the smallest amount of superintendence which proves efficient; while the quantities of the numerous commodities required daily in each locality are adjusted without any other agency than the pursuit of profit. Suppose now that this industrial *régime* of willinghood, acting spontaneously, is replaced by a *régime* of industrial obedience, enforced by public officials. Imagine the vast administration required for that distribution of all commodities to all people in every city, town and village, which is now effected by traders! Imagine, again, the still more vast administration required for doing all that farmers, manufacturers, and merchants do; having not only its various orders of local superintendents, but its sub-centres and chief centres needed for apportioning the quantities of each thing everywhere needed, and the adjustment of them to the requisite times. Then add the staffs wanted for working mines, railways, roads, canals; the staffs required for conducting the importing and exporting businesses and the administration of mercantile shipping; the staffs required for supplying towns not only with water and gas but with locomotion by tramways, omnibuses, and other vehicles, and for the distribution of power, electric and other. Join with these the existing postal, telegraphic, and telephonic administrations; and finally those of the police and army, by which the dictates of this immense consolidated regulative system are to be everywhere enforced. Imagine all this and then ask what will be the position of the actual workers! Already on the continent, where governmental organizations are more elaborate and coercive than here, there are chronic complaints of the tyranny of bureaucracies – the *hauteur* and brutality of their members. What will these become when not only the more public actions of citizens are controlled, but there is added this far more extensive control of all their respective daily duties? What will happen when the various divisions of this vast army of officials, united by interests common to officialism – the interests of the regulators *versus* those of the regulated – have at their command whatever force is needful to suppress insubordination and act as "saviours of society"? Where will be the actual diggers and miners and smelters and weavers, when those who order and superintend, everywhere arranged class above class, have come, after some generations, to inter-marry with those of kindred grades, under feelings such as are operative in existing classes; and when there have been so produced a series of castes rising in superiority; and when all these, having everything in their own power, have arranged modes of living for their own advantage: eventually forming a new aristocracy far more elaborate and better organized than the old? How will the individual worker fare if he is dissatisfied with his treatment – thinks that he has not an adequate share of the products, or has more to do than can rightly be demanded, or wishes to undertake a function for which he feels himself fitted but which is not thought proper for him by his superiors, or desires to make an independent career for himself? This dissatisfied unit in the immense machine will be told he must submit or go. The mildest penalty for disobedience will be industrial excommunication. And if an international organization of labour is formed as proposed, exclusion in one country will mean exclusion in all others – industrial excommunication will mean starvation.

That things must take this course is a conclusion reached not by deduction only, nor only by induction from those experiences of the past instanced above, nor only from consideration of the analogies furnished by organisms of all orders; but it is reached also by observation of cases daily under our eyes. The truth that the regulative structure always tends to increase in power, is illustrated by every established body of men. The history of each learned society, or society for other purpose, shows how the staff, permanent or partially permanent, sways the proceedings and determines the actions of the society with but little resistance, even when most members of the society disapprove: the repugnance to anything like a revolutionary step being ordinarily an efficient deterrent. So is it with joint-stock companies – those owning railways for example. The plans of a board of directors are usually authorized with little or no discussion; and if there is any considerable opposition, this is forthwith crushed by an overwhelming number of proxies sent by those who always support the existing administration. Only when the misconduct is extreme does the resistance of shareholders suffice to displace the ruling body. Nor is it otherwise with societies formed of working men and having the interests of labour especially at heart – the trades-unions. In these, too, the regulative agency becomes all powerful. Their members, even when they dissent from the policy pursued, habitually yield to the authorities they have set up. As they cannot secede without making enemies of their fellow workmen, and often losing all chance of employment, they succumb. We are shown, too, by the late congress, that already, in the general organization of trades-unions so recently formed, there are complaints of "wire-pullers" and "bosses" and "permanent officials." If, then, this supremacy of the regulators is seen in bodies of quite modern origin, formed of men who have, in many of the cases instanced, unhindered powers of asserting their independence, what will the supremacy of the regulators become in long-established bodies, in bodies which have become vast and highly organized, and in bodies which, instead of controlling only a small part of the unit's life, control the whole of his life?

Again there will come the rejoinder – "We shall guard against all that. Everybody will be educated; and all, with their eyes constantly open to the abuse of power, will be quick to prevent it." The worth of these expectations would be small even could we not identify the causes which will bring disappointment; for in human affairs the most promising schemes go wrong in ways which no one anticipated. But in this case the going wrong will be necessitated by causes which are conspicuous. The working of institutions is determined by men's characters; and the existing defects in their characters will inevitably bring about the results above indicated. There is no adequate endowment of those sentiments required to prevent the growth of a despotic bureaucracy.

Were it needful to dwell on indirect evidence, much might be made of that furnished by the behaviour of the so-called Liberal party – a party which, relinquishing the original conception of a leader as a mouthpiece for a known and accepted policy, thinks itself bound to accept a policy which its leader springs upon it without consent or warning – a party so utterly without the feeling and idea implied by liberalism, as not to resent this trampling on the right of private judgment, which constitutes the root of liberalism – nay, a party which vilifies as renegade liberals, those of its members who refuse to surrender their independence! But without occupying space with indirect proofs that the mass of men have not the natures required to check the development of tyrannical officialism, it will suffice to contemplate the direct proofs furnished by those classes among whom the socialistic idea most predominates, and who think themselves most interested in propagating it – the operative classes. These would constitute the great body of the socialistic organization, and their characters would determine its nature. What, then, are their characters as displayed in such organizations as they have already formed?

Instead of the selfishness of the employing classes and the selfishness of competition, we are to have the unselfishness of a mutually-aiding system. How far is this unselfishness now shown in the behaviour of working men to one another? What shall we say to the rules limiting the numbers of new hands admitted into each trade, or to the rules which hinder ascent from inferior classes of workers to superior classes? One does not see in such regulations any of that altruism by which socialism is to be pervaded. Contrariwise, one sees a pursuit of private interests no less keen than among traders. Hence, unless we suppose that men's natures will be suddenly exalted, we must conclude that the pursuit of private interests will sway the doings of all the component classes in a socialistic society.

With passive disregard of others' claims goes active encroachment on them. "Be one of us or we will cut off your means of living," is the usual threat of each trades-union to outsiders of the same trade. While their members insist on their own freedom to combine and fix the rates at which they will work (as they are perfectly justified in doing), the freedom of those who disagree with them is not only denied but the assertion of it is treated as a crime. Individuals who maintain their rights to make their own contracts are vilified as "black-legs" and "traitors," and meet with violence which would be merciless were there no legal penalties and no police. Along with this trampling on the liberties of men of their own class, there goes peremptory dictation to the employing class: not prescribed terms and working arrangements only shall be conformed to, but none save those belonging to their body shall be employed – nay, in some cases, there shall be a strike if the employer carries on transactions with trading bodies that give work to non-union men. Here, then, we are variously shown by trades-unions, or at any rate by the newer trades-unions, a determination to impose their regulations without regard to the rights of those who are to be coerced. So complete is the inversion of ideas and sentiments that maintenance of these rights is regarded as vicious and trespass upon them as virtuous.[2]

Along with this aggressiveness in one direction there goes submissiveness in another direction. The coercion of outsiders by unionists is paralleled only by their subjection to their leaders. That they may conquer in the struggle they surrender their individual liberties and individual judgments, and show no resentment however dictatorial may be the rule exercised over them. Everywhere we see such subordination

---

[2] Marvellous are the conclusions men reach when once they desert the simple principle, that each man should be allowed to pursue the objects of life, restrained only by the limits which the similar pursuits of their objects by other men impose. A generation ago we heard loud assertions of "the right to labour," that is, the right to have labour provided; and there are still not a few who think the community bound to find work for each person. Compare this with the doctrine current in France at the time when the monarchical power culminated; namely, that "the right of working is a royal right which the prince can sell and the subjects must buy." This contrast is startling enough; but a contrast still more startling is being provided for us. We now see a resuscitation of the despotic doctrine, differing only by the substitution of Trades-Unions for kings. For now that Trades-Unions are becoming universal, and each artisan has to pay prescribed monies to one or another of them, with the alternative of being a non-unionist to whom work is denied by force, it has come to this, that the right to labour is a Trade-Union right, which the Trade-Union can sell and the individual worker must buy!

that bodies of workmen unanimously leave their work or return to it as their authorities order them. Nor do they resist when taxed all round to support strikers whose acts they may or may not approve, but instead, ill-treat recalcitrant members of their body who do not subscribe.

The traits thus shown must be operative in any new social organization, and the question to be asked is – What will result from their operation when they are relieved from all restraints? At present the separate bodies of men displaying them are in the midst of a society partially passive, partially antagonistic; are subject to the criticisms and reprobations of an independent press; and are under the control of law, enforced by police. If in these circumstances these bodies habitually take courses which override individual freedom, what will happen when, instead of being only scattered parts of the community, governed by their separate sets of regulators, they constitute the whole community, governed by a consolidated system of such regulators; when functionaries of all orders, including those who officer the press, form parts of the regulative organization; and when the law is both enacted and administered by this regulative organization? The fanatical adherents of a social theory are capable of taking any measures, no matter how extreme, for carrying out their views: holding, like the merciless priesthoods of past times, that the end justifies the means. And when a general socialistic organization has been established, the vast, ramified, and consolidated body of those who direct its activities, using without check whatever coercion seems to them needful in the interests of the system (which will practically become their own interests) will have no hesitation in imposing their rigorous rule over the entire lives of the actual workers; until, eventually, there is developed an official oligarchy, with its various grades, exercising a tyranny more gigantic and more terrible than any which the world has seen.

Let me again repudiate an erroneous inference. Any one who supposes that the foregoing argument implies contentment with things as they are, makes a profound mistake. The present social state is transitional, as past social states have been transitional. There will, I hope and believe, come a future social state differing as much from the present as the present differs from the past with its mailed barons and defenceless serfs. In *Social Statics*, as well as in *The Study of Sociology* and in *Political Institutions*, is clearly shown the desire for an organization more conducive to the happiness of men at large than that which exists. My opposition to socialism results from the belief that it would stop the progress to such a higher state and bring back a lower state. Nothing but the slow modification of human nature by the discipline of social life, can produce permanently advantageous changes.

A fundamental error pervading the thinking of nearly all parties, political and social, is that evils admit of immediate and radical remedies. "If you will but do this, the mischief will be prevented." "Adopt my plan and the suffering will disappear." "The corruption will unquestionably be cured by enforcing this measure." Everywhere one meets with beliefs, expressed or implied, of these kinds. They are all ill-founded. It is possible to remove causes which intensify the evils; it is possible to change the evils from one form into another; and it is possible, and very common, to exacerbate the evils by the efforts made to prevent them; but anything like immediate cure is impossible. In the course of thousands of years mankind have, by multiplication, been forced out of that original savage state in which small numbers supported themselves on wild food, into the civilized state in which the food required for supporting great numbers can be got only by continuous labour. The nature required for this last mode of life is widely different from the nature required for the first; and long-continued pains have to be passed through in remoulding the one into the other. Misery has necessarily to be borne by a constitution out of harmony with its conditions; and a constitution inherited from primitive men is out of harmony with the conditions imposed on existing men. Hence it is impossible to establish forthwith a satisfactory social state. No such nature as that which has filled Europe with millions of armed men, here eager for conquest and there for revenge – no such nature as that which prompts the nations called Christian to vie with one another in filibustering expeditions all over the world, regardless of the claims of aborigines, while their tens of thousands of priests of the religion of love look on approvingly – no such nature as that which, in dealing with weaker races, goes beyond the primitive rule of life for life, and for one life takes many lives – no such nature, I say, can, by any device, be framed into a harmonious community. The root of all well-ordered social action is a sentiment of justice, which at once insists on personal freedom and is solicitous for the like freedom of others; and there at present exists but a very inadequate amount of this sentiment.

Hence the need for further long continuance of a social discipline which requires each man to carry on his activities with due regard to the like claims of others to carry on their activities; and which, while it insists that he shall have all the benefits his conduct naturally brings, insists also that he shall not saddle on others the evils his conduct naturally brings: unless they freely undertake to bear them. And hence the belief that endeavours to elude this discipline, will not only fail, but will bring worse evils than those to be escaped.

It is not, then, chiefly in the interests of the employing classes that socialism is to be resisted, but much more in the interests of the employed classes. In one way or other production must be regulated; and the regulators, in the nature of things, must always be a small class as compared with the actual producers. Under voluntary coöperation as at present carried on, the regulators, pursuing their personal interests, take as large a share of the produce as they can get; but, as we are daily shown by trades-union successes, are restrained in the selfish pursuit of their ends. Under that compulsory coöperation which socialism would necessitate, the regulators, pursuing their personal interests with no less selfishness, could not be met by the combined resistance of free workers; and their power, unchecked as now by refusals to work save on prescribed terms, would grow and ramify and consolidate till it became irresistible. The ultimate result, as I have before pointed out, must be a society like that of ancient Peru, dreadful to contemplate, in which the mass of the people, elaborately regimented in groups of 10, 50, 100, 500, and 1000, ruled by officers of corresponding grades, and tied to their districts, were superintended in their private lives as well as in their industries, and toiled hopelessly for the support of the governmental organization.

LIBERTY OR LAW?
Wordsworth Donisthorpe

To those who realise with satisfaction or with alarm the rapid march of State-socialism in this country during the last half-century, it should be matter of surprise that those who are opposed on principle to legislation of a socialistic character have not, up to the present time, banded themselves into a party organisation or become known by any general party name.

The doctrine of *laissez-faire* is sometimes, it is true, referred to in the speeches of some of our more thoughtful public men, but only as a rule to be dismissed with a sneer as the crotchet of a doctrinaire. It seems to be taken for granted that no one can accept the principle of "let be" as a working rule of statesmanship without at once declaring himself an extremist; we are immediately reminded of the quack with his universal pill, a panacea for all human ills. The reason for this is difficult to see, but it is possibly to be found in the fact that most of those who have openly advocated the doctrine have been somewhat uncompromising and dogmatic. Let us see how far the charge of extremism is applicable to the existing party divisions. The spirit of radicalism is reform – reconstruction on an ideally perfect basis; but there is probably not a liberal living who would at once advocate such thorough, sudden and extreme change. Again, the spirit of toryism is resistance to change, and the maintainance of the *status quo*, but there is not a tory in the land who would resist the removal of every ancient abuse or obsolete institution. Concessions to expediency are not held to be a violation of the principles upon which the chief political parties in the State base their action. Since each member of the tory party desires to retain in *statu quo* far more than he is wishful to reform, individual efforts for change cancel one another in the bulk, and we have a residuum of complete unanimity in favour of keeping things as they are – a tory party opposed in the abstract to every alteration of State-structure. Conversely, and in a similar way, we have a radical party, whose creed in the abstract is modification of structure in every particular.

Now, if the question of State-structure is in process of gradual solution by the friction of diametrically opposed theories, may it not be advisable that the question of State function should be solved in like manner? Already we have a party whose principle is to expand the interference of the State to its utmost limit. If this new radical party should find itself confronted by a still newer party based on the "let be" principle, we fail to see how the charge of extremism should apply more to the one than to the other, or than to the two conflicting parties which to-day are at issue on the equally vital question of State-structure. And this consideration brings into view a new aspect of government by party.

Autocracy labours under this great disadvantage as compared with party government, that the autocrat, be he ever so benevolently disposed, is in the position of a judge who is compelled to try a difficult case without the aid of counsel. Just as by division of labour and consequent concentration of attention the counsel for the defence and for the prosecution urge all that can be urged in favour of the prisoner and against him respectively, their wits being all the time stimulated by the heat of controversy, so the two contending parties in the State, by concentrating their energies on one or other side of the question at issue, thresh the subject thoroughly out in the heat of political agitation, with a strong probability that not an argument will be lost sight of, not a stone will be left unturned, which can in any way affect the final verdict of the country. So that, regarded in this light, it is not only the normal province but the bounden duty of the tory party of to-day to say all that can be said against any proposed extension of the franchise or scheme of county government. It has a permanent retainer to make out the best possible case for leaving the Constitution as it is. No harm can come of engaging counsel for both sides of every question, in order that the pro's and con's may be exhaustively brought to light and carefully weighed one against the other.

Assuming, therefore, that the rise of a "let be" party is a desideratum, let us see if any signs of such a new developement are discernible on the political horizon.

Before making the necessary survey, however, it may be as

well to state as clearly as may be the precise question at issue between the socialists or new radicals on the one hand, and the advocates of "let be" on the other.

When we examine the numerous questions which exercise the minds of those who take an intelligent interest in politics, we find that they fall into two distinct classes – one class relating to the structure or constitution of government, the other to the function or duty of government. These two fundamental questions "What is the State?" and "What does the State?" though standing clearly apart, are usually confounded and treated together. Now, although they may be equally vital, that is no reason for assuming that those who agree upon the one point must necessarily hold identical views on the other. With respect to structure, politicians fall at once into two large and nearly equal parties – namely, those who are satisfied with the existing constitution just as it is, and those who contend that it ought to be more or less modified. Doubtless, the members of this latter class differ also among themselves as to the kind and amount of change desirable, from the red republican, through all the shades of radicalism, to the most timid trimmer that adorns the liberal benches. Their opponents are of opinion that changes are dangerous, or, that at all events, if they must occur, it is best to let them come of themselves, and to retard rather than hasten them on. This party also contains many shades of toryism, from the old-fashioned worshipper of antiquity, who would fain, if possible, reverse the tide of history and undo the evil of modern days, to the so-called liberal-conservative, who deems it wise to bend to circumstances and to float passively on the stream though not to swim with it.

Turn we now to the other great question, "What ought the Government, however constituted, to do?" "What are the duties of the State, be it monarchial, republic or mixed?" And here again politicians may be split up into two great parties. There are those who maintain the greatest possible liberty of the individual citizen compatible with the equal liberty of his fellows, and who disapprove, therefore, of all meddlesome legislation. They would restrict the functions of the State to the adminstration of justice, the maintenance of order, the defence of the country against foreign antagonism, and the collection and management of revenue for these purposes; and leave other matters to take care of themselves.

On the other hand there are those who believe that a well-organised body like the State is, or might be made, the most highly efficient machine for the carrying out of many great and noble schemes for the improvement of the people and the amelioration of their lot. Such are the persons who support State education, State charities, State museums and galleries, State railways and telegraphs, State banks, State post-offices, and even State censors and spies. Such are the persons who would close the public-house at ten o'clock or altogether, and who would convert drunkards by force, who would and do force their medical nostrums upon unbelievers, and imprison those who resist. Such *were* the persons who took into the general charge the eternal welfare of their fellow-creatures, and founded inquisitions to keep them in the right path. All these and a thousand other matters, say they, can be best regulated and managed by the State.

Diametrically opposed as these two parties are, and fundamental as the issue between them undoubtedly is, it is a remarkable fact that they enjoy at present no distinctive appellations; and it is entirely upon difference of opinion concerning State-structure that the existing party divisions are based. Indeed, some persons (even experienced statesmen) appear to be so far carried away by zeal for structural change or resistance to it, as never to give the equally if not more vital question of function a thought. Others, again, care little for the form of government so long as it is easy to live happily and freely under it –

For forms of government let fools contest,
Whate're is best administered is best;

or as the old but less refined saw hath it, "a good horse is never a bad colour."

Men of this stamp have during the last fifty years kept themselves in the background. The battle for equality – the struggles for parliamentary reform, for a re-distribution of seats, for extension of the suffrage, for the enfranchisement of women, for the reconstruction of the House of Lords, and for endless other constitutional reforms and changes – must be fought out when liberty is not in danger. But the very structural changes accomplished since the framing of the first Reform Bill have produced unforeseen effects upon the views of the ultimate governing body with respect to the duties of the State, which effects have been quickened since some fifteen years ago Mr. Disraeli threw open the floodgates still wider to the torrent of democracy. In explanation of this we cannot do better than quote Mr. Pleydell Bouverie. Speaking at the inaugural meeting of the Liberty and Property Defence League he said, "One sees proposals of even eminent men nowadays which, by looking into the history of this country, you will find are strictly allied to the old sumptuary laws and laws for the regulation of labour, and for settling what men are to earn, eat and drink, which are to be found in the statute book 400 years ago. We thought these notions had been exploded as hurtful and foolish, but they are coming to the front again, and I think it is due to the fact that a large amount of political power is now wielded by the comparatively uneducated and ignorant classes. The very mistakes and fallacies which were not recognised to be such by the educated classes 400 years ago, and which influenced their legislation, are again influencing the classes which have recently acquired political power. They are for emulating those old-fashioned acts of parliament; unreasonable and impossible expectations are indulged in; and there is a great desire for ridiculous interference by Act of parliament, which will again have to be exploded by the good sense of those who agree with the gentlemen here." Agitations for constitutional reform in harmony with the principle of equality are giving place to agitations for restrictions on the liberty of one class for the benefit of another, and the liberty of the individual for the supposed benefit of the public. This tendency brings politics home to the doors of those who take but a lukewarm interest in the "levelling" process, and a very keen interest in their own freedom.

Proceeding now with our survey, the first symptom which presents itself of a reaction against the socialistic tendencies of recent legislation, is the establishment of an association for the avowed object of resisting overlegislation, and calling itself the Liberty and Property Defence League. This League has already enlisted the sympathy and support of thousands who have hitherto held aloof from party strife, including some of the best-known representatives of the shipping interest, the railway interest, the land interest, and many others which of late years have been despoiled, harassed, or interfered with, by the philanthropic but inexperienced busybodies of the new school. Now this Liberty League, as it is shortly and popularly styled, has distinctly stated in its publications that it is not a society of extreme doctrinaires, pledged to resist, as a body and also through its individual members, all extension of State-functions beyond their normal limit; on the contrary, its members are free to take any view of any such question as may happen to approve itself to their sense of expediency, while the League as a body will on all such occasions make the best possible case out for applying the principle of "let be" and leaving the matter to private enterprise. As an illustration of the thoroughness and loyalty with which this plan is carried out, we find a member of the council of the League strongly urging upon the government the necessity for a system of State-aided emigration, while the League itself is doing its utmost with his entire consent to demonstrate the mischief of such an undertaking. Similarly, several influential members of the League have already expressed cordial concurrence with suggestions that some action should be taken for ameliorating the lot of the London poor; while at the same time they fully appreciate the efforts of the League to urge all that there is to urge against any proposed legislation with that object. By adopting this broad platform the League has placed itself beyond the reach of those who would stigmatise it as extremist, and at the same time formed what may turn out to be the nucleus of the new party which sooner or later must come into existence as a counter-balance to the State-socialists, who, within the last few years, have shown themselves so dangerously active, and, indeed, aggressive. The common platform upon which members of the League stand is not any hard-and-fast doctrine of the limits of government duties, but the acceptance of the principle that overlegislation is on the increase, and requires to be kept in check. Since this is the bond of union, it follows that it is competent for a person opposed to *any* measures of State interference with individual liberty to join the League, and at the same time to advocate *any other* measure of State meddling which may suit his fancy. The League itself, on the other hand, cannot lend its countenance to any such measure, however well-conceived or popular even among its own members, for in so doing it would stultify itself.

In the abstract, therefore, it may be said that the spirit of the League is one of resistance to any overstepping by the legislature of its normal boundaries. It is the embodiment of the absolute principle of civil liberty, or the greatest possible liberty of each, compatible with the equal liberty of all. Of those who have faith in State-action, it is probable that none follow up the principle to its extreme logical conclusion, and look forward to the time when every man in the land shall have his own inspector to follow him about, to carry his goloshes, and to see that he puts them on before crossing the road; to take notes of what he says; to correct his grammar and his religious opinions when out of harmony with authorised usage; to see that he drinks what is good for him, and no more; to put out his candle at nine at night, and to accompany him twice to church every Sunday. Consistency wavers before such a prospect. An age when there shall be no crime, no drunkenness, no wrangling, not even difference of opinion, and we shall be an orderly people, doing that which is right in the eyes of the majority – the supreme, allwise, and serenely disinterested majority! But if the State-socialists shrink from this outcome of State-idolatry, so also do their opponents shrink from carrying the principle of non-interference too far. Probably, if the members of the League are prepared to accept any working principle at all as to the expediency of any proposed legislation, it will be that laid down by Mr. Bouverie, viz., that the *onus probandi* lies on those who would limit the freedom of the citizen. "The old-fashioned presumption was always that in the case of any interference with liberty, its reasonableness should be demonstrated before it should be adopted; but now-a-days it seems to be the notion that the presumption is the other way, and the burden of proof is on those who have to defend liberty instead of on those who insist upon interference." Yes, till the sweets of bondage are proved it is better to remain free.

The need for such a party was never more urgent than it is to-day, for blink the matter as we may, there is no denying that a new departure has of late been made by the conservative party, the outcome of which it is impossible to foresee. In an apparent bid for the socialist support, opposed though it is to the conservative traditions and practice, there is nothing actually inconsistent with conservative theory. Be this as it may, the die is cast. The conservative party have thrown in their lot with State-socialism. The gloomy and unheeded forebodings of Lord Wemyss, in 1883, are already fulfilled:

"Whereas in commerce freedom of contract is the very breath of its nostrils, the soul of its being; and whereas the commercial transactions in land – that is, the bargains between landlord and tenant – are in the aggregate greater than those of any two or three of the other largest British commercial interests; these bargains are not only to be forbidden in the future, but broken in the past. This is what the two great parties in the State affirmed when, with grateful hearts and cheerful countenances, they, with delightful unanimity passed the second reading of the government Agricultural Holdings Bill. Contracts, not in 'exceptional' Ireland, but here in law-abiding, free, commercial England and Scotland – forbidden in the future and broken in the past! And why? Solely because – disguise the truth as they may under specious phrases, bury it no matter how deep under agricultural commissioners' reports – liberals and conservatives have cast principle and sound economic doctrine aside, and are playing a game of 'grab' for the farmer's vote."

The result of the game will of course depend on the answer to the question, who holds the trump card? And the trump card is not nationalisation of land only, but nationalisation of all wealth. That is the trump card in the game. Hitherto, the part of the conservative has been to throw obstacles in the path of the radical charioteer, while the whig has taken his seat on the box and hampered the driver's movements, endeavouring all the while to damp his ardour with prudent counsel. It now remains to be seen whether the old party of progress-with-liberty can any longer continue to play the rôle of unheeded Mentor to the new party of communism and spoilation. If the whigs, who, anxious not to impede the process of structural reform, have up to the present silently tolerated much overlegislation of which they secretly disapprove, rather than seem to join hands with those who would bolster up effete institutions, do not now come forward and speak out boldly for the ancient rights and liberties of all classes on the time-honoured lines of property and freedom, to whom shall the country look?

Unless, then, the whigs, old liberals, and conservative progressists can find an independent platform on the lines sketched out by the Liberty League, the outlook for the country is indeed a gloomy one.

Now that the masses have tasted power they will strive for more, and it will be a wise precaution to guard democracy from its own defects by limiting the powers of the State, however constituted, and to enact, while yet we are in a position to do so, that all interference of government in matters outside its normal duties shall be a violation of the constitution. So long as the people see us arbitrarily shutting up their clubs, while our own are left open; forcing their children to learn what we were taught instead of what their fathers were taught, namely, their handicraft; closing their places of business on specified days; taxing them for the support of museums, picture galleries, and scientific expeditions, about which they know nothing, solely for our own benefit; in fine, acting as though by our mere *fiat* we could shower luxuries upon them or doom them to starvation – is it very wonderful they should wish to wield this power which can effect so much for good or for evil? If, ask they, we can reduce their working hours to ten, why not to eight? If we can build schools for their children, why not cottages for them? If we can afford to protect them gratis from small-pox, why cannot we pay the doctor's bill when they do catch it? Naturally they argue that capital is better paid than labour, because the labourer is not so well represented as the capital-ist in the House of Commons, and not at all in the House of Lords. When they obtain the reins, then, say they, it will be the labourers' turn. And who shall blame them? They are only taking a leaf out of our book. It cannot be honestly denied that recourse has been had to class legislation for the benefit of the upper classes at the expense of the lower. Have not wages been kept down by law? Has not the price of bread been kept up by law for the benefit of a class? What have shipowners to say about the old navigation laws? But it is not necessary to assign instances when there are hundreds in the recollection of all. Something more than mortal, then, will these new masters be, if, for any nobler motive than enlightened self-interest, they can be induced, with victory within their grasp, to forego the luxury of revenge and the plunder of their quondam taskmasters.

Nor can we lay the blame of this evil example of overlegisl-ation at the door of either party in the State. Both are alike culpable, though, for reasons which are apparent, the radical party chiefly has been made the tool of the rising socialism. Unless, therefore, it can be shown to the satisfaction of the working-classes that the class legislation worked in their own interest cannot in the long run be of advantage to them, but rather the reverse, we must prepare for a long period of sullen Chinese uniformity and mobdespotism, such as has never been known before. And yet individualism has no easy task before it. The enemy is overwhelming in numbers and strongly entrenched. With the old Anglo-Saxon love of liberty and self-dependence on the one side; ranged against it are the not yet extinct class hatred, a thirst for retaliation, and, above and before all, sympathy with suffering and woe. Not that it is necessary to overcome the sympathy, but to convince those who sympathise, that the best medicine for all social ills is liberty: *optima medicina est non uti medicina.* This is in many cases no light matter. Try and convince the recipient of outdoor relief that such relief is inexpedient. Have you seen whole families during the famines in Ireland or India literally starving to death on land from which its owner or usufructuary draws thousands a year? Demonstrate to them that it would be neither wise nor kind to abolish by law the payment of rent. Have you hopelessly watched a crew of stalwart fellows go down on some rotten craft within sight of port? Convince Mr. Plimsoll, and those who think with him, that the seaworthiness of ships is best left to the care of shipowners. Have you known little children of nine and ten sent down into the pit to toil in solitude, in danger, and in darkness for the live-long day? If so, are you sure that the law relating to mines and prohibiting such cruelty is altogether unjustifiable? Is it true that £80,000,000 is annually spent in intoxicating drink in this country? If so, shall we blame those who would do their utmost, by legislation, to extirpate this national curse – drunkeness? Again, it is not pleasant to see the little ones of the people growing up in ignorance of much that is useful and beautiful for the want of elementary teaching. Surely men will not be found capable of forming themselves into an association for the express purpose of resisting all these noble efforts for the amelioration of poverty and weakness.

. Now this question brings us to the remarkable misconception that has somehow got afloat as to the views of individualists with respect to rules and regulations in general. It seems to be supposed that anything of the nature of a rule is in their eyes anathema and maranatha. The radical papers teem with questions calculated to bring ridicule upon those who oppose State-interference in general. It seems to be forgotten that other bodies can make laws besides the State. The Stock Exchange and the Jockey Club at once present themselves as instances of private bodies making laws which are virtually accepted by the whole country. The customs of the Lancashire cotton trade are the finest example of commercial law in the world. Every club, every society and association, makes its own laws, which are sufficiently sanctioned to meet with respect and obedience, quite as uniformly as the laws of the land. And yet the prevailing impression seems to be that only the State can make laws having any binding effect – that without such State rules and regulations everything would be topsy-turvy. Mine-owners and miners would conspire to blow up the mines; shipowners would scuttle their ships, drown their crews, get up a glorious reputation for going to the bottom, and pay double insurance; cabmen would charge at least a guinea a mile; bankers would smother the country with worthless paper; railway companies would smash up passengers and goods, charge prohibitive fares, and ruin their shareholders; theatrical managers would drive all the respectable and monied classes away from the theatres by exhibitions of bad taste; publicans would sit up all night in order to sell a pint of ale; pawnbrokers would charge 60 per cent. a month, and receive stolen goods with alacrity; landlords would keep their farms unlet and uncultivated; farmers would pay more in rent than they could recoup in profit; and everybody would work to death without taking a holiday; in fine, society is accredited with suicidial mania and must be kept in a straight-waistcoat.

The first question asked is, "What! would you allow a thoughtless collier to light his pipe in the workings?" or, "Would you let the railway companies charge what they like?" or, "Would you have all the land thrown out of cultivation?" or, "Would you have all the crops devoured by vermin?" or something equally irrelevant. Now the answer to all these and similar questions is, that it is not the expediency or appropriateness of this or that regulation with which individualism concerns itself. It may be an excellent provision that passenger trains should not run at more than sixty miles an hour, or it may not; if it is, let the companies make such a rule, or let the public refrain from travelling by lines which have no such rule; but let not Parliament interfere in the matter. Again, as to naked lights in a coal pit, is it really believed that colliers are so absurdly reckless of their own lives as to imperil them for the sake of a whiff of tobacco? And even granting that there are a few such dangerous lunatics in the pits, as out of them, is the mine-owner so anxious himself for a meeting with his creditors as to allow such doings if they can possibly be prevented? The plain fact is apart from theory, that before the passing of any Acts relating to mines, the most stringent regulations were in force concerning the use of lights and lamps in the workings – rules not so much imposed by the masters, as agreed to alike by owners, managers, and men, for the common safety. It is the ability to make such rules, to obey them, and to enforce them, which makes the Anglo-Saxon race what it is, a colonising people, a people fit for self-government. And it is the weakening and supplanting of these contractual rules in all departments of activity by rules emanating from a central legislature, which will some day, if persisted in, reduce the Englishman to the level of his continental neighbours. It is not from any horror of law and order, of method and regulation in all things, that individualism is opposed to State interference; on the contrary, it is rather the reverse; it is because it attaches so high a value to these things, and because it fears to see the habits of self-rule crushed out by the enervating effects of grandmotherly government.

In one respect, there is no comparison at all between the contractual regulations made by those chiefly interested, and the State regulations made, so to speak, by outsiders; and that is, in point of economy, the true balance of advantage. It is doubtless more or less dangerous to go into a pit at all; but a law to prohibit coal-mining would be to sacrifice too much for the sake of safety. Again, a safety lamp costs more than a naked candle; but to tolerate the candle would be to sacrifice too little for the sake of safety. There is always a happy medium, and the legislature is not likely to find it. Take shipping – sea-worthiness is a matter of degree; if absolute unquestionable sea-worthiness is insisted upon, the lower-class seaman is ruined; if the cranky craft is allowed, foul deeds for the sake of insurance are rendered possible. Where the line should be drawn is a nice question, and must be settled between the shipowner and the sailor; it certainly cannot be settled by the State without the certainty of a false economy. "To the sea-faring population," writes Mr. Crofts, "the character of each ship and ship's captain are as well known as the performances of every race-horse to the betting fraternity. If a sailor takes employment on a rotten and overladen ship, with a drunken skipper, to whom astronomical reckonings are as Greek, it is in most cases, not because he does not know any better, but because he cannot do any better. Able-bodied seamen with good recommendations and habits naturally monopolise the forecastles of the best ships, where bad characters and Lascars are at a discount. If these latter want to go to sea, their evil reputation does not permit of their being over-fastidious in the choice of accommodation and masters; and the question for them is frequently one of going afloat with a chance of living, or staying ashore with a certainty of starving."

We have no desire to impugn the motives of those honest but misguided philanthropists, who, filled with sympathy for suffering humanity, struggle to mitigate the laws of nature by Act of Parliament. It is not with these men we need quarrel; they are possibly intelligent men of little knowledge, and open to conviction when the truth is stated to them simply; but it is their subtler allies that are to be feared – imposters who trade on the nobler instincts of their fellow-workers, for the sake of place, popularity or pelf. Such men are beneath conviction; frequently they know the futility of their own proposals, but it suits them to pose as philanthropists. Let us name no names, but there be well-known legislators who speak with unction of the rights and wrongs of labour, and who grind down their own work-people with an iron heel. There is such a thing as Brummagem philanthropy; these are the imposters who form the extreme sect of what Mr. Gladstone once called "political quacks."

But the lovers of civil liberty are not without questionable allies, men who are open to the charge of protesting against State interference with the industry in which they are themselves interested, lest such interference should favour their weaker fellow-workers. When we see men whose whole political lives have been spent in plotting against the liberties of the people, suddenly cry out for liberty, more liberty, as soon as their own pockets are threatened, we may know how far to trust such men, and what their alliance is worth. Poor Jack must not be allowed to drink rum, it is bad for him physically and morally, but he may drown, for am I not a shipowner? The wretched miner must be wrapped up in cotton-wool and work no more than four hours a day, but as for the peasant he may rot on my threshold, for am I not a landlord? Let the poverty-stricken be defended against the rapacity of the merciless pawnbroker; but it is preposterous to tolerate the claim of the helpless widow and children whom a railway accident has left destitute, for be it known that I am a railway king. One can hardly blame those demagogues who have already stigmatised the Liberty League as an unholy alliance; sympathy with suffering and hatred of selfishness may have quickened the zeal of these scribblers for quixotic legislation, while their knowledge of political philosophy is too defective to permit of their seeing its futility.

It is unfortunately too true that a consistent individualist must combine knowledge of principles and the courage of his opinions with a certain surgeon-like imperturbability in the presence of the inevitable; he must know how to withhold the iced drink from the parched fever patient; he must be prepared to be accused of selfishness and greed, of hardness of heart and indifference to the sufferings of others, and of hypocrisy in appealing to the lofty principles of liberty for the sinister purpose of bolstering up unjust privileges and monopolies. These charges must be met and disproved, not only in general but in detail.

Next in importance to the formation of the Liberty League comes the late Mr. Fawcett's pamphlet on State-socialism. After passing in view some of the more prominent pieces of proposed legislation of a semi-socialistic character, which are even now within the range of practical politics, judged by the rate at which we have been travelling of late in this direction, Mr. Fawcett concludes his pamphlet in these remarkable words: "In endeavouring to explain some of the consequences which their adoption would involve, we should greatly regret to do any injustice to the motives of those by whom they are advocated. Mischievous as we believe many of these schemes would prove to be, the great majority of those by whom they are advocated are undoubtedly prompted by no other desire than to promote social, moral, and material advancement. The conclusion above all others which we desire to enforce is, that any scheme, however well-intentioned it may be, will indefinitely increase every evil it seeks to alleviate, if it lessens individual responsibility by encouraging the people to rely less upon themselves and more upon the State."

On the whole, we may safely prescribe the late Mr. Fawcett's last word as the best possible antidote to the teachings of the Government for which he was responsible. Mr. Fawcett certainly had the courage of his opinions, for a more merciless critique on the legislation of the last few years could not easily be indited. Perhaps the writer trusted that his colleagues were too busy or too lazy to read his tract, or too "practical" to comprehend it. Or, possibly, he pinned his faith to one little sop in the text, which seems to have been an afterthought, as it has no particular connection with the argument. In order thoroughly to understand the force of this passage it will be necessary to admit that it is a baser action to rob a man of his purse than to abstract a portion of its contents and restore the remainder. Having admitted this, we are prepared with equal readiness to agree "that it has been shown by the Irish Land Act of 1881, and by the Tenants' Compensation Bill for England and Scotland, which is now (1883) before Parliament, that it is possible to confer these advantages (compensation for improvements, &c.) on the cultivators, without bringing into operation *all* the evils which, as we believe, would result from nationalisation." This may be true without much praise being due to the two measures in question. However, if this meagre tribute to the wisdom of these two great socialistic measures is satisfactory to Mr. Gladstone and his radical entourage, it is not for us to complain.

Mr. Thorold Rogers, in his address before the Social Science Congress in 1883, on "Some Aspects of *Laissez-faire* and Control," treated the question historically. But, as he will himself admit, the trust-worthiness of the results of a study of tendencies to a very great extent depends on the length of time during which those tendencies can be shown to have been in operation. Mr. Rogers' conclusion that the general consensus is distinctly favourable to increased State-interference is probably correct for the present time, and it coincides with what has already been said about the recent rapid advance of State-socialism; but to infer from proof of such present tendency that increased Government action is a concomitant of civilisation would, or would not, be justifiable according as the tendency can be shown to be a persistent one, or at least an increasing one throughout the whole range of history. Any shorter period of observation is apt to be delusive; the present prevalence of socialistic opinions in this and other countries can no more be pointed to as part of a universal development, than could the equally remarkable advance of the extreme doctrine of "let-be" thirty or forty years ago. Almost as philosophically might the marked revival of that doctrine during a recent period in England be cited in support of the doctrine of individualism. Now, if we take English constitutional history as the subject of our examination, we shall find that so far from being on the increase, State-interference with individual liberty has been a constantly diminishing quantity. We have but to cast our eyes down the statutes of the Plantagenet period to discover in what numberless private concerns the State intruded, with which no modern Government would dream of meddling. The price of corn, the wages of labourers, the importation of coin, the manufacture of beer, the rate of interest on loans, attendance at divine service, and a thousand other matters were carefully supervised by the State. A statute of Henry VIII. goes so far as to forbid the use of machinery in the manufacture of broad-cloth, a law which drove a good deal of the woollen trade to Holland, where the "divers devilish contrivances" were under no ban. Why, there are actually early English laws setting forth with what amount of energy and thoroughness the ploughman shall plough each furrow. Further illustrations are unnecessary, for it will be admitted by any candid reader of history, that, on the whole, the endency to State-interference diminishes with the evolution of societies. The slight reaction observable in our own day seems to be satisfactorily explained in the passage already quoted from Mr. Pleydell Bouverie's address at the meeting of the Liberty and Property Defence League, and need not be further dwelt on. The evil will disappear only when the newly enfranchised classes perceive, not only that they will themselves suffer from restrictions on free action, but that they will be the first and the worst sufferers. When Mr. Rogers descends to the particular instances of what may be called modern socialistic legislation, he seems to be anxious and able to find some special justification for each in its turn. Mr. Rogers is quite incapable of prostituting science to the defence of party, and yet anyone might be forgiven for thinking otherwise to whom Mr. Rogers' writings were previously unknown. The Factory Acts are good, he says, because they result in the restraint of waste. It might easily be shown that the economy of labour has been indefinitely postponed by the operation of the Factory Acts. "The doctrine of *laissez-faire* is absolute in the case of contracts for the use of labour, *except in cases where –* " and then comes a string of exceptions apparently cast in general language for the purpose of justifying the Acts just named, the Truck Acts, the Act of 1883 for prohibiting the payment of wages in public-houses, and other similar interferences with individual freedom.

We are not going to defend the tally-shop, though many a poor wife has cursed the day since when her husband's wages, instead of being paid in groceries and household stores, were paid in cash to be spent in drink. What is of more importance to note is, that where workmen as a class were thrifty and steady, as in the mining districts of Durham and Northumberland, the truck system died a natural death without any need for State intervention. Similarly, the fishermen in several of the east coast ports have put a stop to the system of paying wages in the public-house in a very simple manner; by steadily refusing to order liquor, or even to drink it at the expense of another, they have made it unprofitable to the publican to give the use of his premises for the purpose. Men who have not the strength of mind to act thus will not be made more self-reliant or more fit to wrestle with the many temptations of the world by being put into leading-strings and kept out of sight of beer. With respect to the free choice of a calling, Mr. Rogers agrees "that the aggregate of industry sorts itself best in the interests of all when the process is left to perfectly free action." But this excellent generalisation goes too far for him; it condemns much recent legislation; consequently a qualifying clause must be introduced to justify it, so that the rule now reads, "the aggregate of industry sorts itself best in the interests of all when, *certain obvious conditions being satisfied and precautions taken*, the process is left to perfectly free action." One of these precautions seems to be the State-examination of everybody in order that "adequate evidence should be given of professional competence." "The impulse" says Mr. Rogers, "is towards the creation of new professions with special tests of proficiency; this is the case with the art of the dispensing druggist, of the surveyor, of the elementary schoolmaster," and he might have added, of the skipper and second hand of fishing-boats. No doubt some ingenious philosophical excuse will be found even for the Fishing Boats Act before long. The enforcement of professional responsibility by law is a totally distinct question, and rests on the answer given to a deeper question than that concerning the demarkation of State functions. When we come to the railways, Mr. Rogers seems to have some difficulty in finding any sound or even specious reason for making them an exception to the general rule. "The case of these *adventurers* is most peculiar," he says. "The directors and shareholders of the existing companies vote in Parliament against rival lines without pretending to consider the public good."

We believe the brewers as a class do not support local option bills; it is hinted that the bishops are somewhat biassed in favour of the established church; and landowners are not always agitating for a heavy land-tax; but the charge against the railway directors appears to be, not so much that they consider the interests of their own class first, after the manner of others, but that they have not the decency to *pretend* to put the interests of plasterers, tanners, physicans, &c., &c., before their own. So the railways "and are to be brought under increased State-control, the Act of last session [1883] (the so-called Cheap Trains Act) is only an instalment in the direction of this control." The answer to this same Act is the formation of a Railway Shareholders' Defence Association, just as the Vigilance Association of San Francisco was the natural reply to the outbreak of lawlessness and immorality in that rising colony. Reasons are also forthcoming for the violation of the "let-be" principle in the matter of agricultural holdings, of homes for the poor, of places of entertainment and refreshment, of education, and of sanitary arrangements. With respect to education, Mr. Rogers is candid enough and paradoxical enough to admit that "it is of no material or economical benefit to the recipient;" and since we force it upon others solely for our own benefit, at some loss and inconvenience to themselves, we have no right to charge them anything for it. Many people will agree that *if* education is to be compulsory, it should certainly be free, but they will underline the word "if."

On the whole, Mr. Rogers' address is worth careful study, and though he seems to favour the readjustment of organic evils by rule-of-thumb, on the Chinese-lady's-shoe principle, rather than trust to natural selection, still his special reasons for special suspensions of the laws of nature are invariably ingenious and suggestive, and the address itself is evidence of the reviving interest taken in the question with which it deals. When, therefore, Mr. Rogers concludes by saying, "It is scarcely likely that the new Liberty and Property Defence League will be able *for some time* to counteract this tendency," we are justified in hoping that when that time arrives Mr. Rogers will be found in the ranks of the anti-socialists.

But perhaps the strongest evidence of this reviving interest is to be found in the apologetic tone adopted in Lord Salisbury's article on Labourers' and Artisans' Dwellings in the *National Review* for November, 1883. "Some persons," he writes, "may be disposed to enquire at the outset whether it is right that Parliament should interfere at all. I see a statement in the newspapers that the Liberty and Property Defence League are preparing to denounce any such interference as unsound in principle. I have the greatest respect for the League. They preach a wholesome doctrine, and necessary for these times. But if this account of their views is a true one, I think they have in this instance gone further than sound reasoning and the *precedents of our legislation* will justify. At present no proposal has been made, as far as I know, to give assistance for this purpose except by way of loan, and surely it cannot be maintained that loans for public objects are against the *practice* of this country, because their first effect may be to promote the interest of individuals. Without entering upon disputable ground by quoting Ireland and the West Indies, it is sufficient to recall the advances made by various governments, but especially by that of Sir Robert Peel, for the extension of drainage in this country. A very large sum was advanced to landlords at an interest which secured the State from loss, but lower than their own credit would have obtained. It was duly paid after having done its work. That work was in the first instance to increase the rental of the land, and, in the second, undoubtedly it served the useful purpose of giving employment under the agricultural depression caused by the repeal of the Corn Laws, and of increasing the general production of the country. In the case before us also the loan would be justified by imperious considerations of public policy, even if all thoughts of humanity were cast aside. These overcrowded centres of population are also centres of disease, and successive discoveries of biologists tell us more and more clearly that there is in this matter an indissoluble partnership among all human beings breathing in the same vicinity. If the causes of disease were inanimate, no one would hesitate about employing advances of public money to render them innocuous. Why should the expenditure become illegitimate because these causes happen to be human beings? But this unhappy population has a special claim on any assistance that Parliament can give. The evil has in a great measure been created by Parliament itself. If London had been allowed to go on as it was half a century ago many benefits of vast importance would have been lost, but the intense competition for house-room would not exist and the reformation of "rookeries" would have been a much less arduous task. But improvements on a vast scale have been made, and those improvements in too many cases have only meant packing the people tighter. New streets, railways, viaducts, law courts and other public buildings, made compulsory under the authority of Parliament, have swept away the dwellings of thousands of the poor, and in that proportion have made the competition more intense for those that remain. Many tenements have let for a high price, which, if artificial compression had not been used, would have found no tenant. Under these circumstance it is no violation, even of the most scrupulous principles, to ask parliament to give what relief it can. *Laisse-faire* is an admirable doctrine, but it must be applied upon both sides."

Whether loans for public objects are, or are not, against the *practice* of this country is hardly relevant when we are discussing the wisdom of the plan. This country, like most other countries, is occasionally guilty of foolish practices, and what we want to know is, not what the State has been in the habit of doing in the past, but what it ought to do in the future. As to the advances made under Sir Robert Peel to landlords for drainage purposes at a lower rate of interest than their own credit would have obtained, the question is, was this effected without loss to the country? That the State was duly repaid with interest in full may be quite true, and yet the country may have lost heavily by the transaction. The interest on State loans has to be paid for out of taxation; and the question is, would the money intercepted by the State for these purposes have found its way into more remunerative channels than the three per cents. or not? And in any case, would the wealth so intercepted have fructified at a greater rate in the hands of the people than on the fields of the landlords? There is at least this to be said, the capital which is invested by the private enterprise of the people does, as a fact, on the average realise over three per cent. per annum, whereas the investment on drainage was after all nothing less than a speculation which was justified only by success. It might have been a colossal failure. Perhaps the worst that can be said of this speculation is, that its good luck has elevated it into a very dangerous precedent. The amount of risk involved in it was accurately measured by the interest which the landlords would have had to pay if they had borrowed the money on their own credit. "If," said the late Mr. Fawcett, "the State makes loans in cases where they cannot be obtained from ordinary commercial sources, it is clear, that in the judgment of those best qualified to form an opinion, the State is running a risk of loss." As to the useful purposes of giving employment, could a more dangerous doctrine be formulated?

Lord Salisbury's chief argument for State-interference in this direction is based on a complete misapprehension of the position of the "let-be" school. It amounts in effect to this. These London slums are *foci* of pestilence; if similar dangers were due solely to inanimate causes, you would not hesitate to spend the public money in their prompt removal. Why, then, should you refrain from doing so merely lest one wretched class of the community should be accidently benefited at the expense of the remainder? Why, indeed? But that is not the reason for objecting to the expenditure. Lord Salisbury is mistaken when he says "that no one would hesitate if the causes of disease were inanimate." They would and do hesitate, and more than hesitate, they strongly protest. But their reason is the most profound distrust in the efficiency of State machinery for these and all similar purposes – absolute disbelief in the power of the State to effect the desired object. There is no doubt whatever that Parliament has already done much in the way of aggravating the evil, and in making "improvements which in too many cases have only meant packing the people tighter." Therefore, although it may be "no violation of the most scrupulous principles to ask Parliament to give what relief it can," it is nevertheless permissible to doubt if Parliament can give any, and to protest against throwing good money after bad. The problem to be solved is, how to build and fit out a £75 tenement for £30 or £40; and we have only to look deep enough into all the schemes propounded with a view to its solution, to find that the key to every one of them is plunder more or less disguised. The promoters of the urban scheme would continue to compel the ratepayers to buy land at a guinea a foot, and to sell it to the philanthropists for five shillings. The friends of the suburban scheme have more respect for the pockets of the ratepayers; they would organise "a system of cheap trains," in other words, they would compel the railway companies to carry certain classes of passengers at a dead loss. Whether this is done after the manner of Dick Turpin, or on the model of the so-called Cheap Trains Act matters little. Whether shareholders are to be robbed in the old-fashioned style, or tricked out of their rights by an obscure Act of Parliament, is a question for those whose policy is spoliation with decency. The passenger duty had been condemned by all parties on grounds of justice and expediency, and the companies had been given distinctly to understand that the tax would be abolished as soon as the state of the revenue justified the sacrifice. On the faith of this understanding the companies refrained from further agitation in the matter, until they are informed that they are at last to receive part of their admitted rights, *on condition* of their carrying a certain class of persons over their lines at an unremunerative rate. There may be other schemes already before the public, and no doubt several others will crop up in response to the recently stimulated demand, but of this we may rest assured, that plunder underlies them all. We are of opinion that if anything was wanted to demonstrate the utter hopelessness of any attempt to improve the dwellings of the poor by State help, that want has been met by Lord Salisbury's own very able analysis of the position. The difficulty to be overcome is summed up in these words, "Until their wages rise they cannot pay for the bare cost of decent lodging such as existing agencies can offer."

The ablest contribution to the science of politics which has appeared since the publication of Mill's "Liberty," and Spencer's "Overlegislation," is unquestionably Lord Pembroke's article on "Liberty and Socialism" in the *National Review* for May, 1883.

The writer begins with an analysis of the causes which have led to the rapid decline in popular favour of the doctrine of *laissez-faire* during the last two or three decades. "A few years ago the doctrine of non-interference seemed to be paramount in English politics, and any one who ventured to prophesy that there would be a reversal of public opinion before the end of the century was ridiculed as a crocheteer and an alarmist." And yet only recently the *Times* is found maintaining that "the doctrine of *laissez-faire* is as dead as the worship of Osiris." "Amongst other things that helped to bring about the reaction," says Lord Pembroke, "was the fact that it had been an era of continual political reform. Laws and institutions that the country had outgrown, had to be removed; restrictions that our wiser knowledge had shown us the folly of, had to be swept away. One would hardly have supposed that this process could have been favourable to a belief in the efficacy of interference. But, however strange and unreasonable, it is undoubtedly true, that in many minds this purely liberative and destructive course of legislation has given rise to the notion that perpetual meddling by Act of Parliament is necessary to prevent stagnation – that unless our legislators keep stirring things up progress will stop; that what is called on platforms "beneficial legislation" is a kind of stimulating manure indispensable to the national growth. To those who hold this profoundly foolish, but by no means uncommon view, the very name *laissez-faire* implies dereliction of duty, and thereby stands condemned." Who cannot bear testimony to this strange confusion of ideas? Because repealing or undoing Acts of Parliament are themselves called legislation, they are frequently adduced as proofs of the efficacy of legislation. Should the question be asked at a public meeting, "What good has ever come of legislation yet?" someone is sure to reply, "Look at the repeal of the corn laws." It is more than probable that the expression *laissez-faire* is still commonly understood in its oldest sense to mean, Let things alone, let them drift, let that which is filthy be filthy still. There is no doubt that this is the sense in which it was used by the French Minister of State who first gave the phrase political currency. And this may be another cause of its present unpopularity. Another vulgar notion, which is thoroughly disposed of in Mr. Herbert Spencer's "Overlegislation," is the erroneous one that if the maxim is carried out the duties of the State will necessarily be reduced to nil, and there will be no further use for a legislature. To those who are acquainted with the chaotic state of the English law and its ponderous procedure, this mistaken notion will not require disproof. The reform, completion, and codification of the law will supply material for many an abler Parliament than any we have yet sent to Westminster.

Lord Pembroke makes search for a simple principle which shall "limit the rights of society against the individual, and of the individual against society – a principle which if it cannot, owing to the limitation of human knowledge, completely solve all difficulties, will at least prove a true guide in all cases in which we can see correctly how to apply it." The search is fruitless, and the discovery is pronounced impossible. "I can no more imagine a principle that would tell us in every case the limits of individual and State rights, than one that would tell us in every case whether the dictates of egoism or altruism are to be obeyed." The principle attributed to the school of Spencer and Von Humboldt, viz., "absolute freedom for each, limited only by the like freedom for others," is examined and discarded as only "an undue straining of language." "If by any effort of ingenuity it be stretched wide enough to be made the true rule in all known stages of human progress, it is evident that its width of interpretation would make it quite worthless as a practical guide to us. If, on the other hand, it is admitted that it could not apply as a wise practical rule to all these phases, or even to any one of them that has yet been known – and it is only claimed that it is an ideal principle towards which progress is constantly tending, and which may become of universal application when men are very different from what they are now – its equal uselessness to us in the present day as a practical guide or test is no less plain." And, as a test of its value as a practical guide, the writer asks those who hold it to consider how they propose to apply it to the law of marriage. "Are they prepared to abrogate this greatest of all interferences with freedom of contract, and do they hold that such a reform would bring a preponderance of benefit in our present state of civilisation? If, on the other hand, they declare that the principle of absolute freedom for each, limited only by the like freedom of all, does not condemn such a law, I am puzzled to guess what form of State regulation it is capable of defending us against. We must not loosen or tighten its interpretation to suit our convenience." The writer reverts to this awkward question of marriage; "I think," he says, "we have a right to ask those who regard this as an infallible practical rule whether they are prepared to adhere to it in this instance? If they answer in the affirmative, as Von Humboldt did, most people will have a strong opinion about the soundness and wisdom of the principle." Now, without in the least disputing Lord Pembroke's right to ask this crucial question, the extreme individualist may with equal right decline to answer it. Clearly he must either admit that the marriage law is an exception, which upsets the trustworthiness of his principle, or else he must express the contrary view; in which case there can be no doubt that "most people will have a strong opinion," not only about the soundness of his principle, but also about the desirableness of his acquaintance. And, unless he is prepared to pose as a martyr to his political doctrines, he had better keep his mouth shut. His interrogator may, from that, possibly infer his inner admission, but it is surely cruel to demand an answer to such a question in the market-place. Perhaps Lord Pembroke's own opinion upon this point would be interesting, and since he will admit that we "have a right to demand it," he will doubtless favour us with it on the occasion of his promised return to this subject.

We have already explained that we do not see the necessity of proclaiming ourselves absolutists in the matter of State functions, any more than in the matter of State structure, so that we do not feel called upon to face the ordeal prepared for us; but when Lord Pembroke confidently asks, "Yet will anyone contend that the abolition of prescribed cab fares would be an improvement?" we may venture to point out, not only that the suggestion has been seriously made, but that it has actually been carried out in practice in the city of Liverpool, and succeeded remarkably well. We cannot follow the writer through his extremely interesting and profound examination of the application to the concrete of Mr. Spencer's division of State-action into negatively-regulative and positively-regulative; but we are quite ready to admit that until this part of the essay has been carefully considered and fairly answered, individualists of the absolutist school, of whom Mr. Auberon Herbert is the able, albeit somewhat Quixotic, chief in this country, must rest content to sit in the cool shades of speculative philosophy, and leave the field of practical politics to the gifted exponent of the principles of the Liberty League.

"Experience and observation will enable us to frame rules and principles that will become wider and more general with the advance of political science; and if, in this science, the first principles should be the last things to be discovered, we should remember that it will prove no exception to the general rule." This is the outcome of Lord Pembroke's study; and it is in complete harmony with the teachings of inductive philosophy. There can be little doubt that the marked revival within recent times of the "let-be" doctrine is in great part due to this and other publications of the League. And it is noteworthy that the discussion has emerged from the cloisters and reappeared on the platform. Mr. Goschen is known rather as a shrewd and observant statesman than as a student of abstract science; and it is gratifying to find him addressing an Edinburgh audience on such a topic as *laissez-faire* and Government interference. Let us hope that the wise words of warning uttered in Edinburgh will pass far beyond the walls of the Philosophical Institution, and have weight with thousands to whom the vaticinations of a statesman are both more accessible and more convincing than the dispassionate arguments of a philosopher. "The dangers in the road of social reconstruction under Government control were so grave that they could scarcely be exaggerated; dangers arising not only from the serious chance of inefficiency in the methods chosen, but from the transfer of responsibilities by the establishment of national law in the place of individual duty; from the withdrawal of confidence in the qualities of men in order to bestow it on the merits of administrations; from the growing tendency to invoke the aid of the State, and the declining belief in individual power." Mr. Goschen appears to derive some comfort from the reflection that, *pari passu* with an increased demand for State interference, goes an increased tendency towards decentralisation. "The transfer of work in the way of interference from the central body to local authorities diminishes the extension of central power and patronage, which is a most undesirable accompaniment of increased Government action; it reduces the number of the army of men whom the central authority are compelled to employ; it eases the work of the Government; it imposes public functions on different classes of citizens; it interests an additional stratum of society in public business; and lastly, it provides to some extent a safety valve against possible tyranny on the part of an all-powerful class. *If* the extended demand for Government interference is to be progressively satisfied, it is earnestly to be hoped that we may proceed *pari passu* on the lines of decentralisation." We fail to see that decentralisation can be an antidote to democratic despotism. What is the use of reducing the number of central officials if ten times the number is to be maintained by the local authorities? Why ease the work of a Government which will only make use of its increased opportunities to devise new mischief, simply in order that local bodies may help to do it? Why impose public functions on new strata of society, when those functions are abnormal and despotic? If we are to have a despot, myriad-headed or otherwise, the more central, cumbrous, and unwieldy the machinery through which it has to obtain its ends, the better for its victims. The tyranny of the Sultan is as nothing to the tyranny of the pashas. The larger the area from which the central body is drawn, the greater the number of conflicting interests which it is necessary to reconcile before the desired policy can be carried out, and the better the chance of its being emasculated during the process. Local despotism is the worst despotism. Decentralisation cannot go further than the family; and what kind of local government is more loathsome than the unchecked rule of a brutal paterfamilias? Local option, in regard to liquor and to other matters, in part and parcel of a system of decentralisation which, for the trampling under foot of private liberty, and the crushing out of individuality, has no equal among modern forms of government. When the normal functions of the central legislature, and of provincial legislatures down to the municipality, have been defined and approximately adapted to the age, then, and then only, is decentralisation compatible with civil liberty.

Let us conclude by answering the question with which Mr. Gladstone succeeded in puzzling some Derby working-men on the occasion of their presenting him with a china service. "How," he asked, "is the time of the House of Commons to be economised?" Our answer is simple: "Let the House of Commons mind its own business – thoroughly and exclusively."

EMPIRICISM IN POLITICS
Thomas Mackay

> The Conservative Party has always leaned, perhaps some-
> what unduly leaned, to the use of the State, so far as it
> could properly be used, for improving the physical, moral,
> and intellectual condition of our people, and I hope that
> mission the Conservative Party will never renounce.

THE historical accuracy of this statement, made by Lord
Salisbury on a recent occasion, will not be disputed. With
equal justice the same declaration could be made by the other
political Party. Hitherto no Party has attempted to remove
the ambiguity which lurks in the words "proper use." The
sentiment above quoted presents a very fair description of
the empiricism which has always characterized our political
conduct. A "proper use" has been given concrete definition
by the exigency of Party politics, when some sectional interest
has to be conciliated; or, it is interpreted so as to cover
those advantages which the majority for the time being is not
ashamed to take for itself. There is no pretence that our
political conduct is guided by scientific principle. Our system
is based frankly on a representation of interests, not on a
representation of wisdom. Hitherto, interests have been
somewhat evenly balanced and revolutionary changes have
been impossible. Such growth as has taken place, has, for
the most part, been the result not of legislation but of natural
social causes. The ascendency of the masses has now disar-
ranged the balance of power, and their view of what is
"proper" in the use of the State seems likely to be productive
of startling changes.

The Socialist theory of life, which has received formal recognition at the Trades Union Congress, is not a rejection of
Lord Salisbury's maxim, but rather a driving to its logical
conclusion the theory and practice of government which,
without much practical inconvenience, has hitherto prevailed
in our national councils. The paternalism of the Conservative

Party (to use a now historical term) is a limited paternalism choosing its objects of patronage, partly from electioneering motives, and partly from a genuine belief that the mechanism of society can be improved by the frequent intervention of the State. The paternalism of the Socialists, like Aaron's rod, has consumed all other paternalisms. Under the impulse of the new democracy, which puts its own interpretation on the word proper, the free development of society, which has hitherto been but little hindered by our political system, is being checked on every side. The State is now to administer, not merely to protect our daily life.

It is not surprising that this new development of a time-honoured practice should at once throw us back on an examination of first principles. The Socialist interpretation of this world-old theory of life, if it has done nothing else, has attracted attention to a new theory of life and of society which has been worked out by a great scientific thinker, apart from the stress and prejudice of practical politics. The present generation is confronted for the first time with a new social creed, which rests on the belief that the beneficent adaptations of civilized life have been created, and can be altered for the better, by the free intercourse and experience of the units which compose society, and by that means only; that morality, a sense of justice, a love of one's neighbour, and all the higher instincts of mankind are the natural outcome of such measure of freedom as the race has enjoyed; that the baser motives of the lower stages of development can only be controlled by the salutary rules of social discipline apprehended, approved, and voluntarily accepted by the individual will. The assumption that hatred and warfare is the natural relation between individual men is manifestly untrue. The desire for social organization is a human motive at once primitive and passionate, but the law of harmonious organization can only be discovered; when discovered, can only be adopted; and, when adopted, can only be continuously upheld and extended by the experience of human beings moving freely in their social environment. Attempts to improve the delicate mechanism of the harmonious progression inherent in a free society, by the forceful action of the State, must result in reaction and hinder the growth of true social instincts. This antithesis between Society and the State, of which the foregoing is a very imperfect expression, involves, I venture to assert, a new theory for the guidance of political conduct. It is presented, for the first time in its completeness, by the life-long labour of Mr. Spencer.

The fact that this doctrine has at present little or no influence within the walls of Parliament, or with the majorities who send representatives there, is not matter for wonder. Practical politics are not governed by theory. Theory only influences men's minds when it offers an explanation of an experienced inconvenience. The old Radical Party abolished aristocratic paternalism, and as a result the country entered on a long spell of prosperity. It is impossible to create privilege for all, and the new Radical Party now vies with the Conservative Party in exercising paternalism over those sections which, for some reason or another, seem most urgently to require it. We have hardly yet begun to realize the inconvenience of this course. Until that day arrives, the voice of the philosopher is as of one crying in the wilderness. Here it might be well to guard against misconception by the admission that, in a sense, political action must be empirical: in the sense, namely, that it must be tentative and opportunist towards a goal which is or should be more or less definitely and scientifically conceived. Whether the ideal of Karl Marx or of Mr. Spencer is our aim, it is obvious that violent change, in its pursuit, is not practicable. Politics have to do with the intermediate steps by which, in our advance towards an ideal, we endeavour to extricate ourselves from the result of errors in the past, or press forward on what we believe to be the path of progress. On such intermediate steps there is room for men who hold the same ideal to differ. Thus some, who are convinced Socialists, have disapproved of attempts to use the Poor Law as a means of equalizing the fortune of the rich and the poor. Or, again, convinced Free Traders have questioned the wisdom of commercial treaties and "most favoured nation" clauses. Such differences, however, are of minor importance, and need not destroy the definite outlines of our conception of the law of progress.

Further, it will be argued, that it is the business of the Statesman to compromise between two extreme opinions, and it may be admitted that compromise, which in theoretical opinion is often the slovenly device of an indolent intellect, must in action be at times gratefully accepted, provided always that compromise is not merely another word for surrender.

In the present controversy do circumstances make compromise possible? Those who talk of compromise seem not to realize that the knell of the period of compromise has sounded. The era of Constitutional Government, where power was so nicely balanced that the authority of Government was too weak to overbear the living and growing organism of natural society, is drawing to a close. We are falling under the rule of a tyranny more absolute and unrelenting than anything the world has ever seen. The hopes and delusions of the Socialist Party will not be satisfied by such jettisons of ransom as our Statesmen all appear willing to make. It will point triumphantly to the concessions already made, to the belief which statesmen profess in the healing power of legislation, and will take no denial, and as an argument *ad homines* this position is unassailable.

It is no longer a question of compromise, but of absolute surrender. The wolves of socialism will not be bought off with the trumpery concessions with which modern statecraft tries to appease them. The principle of government which Mr. Cleveland has euphemistically called paternalism means simply the Party in power jobbing the resources of the country to feed its own pack of wolves. The Socialist Party, perfectly fairly from its own point of view, hunts all political parties with contemptuous impartiality. By tentative and experimental steps we are drifting into socialism, an intolerable condition from which some future generation will set itself free by violence and revolution. To this approaching ruin, there appears to be but one possible barrier, a disillusionment of men's minds in the possibility of advancing progress by the coercive violence of legislation, and a juster appreciation of the truth that the forces which make for civilization and justice are inherent in a free society, and are the direct antithesis of the empirical regimentation of an artificial state.

In these days, when it is the business of a Statesman to follow and not to lead, the difficulty of popularizing a scientific view on a public platform is not lightly to be overcome. Still the logic of time and of events may shortly prove more convincing than many treatises of philosophy. A drowning society may catch at what seems to it a straw, and find it an instrument of salvation. Let us hope that the Party of rescue will not arrive too late.

I have maintained that at present practical politics are not scientific. In a remarkable volume of essays[1] by the late Sir Louis Mallet, it is argued that the only scientific political Party which has ever attained prominence in this country was created and led by his friend and teacher, Mr. Cobden. Sir Louis Mallet explains that it is a popular misconception to suppose that Cobden confined his advocacy of Free Trade to matters of international commerce. Rightly understood, the creed of Richard Cobden applied to the whole economic organization of society, and for this reason Sir L. Mallet calls his volume *Free Exchange*, a title which accurately represents the teaching of the great Statesman whose memory he sets himself to vindicate. What truth there may be in this attempt to make Mr. Cobden the anticipator, as it were, of the political philosophy of Mr. Spencer, it is not necessary to determine. Cobden was a practical man and did not trouble the constituencies with more philosophy than was essential to his argument; but Sir Louis Mallet's testimony is conclusive that his views were in advance of his time. It is the fashion now to say that the opinions of Cobden and his school are dead and buried. There is something suspect in this parrot-like vociferation that suggests mere servile adulation of the powers that be, and a growing uneasy conviction that time will vindicate the memory of Cobden as the only great practical Statesman which the new industrial era has yet produced. Whether his philosophy be right or wrong, it is every day becoming more apparent that the only barrier against the advance of Socialism will be found in a rehabilitation, on a larger scale, of the principles which he succeeded in persuading his countrymen to apply to the limited sphere of international trade.

It is an error to represent that the principles which underlie the great work of Cobden have ever had a wide or paramount influence in our political action. The application of them has been confined to the sphere of international trade. It is therefore an absurd misrepresentation to attribute all existing shortcomings in our social system to the doctrines of the so-

---

[1] *Free Exchange*, by the late Right Hon. Sir Louis Mallet. Kegan Paul and Co., 1891.

called Manchester School. It is worth while to enquire what has brought about the alleged unpopularity of these opinions. The causes are simple and appear to be on the surface. The time was not ripe. Cobden's theory, whatever his esoteric doctrines may have been, was, with his supporters at any rate, rather a happy inspiration than a fully developed system of politics. Leaders arose within the Liberal Party, who, while ready to join in attacks on a class to which they did not themselves belong (a fault which justly or unjustly has been attributed to Cobden himself), were incapable of appreciating the far-reaching consequences of accepting the principle of Free Trade.

Speaking to an audience of Non-conformists, Mr. Balfour described the

> Theory of what is commonly called individualism, in which they laid it down, no matter what constitution you had, the State as a State could not do very much for its existence, but what had to be done must be done by the individual himself and not by the government representing the community as a whole. That view, as you all know, reached its best expression in Mr. John Stuart Mill's writings, and others among that school, to whom I said before we owe a great deal, but it was necessarily and essentially of a transitory character.

These words contain a great and as I venture to think, a most important misconception. Mill was by no means a representative of the scientific Liberalism of Cobden and his school. Mill's authority has, without doubt, largely influenced the thought and political conduct of his generation, but I suspect when history comes to be written it will be found that the so-called philosophical Radicalism of Mill was the force which, seemingly from the inside, broke up, for the time being, the authority of the Manchester School of Politics. As a proof of this, it may be remarked that the greater portion of *Free Exchange* (the volume of Sir L. Mallet already mentioned, the most authoritative literary document as to the esoteric teaching of Cobden) is occupied with a hostile criticism of Mill. Mill is the author of the "unearned increment" agitation. From the point of view of his school, Sir L. Mallet deals with this absurdity in a most effective and conclusive manner. Mill also has reaffirmed (under the guns of the enemy, which in the days of his master Ricardo, had not been unmasked) the doctrine that labour is a cause of value. The fallacious theory of value of which this opinion is a part has been avoided and exposed by the truer insight of the French School, by Condillac and Bastiat, and by its English representatives, Archbishop Whately and Mr. Dunning MacLeod. To this school we must look, Sir Louis Mallet justly argues, for a rehabilitation of the "shattered science" of political economy.

Intellectually, then, the position of Mill is that he has surrendered to the Socialist Party the most important and impregnable strategical position. His great authority, moreover, has prevented the esoteric doctrine of Cobden from permeating the mind of the Party, while it has given philosophic sanction to a portion, at any rate, of the Socialist pretensions, and to that conversion of the Liberal Party into a Socialist Party which is taking place at the present day. This was the natural bent of his character. If the argument in favour of confiscating the so-called unearned increment in the value of land is to hold, it is obvious to the meanest capacity that the same line of reasoning must apply to the unearned increment in all other forms of private property. This is a necessary corollary of which the Socialist, logically enough, makes abundant use.

The private appropriation of value is an instinct inseparable from human society; it is the only alternative to general scramble. Property does not, and cannot vest in those who are the cause of its value. The cause of its value is the demand of those who do not possess it. Increments of value are never *earned* by their owners. In every case they are due to demand, *i.e.*, to the action of those who are not the owners. Much labour and ingenuity may have been bestowed to make a product, but value is created only when, and if, the effort has been directed to meet a commensurate demand, which may have been ascertained beforehand, or be altogether unexpected; if this demand is not present, the product is valueless (except perhaps for home consumption, a case so rare in modern industry that it may fairly be neglected).

The problem therefore is not how best to appropriate one particular form of "unearned increment." It is rather how best to distribute the unearned increment and decrement which must arise in all the products of industry by reason of the variations of demand and supply. The unanimous verdict of civilized society has hitherto replied; – by means of the institution of private property. Such collectivism as is practicable in the good things of this life is brought about by the sub-division of labour and enterprise, and by the right of free exchange. Further, a large measure of collective enjoyment is assured by the fact that there is no limit to the production of wealth, and no bar to the ownership of property by the labouring class. Property ceases to be an object of bitter contention when all have some, not necessarily an equal enjoyment therein. What we require therefore is not the breaking up and destruction of property already accumulated or the tenures by which it is held, but an increased production of wealth and an abandonment of the fallacies of collective ownership, which are fatally hindering the acquisition of property by our poorer classes.

Absolute ownership of property, we are sometimes pedantically told, is unknown to English law. Sir William Harcourt is the latest champion of this mediæval Socialist doctrine. In his letter on the Budget he argued that private property and inheritance are enjoyed merely by favour of the State, which, therefore, has a prior title to every man's property. One might as well argue that practical legislation can be based in this nineteenth century on the precedent of the Rape of the Sabine women, because antiquaries find in our marriage customs reminiscence of marriage by capture. Against this doctrine and all that follows from it believers in human progress are bound to protest.

Sir W. Harcourt's doctrine, however, holds the field at Westminster. Wealth and property are the sport of the empirics who assemble there. The Conservative Party has never professed to be a Party of principle. At one time resistance to change was its animating motive. When this attitude seemed desperate, Mr. Disraeli educated it. It has resisted the removal of many restrictions and finally removed them of its own accord. The more intelligent members of the Socialist Party are aware that their theory is inconsistent with Free Trade, and before long they will indoctrinate with this opinion the Liberal Party, which they have absorbed; it is not, therefore, improbable that, in the not very distant future, the Conservative Party will defend us against Protection just as keenly as it supported it half a century ago. In the meantime, however, the policy of the Conservative does not appear to be inspired by any intelligible principle. Mr. Disraeli has been succeeded as pedagogue by Mr. Chamberlain, who is teaching the Party to deck its shop windows with a feeble imitation of the goods offered for sale by the Socialist Party.

Knowing what politics have been, and what, it is assumed, they probably must be, plain men are not surprised or much disposed to complain, though they may occasionally express a wish that the national game could be carried on at the cost of the protagonists themselves. They appear to have grown accustomed to the public sale of their interests. Will this apathy continue? It will appear a paradox to argue that it is likely to continue just so long as the delusion lasts that to resist Socialism is selfish. Selfishness is a subordinate motive, a motive if not exorcised, at least transfigured by the discipline of centuries of social experience. That the Procrustean methods of Socialism will rewaken again the baser instincts which human character, in its ascent, has out-grown, is a truth too obvious to be denied by the observant student of events. Meanwhile, paradoxical though it will appear to the political pessimist, it is argued with some confidence that a strenuous resistance to Socialism will not be raised till the true unselfishness of such a course is brought home to the conscience and conviction of mankind. We have no just cause to be ashamed of human nature or to be disheartened as to the possibilities of progress guaranteed to us by its free development. On the contrary, it is this view which should kindle our enthusiasm, while relentless hostility should be offered to the cynical suspicion which seeks to fetter the free development of our nature by arbitrary restraints, and to smother it in a formalism which neither quickens nor inspires. The pace of reckless legislation is now being hurried, and it remains to be seen whether, on the one hand, a truer appreciation of the righteousness of resistance or, on the other, a rekindled instinct of self-preservation will not find a new rallying point in defence of society, a new watch-word of "No Paternalism but equal liberty for all before the law."

With a view of bringing into still clearer relief this antithesis between Society and the State, let me contrast, in a concrete instance, the way of the politician with that natural development which offers, as I believe, the truer and more permanent remedy.

Speaking at Edinburgh in October, Lord Salisbury referred to the question of Poor Law reform, more especially with regard to Mr. Chamberlain's proposal to add to our present established system of legal relief some new form of assistance to the aged. He said:

> The Poor Law – that is to say the question of dealing with the old – has been, as you know, an old question and Conservative grievance. In old time the Conservatives were very suspicious of the action of the Poor Law, and again and again they have taken action against it . . . At that time, the economical school was perhaps unduly imperious, and all such ideas were rejected. They are entertained more freely now, and I believe they are entertained with justice, and there is nowhere where they can be recommended with greater confidence than here in Scotland . . . I think that problem (*i.e.*, the maintenance of the aged) is one which awaits solution and which will press heavily upon the best-intentioned and the most careful legislators of the future . . . I do not attempt to bring you into details. I merely wish to point out to you that this greater generosity in favour of the old and impotent is in analogy to and pursuance of the best traditions of Scottish relief of the poor, and nowhere should such proposals be listened to with so much sympathy and respect – so much support – as here.

This language deserves most careful analysis. There is first to be noted the terrible pessimism which assumes not only that the natural organization of society is a failure, that the distribution of wealth, the bonds of family affection and social benevolence have failed, but that they are doomed to perpetual failure in the future. *Sans phrase* the Poor Law is identified with the question of dealing with the old. Is this all that modern civilization can offer? The old must starve, unless we resort to the enforced contributions of the rate-payer! Is this so certain, so irremediable that we should legislate to stereotype this condition and to render unnecessary the practice of thrift, the exercise of filial affection, and of social benevolence? These virtues we have learnt to regard as the mainstay of civilization.

For so the whole round world is every way
Bound by gold chains about the feet of God.

Are these saving graces to be replaced by the virtue of punctually paying the rate-collector?

With regard to the action of the Conservative Party in the past, the country will remember with gratitude the conduct of that true patriot, the great Duke of Wellington. With all his love of the old order of things, the strong common sense of the Iron Duke pushed aside the shallow sentimentalism of some of his followers, and gave a consistent support to the Poor Law Amendment Act introduced by a Liberal Government and passed into law by the first reformed Parliament.

Can it be, as Lord Salisbury argues, that there is a disposition now to go back on that policy? By abolishing out-door relief to the able-bodied, the Poor Law Amendment Act has restored independence to the working classes of this country. It is argued – nay, it has been proved to demonstration, that, where boards of guardians refuse to take responsibility for the maintenance of the aged except by offering relief within the walls of the union house, the aged are provided for by additional thrift and by a quickened spirit of family affection and social benevolence. This is a drastic remedy, some will say, impossible for a politician. So be it, no one has asked the politician to appear as spokesmen for an unpopular opinion, however self-evident and salutary it may be, a much humbler request is preferred, namely, that if they will not lead us on the true path of escape, they will at least be neutral, and refrain from putting themselves at the head of the mob that shouts loudest for a return to the bondage and flesh-pots of Egypt.

Again, there is the assumption that the solution of the problem – the maintenance of old age, belongs to the province of the legislator. What warrant is there for this? The duty of providing food and clothing and the necessaries of life has been discharged, on the whole successfully, by the natural instincts of self-preservation, by the natural affection of the family, and by that larger spirit of philanthropy of which this suicidal proposal for substituting Poor Law relief for a voluntary exercise of charity is a misguided, and, as we may hope, a temporary aberration. If it be wise and statesmanlike to relegate old age to the tender mercy of the law, if it is possible to bring on the millennium by increasing our taxation in a spirit of enthusiastic philanthropy, surely we ought not to stop with this trifling reform. Admittedly, on all hands, a wider distribution of property or of its advantages is desirable. If we can deal with old age by means of this short cut, why should we hesitate to deal with the evils of widowhood or orphanhood, of sickness and every other infirmity to which flesh is heir? Surely if reform can be made in this way, we should, with enthusiasm, and at once, embrace the whole theory of Socialism. With a perfect consistency our Socialist friends are ready to apply the method foreshadowed in Lord Salisbury's speech to every relation of life, nor do we see what logical answer can be made by those who accept Lord Salisbury's premises.

Nor, I venture to think, will Lord Salisbury's interpretation of the "best traditions of Scottish relief" prove very acceptable to the majority of Scotsmen. One would gladly believe that in Scotland, even now, there is no lack of generosity towards the old. A compulsory assessment for the relief of the poor was not universal in Scotland till 1845, and to the present day there are parishes where the relief of the poor is still retained in the hands of the Kirk Session.

Since that time a proverbial remark has come into vogue, that "thrift went out with the New Poor Law." The older, nobler and more indigenous tradition of Scottish relief would take us back to the time of Dr. Chalmers and his gallant attempt to keep the devastating influence of a compulsory Poor Rate away from his parish in Glasgow. To give his own words, –

The knowledge of a compulsory provision operated as a disturbing force both on the self-care and on the sympathies of Nature. Remove that provision; and these principles were restored to their proper force or orginal play. The body politic of our parish was put into a better condition, and all its evolutions went on more prosperously than before – not by any skilful mechanism of ours, but by the spontaneous working of Nature's previous and better mechanism.[2]

[2] *The Sufficiency of the Parochial System, without a Poor Rate, etc.*, by Thomas Chalmers, D.D., LL.D., Professor of Theology in the University of Edinburgh, etc., etc.

History seems to repeat itself. Dr. Chalmers' experiment was abandoned not because it failed, but simply because it was overwhelmed by the introduction of a compulsory Poor Rate. First its opponents denied its success, then they admitted its success and attributed it "to the marvellous and præternatural strength of the projector." This last is an argument which both Mr. Booth and Mr. Chamberlain have applied to the often quoted dispauperization of Bradfield.

In the work of abolishing legalized charity," Dr. Chalmers says elsewhere, "the heaviest conflict will not be with the natural poverty of the lower orders, but with that pride of argument, and that tenacity of opinion and all those political feelings and asperities which obtain among the higher order." As to the poor themselves, the voluntary parochial system which he advocated would, he said, "put them, and that chiefly out of their own capabilities, into a far better economic state than any legal or compulsory system of relief ever has, and, we shall add, ever can do.

To the pessimism of Lord Salisbury, his countrymen will, I think, prefer the exalted faith in human destiny professed with such unfaltering conviction by this genuine and high-minded Scotsman. In speaking of the abandonment of his system, when overthrown by the legislating politicians of the day, he sums the matter up as follows:-

This has long awakened my bitterest regret; but it cannot shake my confidence. Even one decisive experiment in chemistry will establish a principle that shall remain an enduring certainty in Science – even though an edict of power in the spirit of that blind and haughty Pontiff who denounced the Copernican system should forbid the repetition of it. My experiment has been made and given forth its indelible lesson, though my experimentalists have been disheartened and scared away. This no more invalidates the great truth which they have exemplified so well, than a mandate of intolerance can repeal a law of physical nature, or change the economy of the universe.

History again repeats itself. "Experimentalists" at Bradfield, Brixworth, Oxford, S. Neots, at Manchester, at Whitechapel, Stepney and S. George-in-the-East, have demonstrated the capacity of human nature for independence. The spirit of the blind and haughty Pontiff still animates the legislator. Mr. Fowler's vaunted reform, the Local Government Act of last Session, has added perhaps a few more sinister influences, but practically leaves the problem where it was.

During the discussion of that measure statesmanship was represented by the rather feeble spirit of chicane, which underlies the remark made by one of the ministers in charge of the bill. He defended the merging of Poor Law Boards in District Councils on the ground that it was undesirable that popular elections should turn directly on questions connected with the administration of relief. Before it can be trusted the oracle must be hood-winked, or at least prevented from concentrating its attention on one subject at a time. There is truth in the contention (though one hardly expected to find Saul among the prophets) that the only chance Society has of surviving the encroachment of the State is that the executive will be reduced to impotence by the multiplicity of conflicting, irreconcilable interests, and by the unmanageable accumulation of problems which credulous devotees present to the great Fetish for solution.

Under such circumstances movement in the right direction is not likely to be inaugurated by politicians, but this haste to lead the rout into deeper and deeper quagmires of dependence, cannot fail to awaken the "bitterest regret," though it cannot shake the confidence of those who still cherish a belief in the dignity of human life.

From what degenerate source, Scotsmen will wonder, has Lord Salisbury derived this picture of the best tradition of Scottish relief. Let me appeal from this caricature to a more authentic document. Galt in his *Annals of The Parish* has given a most faithful and characteristic portrait of Scottish manners as he knew them in the beginning of the century. Like the native product, his humour is most frequently dry and caustic, its true kindliness but rarely finds expression; for this very reason, it rings all the truer when it falls into a gentler vein of sentiment. The narrator of the following incident is the minister of the parish. He relates how he was sent for to see Nanse Banks, the old schoolmistress. He found her "sitting in the window neuk reading the Word." A chair was set ready for the minister and

"I discerned that there was something more than common

to happen, and so it appeared when I had taken my seat." "Sir," said she, "I hae sent for you on a thing that troubles me sairly, I have warsled with poortith in this shed, which it has pleased the Lord to allow me to possess; but my strength is worn out, and I fear I maun yield in the strife," and she wiped her eye with her apron. I told her, however, to be of good cheer, and then she said that she could no longer thole the din of the school, and that she was weary, and ready to lay herself down to die whenever the Lord was pleased to permit. "But," continued she, "what can I do without the school, and, alas, I can neither work nor want, and I am wae to go to the Session." I comforted her, and told her ... that the Session was in her debt. "I would rather, however, Sir," said she, "try what some of my auld scholars will do, and it was for that I wanted to speak. If some of them would but just, from time to time, look in on me, that I may not die alane, and the little pick and drap that I require would not be hard on them. I am more sure that in this way their gratitude would be no discredit, than I am of having any claim on the Session."

The worthy minister of course acted on this pathetic sugges-tion, assistance was readily obtained from grateful scholars and friendly neighbours, and the few remaining days of the aged schoolmistress were tended with watchful and solicitous sympathy.

There is no reason to suppose that Scottish human nature is altered so much for the worse. Thrift may have gone out with the new Poor Law, but it has not gone beyond recall, and it is possible to hope that some kindly instincts of human nature have survived its ill-omened advent. There is nothing, we venture to sav. remarkable or extraordinary in Galt's presentment of old-fashioned Scottish charity. With the unerring instinct of a true artist, the story is told in the delib-erately prosaic language which he knew to be the proper vehicle for the Annals of the Parish. It never occurs to him to speak of generosity. This is left for those who seem to believe that these kindly instincts have followed the virtue of thrift into limbo, and that a proud and patriotic people can show its generosity by relegating the aged to the care of the Poor Law.

It is usual to meet these arguments in favour of what Mr.

Huxley, with his happy talent for phrases, has called Administrative Nihilism, with the remark, We must do something, we must offer to the constituences some positive programme. It is, however, a misconception to suppose that this advocacy of restricted State action proceeds from indifference to human suffering or a desire to prevent human energy from labouring to find remedies for our social difficulties. To express a preference for what seems to us a practicable method of reform rather than for a method which seems impracticable is only natural. Our decision may be at fault from ignorance or from error, but it is not dictated by indifference; and, to refer again to the concrete instance of Poor Law administration, the plan of action here advocated in this particular sphere undoubtedly requires energy, devotion and continuous labour far beyond what is needed in agitating for political changes. To enter on a struggle such as that described by Dr. Chalmers, with the deliberate purpose of restricting and removing the insidious influence of legal relief, and so re-creating the manhood of the pauper and quickening the virtue of benevolence into a more intelligent and active operation, is by no means an enterprise characteristic of a policy of "do nothing." It may be a wrong policy, but it does not arise from indolence. The difficulties of such a programme have been correctly described by Dr. Chalmers. It is, he believed, a right and therefore an easy solution. Its difficulty is due to the inveterate tenacity of a false belief. Elsewhere there is no lack of human energy and enthusiasm, and it is impossible not to experience some bitter regret that so much of it should be wasted in the unprofitable mumbling of political shibboleths now void of meaning. It would be easy to name other spheres of action where there is need of intelligent, disinterested and unremitting labour. Dispauperization means the restoration of independence, not the abolition of poverty; that is the next step. The whole question of working-class investment is full of problems of the highest importance; most pressing, perhaps, among these is the organization of a cheap system of credit. In England the useful institution of co-operative banks is in its first infancy. Yet, as Mr. Wolff has clearly shown us from the example of other countries, it is an instrument most potent and beneficent, in helping to spread the advantages of property over an ever widening area. Again, there is room for endless experiment and for the exercise of the highest constructive ability in devising terms of industrial peace between labour and capital which will satisfy the legitimate claims of both.

This aspect of the subject cannot be pursued further now, but enough has been said to indicate, if not to establish, my contention that an unwillingness to have resort to legislation has a necessary counterpart, namely, a desire to expend energy in the more profitable field of voluntary public service; and with such a fruitful and promising field of labour lying open, I am compelled yet again to express a feeling of "bitter regret" that so much of the energy of the nation is engaged in pursuing the illusory phantom of a legislative millennium. If this enthusiasm could be more wisely directed into profitable channels of voluntary action, we should be within measurable distance of great and far-reaching reforms.

Section 2

Moderate Individualism

LAISSEZ-FAIRE
AND GOVERNMENT INTERFERENCE
George Joachim Goschen

I HAVE chosen "Laissez-faire and Government Interference" as the subject of my address to-night, because among all the complicated social and economical phenomena of the present day, none appears more interesting or of deeper importance for philosophers, economists, politicians, and, indeed, for all students of the varying aspects of our national life, than the changes which have occurred and are daily occurring in the relations between the State and individual liberty. None of us can be blind to what is passing around us in this respect. Whether we look to the events of successive years, to the acts of successive Parliaments, or to the publication of successive books, we see narrower and narrower limits assigned to the application of the principle of "Laissez-faire," while the sphere of Government control and interference is expanding in ever widening circles.

The extension of State action to new and vast fields of business, such as telegraphy, insurance, annuities, postal orders, and parcels post, is not the most striking feature. What is of far deeper import is its growing interference with the relations between classes, its increased control over vast categories of transactions between individuals, and the substitution in many of the dealings of trade and manufacture, of the aggregate conscience and moral sense of the nation, for the conscience and moral sense of men as units. The parent in dealing with his child, the employer in dealing with his workmen, the shipbuilder in the construction of his ships, the shipowner in the treatment of his sailors, the houseowner in the management of his house property, the landowner in his contracts with his tenants, have been notified by public opinion or by actual law that the time has gone by when the cry of "Laissez-nous faire" would be answered in the affirmative. The State has determined what is right and wrong. what is expedient and inexpedient, and has appointed its agents to enforce its conclusions. Some of the highest obligations of humanity, some of the smallest businesses of everyday life, some of the most complicated transactions of our industrial and agricultural organisations have been taken in hand by the State. Individual responsibility has been lessened. National responsibility has been heightened. Reliance is being placed on the efficiency of new forces, and on the application of new principles. The attitude of the public towards "Laissez-faire" on the one hand and State action on the other has entirely changed.

I wish it were in my power to present you with a history of the ups and downs of the principle of Laissez-faire" in popularity and prestige. I wish I could place before you how it has fared at the hands of successive generations since the time when first, in protest against the unbearable interference of Government in all and every department of industry, and against a tyrannical control over the majority of the transactions of life, the cry was raised in France, more than a hundred and thirty years ago, by champions of freedom of trade and freedom of labour, "Laissez-nous faire, laissez-nous passer." "Give us freedom of action and freedom of movement." In the present day of its declining popularity, let it not be forgotten that this principle owes its origin not to hard and impassive theorists and cold-blooded economists, but to a school of ardent and almost revolutionary social and philosophical reformers, the Physiocrats as they were called of the eighteenth century.

I wish I could say more on this head. "Laissez-faire" deserves some gratitude. The names of men who have rendered untold services to liberty in all its branches are associated with the story of its development, but I have neither the leisure nor the knowledge for such a historical review. I commend it to the attention of more learned economists. I have read most instructive separate chapters, in books on political economy, on the various stages of the controversy between the advocates of the principles of natural liberty and those of State control. But the subject is so vast as to deserve not only incidental treatment, however able and lucid, in a general work – it is well worthy of a book to itself.

Most writers on "Laissez-faire" have occupied themselves mainly with discussing the proper limits of the functions of Government. In so doing they have been compelled to analyse the various possible forms of State interference, to classify them in groups under certain heads, and to examine what were indispensable functions and what optional. Such analyses and classifications have great attractions, especially if they lead to generalisations which can be clearly stated and easily grasped (a result, however, which I fear has never been accomplised in the case of "Laissez-faire"). But if I were to attempt such a task to-night, I should most surely fail to compress within an address such as this even a bare catalogue of the different groups of legitimate or illegitimate functions of Government accompanied by the shortest summary of the arguments on either side. I propose, therefore, turning aside from the abstract and theoretical speculation, to confine myself in the main to an examination of the causes of that wider actual application of control, and that growing disbelief in the efficacy of the action of natural liberty which are giving a fresh character to so many features of our economical, social, and even national life. I should further wish to pass in short review some of the possible consequences of the course on which we are travelling so fast.

I need scarcely remind you that the causes of this revolution in public sentiment have been complicated and various in the extreme; but, amongst the many contributing influences, some stand out clear and prominent.

Foremost amongst them I discern an awakening of the public conscience as the moral aspects of many sides of our industrial arrangements – rising doubts, less as to the efficiency of existing organisations for producing wealth (though this, too, has been called in question), than as to their compatibility with the humane requirements of improving civilisation. The existence of facts previously unknown or ignored has been revealed in striking colours, the public sense has been stirred, and emotions caused which demanded the application of immediate and direct remedies. I hold the principle of "Laissez-faire" to have lost favour, chiefly owing to moral considerations, to the assertion of the claims of other than material interests, and to a growing feeling that it is right deliberately to risk commercial and industrial advantages for the sake of reforming social abuses, and securing social benefits. Professor Rogers, in his late able address on "Some sides of Laissez-faire," makes the very striking suggestion that all interferences with freedom of action or contract, which have stood the test of experience, have had, more or less distinctly, the aim of husbanding industrial resources, by restraining the waste of them, and have achieved that result.   He cites the Factory Acts in illustration of his point.   The Education Acts might similarly, and with much reason, be quoted as due to the desire to augment our industrial power.

But I believe that, certainly in the case of the Factory Acts, and to a great extent in the Education Acts, it was a moral rather than an economical influence, the conscientious feeling of what was right rather than the intellectual conviction of ultimate material gain, the public imagination touched by appeals to our higher nature, which supplied the tremendous motive power necessary for passing laws which put the State and its inspectors in the place of father and mother as guardians of a child's education, labour, and health.

I trust I shall not be misunderstood.   Arguments based on the deficiencies of our national education, which prevented us from competing with other countries, have been urged over and over again, and they have prevailed, apart from any moral influences, in causing the foundation of many Government educational establishments, besides the primary schools.   But although these establishments *offer* teaching, they do not *compel* it; they give inducements and certificates, and they belong less to the category of control or interference than to the category of services performed by the State, which would not otherwise be performed at all.   What I wish first to insist on is that the victory of the principle of compulsion over the principle of natural liberty could never have been gained except by a moral force.

Numerous other instances will at once occur to you of the result of the awakening of the public conscience.   You see its effects in the legislation respecting ships and sailors, the prevention of accidents in mines and manufactories, the curtailment of hours of labour, the employment of women and children underground, the state of canal boats, unsanitary dwellings.   All the Acts of Parliament relating to these subjects have been based mainly on moral grounds.   In the case of many of them, arguments from expediency have not been wanting, but the stimulus has been given by the sense of moral right.

Take the case of legislation which followed on Mr. Plimsoll's crusade.   The public and Parliament were moved by the startling numbers of sailors who perished, apparently from remediable causes, in the course of a single year. Such a wholesale loss of human life must be stopped at any cost. No arguments as to the possible effect of stringent legislation on the fate of British shipping would have been listened to. They would have been brushed aside. An incredulous and impatient attention was given to pleas contending that the proposed legislation might not be effectual for its purpose, or that the facts were exaggerated, but no arguments could have stemmed the tide. The State must act; the State alone could be trusted. Its agents must assume the responsibility. "Laissez-faire" had been tried and found wanting. The ship-owners must henceforward conduct their business under Government control.

Events in this instance marched rapidly and in a striking form. But the history of the laws relating to merchant shipping is but a duplicate of other similar legislation. The doctrine of "Laissez-faire" meant that a man's own interest is one of the surest factors in the production of wealth; but if, in the pursuit of individual interest, it was proved that the safeguards for the security of the interests of others in life or limb were insufficient, the public demanded that restraint should take place. The plea has not failed to be put in, that the power to inflict injury or risk on the employed did not lie in the hands of the employers alone; that the employed might refuse to serve masters whom they could not trust; that self-interest, however selfish, would ultimately have to yield to the influences which would be brought to bear upon it; that to relieve the employers of responsibility would lessen some securities, though others might be offered. But, in my judgment, it has become, wisely or unwisely, a matter of conscience with the public, that it cannot stand aside when calamities occur; that the indirect action of other influences is too slow, or too uncertain; that in its own action alone it can find the satisfaction of its conscientious scruples. In view of this attitude of the public mind, I have spoken of the substitution of the conscience of society and national responsibility for the conscience of individual men.

The striking advance of the temperance movement is of course another instance of the influence of moral feeling – moral feeling so strong and deep, as to become almost deaf to arguments as to the rights of individuals. Champions of this cause are, again, perfectly entitled to plead from their point of view that true expediency is on their side, and that even the wealth of the nation suffers from the wide prevalence of drunkenness.   No analysis of motive is ever exhaustive and few are accepted as just, but I contend that the evils excited by the degrading effects of drunkenness, the sympathies awakened by the innocent sufferers from the vice of others, the disgust at the existence of a national scandal, have had infinitely more power than any other motive in bringing the country up to its present point in respect of preparedness for legislation which would have been absolutely impossible a few years ago.   Liberty is made to yield to the claims of morality, but, in this country at least, it is seldom, if ever, sacrificed to grounds of expediency alone.

I need scarcely say more as to the extent to which the principle of natural liberty has been attacked on the ground that, sound as it may be as a system for *producing* wealth, it stood condemned as permitting certain abuses, and leaving certain deficiencies unsupplied, to which the public must have an immediate and direct remedy.

Another not dissimilar cause has been undermining "Laissez-faire" on parallel lines.   The charge is laid against it that whether or not it succeeds in *producing* wealth, it fails in bringing about a sound and just *distribution* of wealth.   Freedom of action on the part of individuals and classes is accused of leading to abuses and dangers in this respect to which it is alleged in some quarters the State ought and could apply a remedy.   The prosperity of the country is examined and analysed.   Certain classes are said to be prosperous and to have become richer and richer, others have not prospered equally, some have not prospered at all.   This inequality of progress has happened under "Laissez-faire."   Post hoc, propter hoc.   The State should try its hand at what natural liberty had failed to do.   Under this process of reasoning it is argued that "Laissez-faire" is a perfectly natural motto for capitalists, manufacturers, landlords, and tradesmen, and the cry is raised, "they have had their way, and see what has come of it!"

I need not dilate on the searching inquiry which at once suggests itself as to many of the facts alleged in these arguments, and as to the connection between the alleged cause and the alleged effects.   It may be asked whether there are not other causes at work which account for the alleged effects, whether any system is feasible by which the distribution of wealth can so be regulated as to satisfy an abstract standard of justice, and whether, if the State goes very far in regulating the distribution of wealth, the amount of wealth to be distributed may not be reduced to such an extent as to cause almost universal loss. I simply allude to such questions lest my silence with regard to them should be misconstrued, and I would very earnestly entreat all who hear me to remember that the limits into which I must compress my remarks prevent me from introducing countless qualifications and explanations which the complicated nature of my subject really demands. I must appeal to the candour and indulgence of my critics in this respect, and beg them to believe that if I omit many considerations of great importance it does not follow that I have ignored them. Time prevents me from entrenching my position as I go along.

The profits derived from land are the form of wealth, the distribution of which has thus far excited the most attention. The land agitation (to use the popular phrase) in England and Scotland (I will touch on the Irish Land Act separately), I take to be an insurrection against the principle of "Laissez-faire," as failing to secure justice to the tenant in the distribution of the aggregate profits derived from the partnership between land, capital, and labour. You will observe how the word "justice" is constantly used. It is assumed that, apart from what men agree to, there is an abstract standard of distribution, within the limits of which, but only within the limits of which, free contract is to be allowed.

But the question between landlord and tenant as to agricultural improvements sinks into insignificance by the side of a point of vast importance which is now being raised as to the relations between landowners and the community at large. The wealth which has accrued to the owners of land, including the owners of the sites on which towns are built, is being denounced as one of the gravest social and economical misfortunes which befall societies. It is important to recollect that this view, advanced with much ability and enthusiasm, is not raised simply as regards land in the United Kingdom. The question has been started in a much broader form. "Is it right that in California or in any new country individuals should buy up the sites of towns, or secure vast estates by purchase, and speculate with them till the community is driven to take them off their hands at incalculable profits?" That is the position taken up by the advocates of the nationalisation of land. Not only is freedom of contract in respect of land ownership to be limited, but land is to be withdrawn altogether and absolutely from the domain of purchase and sale. Such is the extreme proposal, but principles are involved likely to give rise to far more practical discussion than the plan as a whole. It would be incredible that even a very advanced democracy would accept Mr. George's scheme as it is put forth, but the right and duty of the State to control and limit the profits arising from the monopoly of land is insisted on in influential quarters as part of a practical programme. And it is argued that this object can be partially attained without recourse being had to more startling methods, by a system of special taxation. The imposition of taxes has often been used for other than revenue purposes. Where protection to native industry is demanded, the machinery of the taxgatherer furnishes a convenient instrument ready to hand; and similarly the hand of the State is to be invoked to secure a distribution of wealth on new lines and principles. Nor are these ideas to be applied only to the owners of land. Liberty in making testamentary dispositions is charged with producing such accumulations of wealth as are contrary to the general interests. Here again it is suggested that taxation will do the necessary work. A judiciously revised system of death duties is to be the answer of the community to any death-bed desire of "laissez moi faire."

Special demands by some classes of the community for curtailment of the limits within which they may make bargains, special demands by the State on the increment of value accruing to land by the progress of the community, a graduated income tax to prevent the accumulations of fortunes during lifetime, death duties so arranged as to prevent accumulations amongst heirs – such are some of the vast views which are being brought to the front, in all of which Government interference is to take the place of "laissez-faire" in the distribution of wealth.

Let us turn to a third cause. As society becomes more complex, more crowded, as conflicting interests jostle each other more and more, so will the cry for more regulation become louder from day to day. Till some years ago the

street traffic in the metropolis regulated itself. The rules of
the road were held to suffice. The stream of vehicles passed
to and fro under a very wide application of "laissez-faire"
and "laissez-passer." But when blocks became more frequent,
collisions more numerous, street accidents more and more a
common occurrence, the cry arose for the police. Society in
the shape of two policemen stationed itself in all the important thorough-fares. Coachmen were stopped, drivers
directed, foot-passengers assisted, refuges constructed. Freedom of passage ceased. The principle of individual liberty
yielded to organised control. Similarly on the highways of
our industrial traffic, and in the movements of society along
its various tracks, it would appear that collisions became so
frequent, and accidents so numerous, complications, crowd-
ing, and disputes so intolerable, that the police of the State
are summoned at every turn. Regulations unnecessary and
odious in a simpler state of civilisation not only became
acceptable, but were loudly demanded.

If this be in truth a contributory cause, it may furnish an
explanation of a phenomenon which has often struck me as
remarkable, and requiring explanation. How is it, I have
often asked myself, that while the increasing democracy at
home is insisting with such growing eagerness on more control by the State, we see so small a corresponding development of the same principle in the United States or in Anglo-
Saxon colonies? It is clearly not simply the democratic spirit
which demands so much central regulation. Otherwise we
should find the same conditions in the Anglo-Saxon democ-
racies across the seas. Other causes must be at work in the
United Kingdom. On the one hand, the philanthropic and
sensitive element is always infinitely stronger in the old
country; and, on the other hand, its civilisation is more complex, more crowded, more honeycombed with anomalies,
more running into extremes. The colonies have more breathing space. There, individual energy can expand with less
encroachments on neighbours' interests. There, movement is
freer, and the first instinct of man for untrammelled liberty,
confidence in himself, and in his power to shift for himself,
and hold his own, have not yet yielded to the acquired taste
for that regulation, control, interference, and inspection with
which the most independent-minded nation in the world is

rapidly being inoculated as an outcome of the latest form of its civilisation.

While society in the old country, as I have shown, thus demands the aid of the State to expedite and further its transactions by regulating and organising them, the movement is stimulated by a further cause. The successful performance of a certain set of duties by a public department inspires its administrators with the natural desire to extend their sphere of acknowledged usefulness. Ambition for more work is a sentiment not confined to those whose pecuniary self-interest prompts them to enlarge an industry which is a source of personal profit. Nor, when it is exhibited by public servants, need it be cynically attributed to a thirst for more power, patronage, or importance. I have had some experience of the qualities of civil servants of the Crown. It is a mistake to credit them with any tendency to scamp their work. On the contrary, the leading men amongst them, the flower of an honourable profession, who rarely reap sufficient acknowledgment at the hands of the public, who are often debited with the failures, but less often credited with the successes of their department, show the keenest desire for adding field after field to the region in which they labour. No country gentleman covets more earnestly bits of land lying outside of, but adjoining, his estate, than the energetic heads of departments, whose work has succeeded, covet an extension of the limits of their activity. You may remember how the desire of the Post Office authorities for the acquisition of the telegraphs almost developed into a passion.

Again, the Post Office succeeded in Savings Bank; why not try their hand at banking? Their distribution of letters gave widespread satisfaction; why not distribute parcels also? And if banking and annuities, and savings in every form, why not insurance also? As to the public, it gladly accepts any immediate and palpable boon from a department which has served it well. I do not contend that the demand of the public for that regularity, security, and, above all, universality, that carrying the conveniences enjoyed in populous centres into remote nooks and corners of the country, which it is believed central agencies alone can secure, has not contributed largely to this acquisition by the central authorities of many businesses hitherto left to local and private enterprise. Indeed, it may be cited as a separate and very notable cause. But, believe me, the stimulus comes also from the departments. Nor is it unimportant to bear this tendency in mind. The more the public puts upon civil servants, the more will civil servants offer to do for the public.

Perhaps I have dismissed the wish of the public for the performance of such duties as telegraphing and carrying parcels in too few words, considering the important bearing it has had on the extension of Government activity. But it lies nearer the surface than the other influences which I have described. And I was about to say that it concerns that branch of Government functions on which there has been some degree of agreement, namely, those which the Government, from the fact that it has agencies of its own throughout the country, can clearly perform with the greatest advantage; but this suggestion would not command universal assent. For instance, the propriety of the degree to which it has attempted to extend its insurance and banking business has often been called into question.

One cause of a more exceptional character than those broad causes with which I have hitherto been dealing ought scarcely to be omitted in the enumeration I have made. Government interference may sometimes appear the only *deus ex machinâ* for the immediate solution of some political or other difficulty, of which the instant termination is demanded by high reasons of State. Of all recent legislation, the Irish Land Act is probably the most gigantic invasion of the principle of Laissez faire in recent times. The call for the substance of that Act was clearly due in great measure to one of the causes which I have already discussed – dissatisfaction on the part of the Irish with the distribution of the joint product of land and labour; but the Act was avowedly not based simply on the intrinsic merits of the case. Heroic remedies were required for an exceptional and almost revolutionary state of things; and the knot which for centuries had become more and more inextricably tangled could, in the judgment of those who were responsible, be only cut by the State. But here again, as in other cases when the ball has been set rolling, the new departure is in the strictest sense of the term a departure only. It is not an arrival, not a terminus. An isolated act of heroic legislation cannot be limited by the declarations of it authors. It has its effect on the public mind, on the beliefs entertained as to the general functions of the State. I am speaking simply as an economist, and a student of contemporary history, to members of a philosophical institute. Within these walls we are not concerned with political parties. We know no party questions. But an account of the present situation of the principle of Laissez-faire would not be complete if all allusion to legislation, which so materially affects it, were omitted. For better or worse the Irish Land Act is a landmark in the history of the accelerating rate of Government interference; and the force of the precedent, and of its effect on various classes, cannot be ignored.

I have endeavoured to put before you several powerful causes of the change in the public mind, which I am attempting to explain. But I venture to think that the degree to which, in these last years, these influences have been operative, is due to a further cause of a very important and significant character. Trust in the action of the State would never have developed to the extent to which recent legislation, and still more the actual demands for much more drastic legislation, proves it to have grown, if the organisation of the State had not undergone very material modifications. Changes in the distribution of political power have produced changes in the manner in which the action of the State is regarded. Control by an oligarchical Government would have been repugnant to the feeling of the commercial classes. Control by a Parliament mainly influenced by the commercial and capitalist classes would have inspired little confidence in the mass of the people. *Pari passu* with the development of more democratic conditions, a demand by the awaking democracy for action on its behalf was a not unnatural result. So long as legislation involving minute Government interference could be regarded simply as paternal legislation, it excited, not confidence, but distrust. The people of this country have never wanted the State to be parental. Now, when the State is invoked, it is not invoked as a parent, or as a beneficent master; it is invoked as the agent, aye, as the servant, of the people's will. From this point of view the movement is essentially democratic. Society wants its representatives to act on its behalf. Society demands to control the individual. The movement is distinctly socialistic.

I cannot conclude this review of the causes of the present intense demand for Government interference without alluding to the burning question of the housing of the poor. In this case nearly all the causes which I have noted, combine to create the demand – a public sense of moral responsibility, dissatisfaction with the present distribution of wealth, complications arising from the crowded state of society, and the belief that Government is the only *deus ex machinâ* to solve an almost insoluble problem. I include dissatisfaction with the existing distribution of wealth, for no candid observer can ignore that the high profits realised by the landlords and the extreme poverty of many of the tenants are strong elements in the present agitation. But what will carry this movement forward to an actual experiment, as it has carried others, will not be expediency, though arguments based on expediency will be most powerfully urged, nor the agitation of those who have to pay exorbitant rents, but a wave of deep and strong feeling passing over the public mind.

I agree with Lord Salisbury that the principle of Laissez-faire cannot be pleaded in bar of all action in the matter. A most complicated situation has been created, partly by acts of the Legislature itself, in which "natural liberty" scarcely exists; and it is clear that there are many parts of the subject with which, under any theory of Laissez-faire, the State is competent to deal. But the first question to be decided will be, whether the State is simply to appear on the stage in a benevolent character, placing national resources, in loans or otherwise, at the disposal of persons prepared to build houses for the poor; or whether the true beginning is not to insist on a sterner and more thorough enforcement of individual responsibility. To my mind the argument is almost irresistible, that it is as just to prevent, and if necessary to punish, houseowners who let out rooms unfit for human occupation, as tradesmen who offer putrid food for sale. Tenants may knowingly, in their inability to procure other accommodation, take such rooms and pay famine prices for them, just as the extremely poor might knowingly buy bad food. But this does not relieve the owner of his responsibility, nor can the State permit the evils of a virtual monopoly to be intensified by that monopoly being used in a manner destructive of health and morality. Two evils have to be met: the existence of vast tracts of buildings, partly themselves dangerous to health, partly so occupied and crowded as to be dangerous to health, and secondly the absence of sufficient suitable dwellings. The State is more capable of dealing with the former than with the latter, and here is the key to the situation. No element in the whole matter is more important than how, and at what price, sites can be obtained. The readiness to embark capital will depend on the cost of sites. It is possible that when purchasers, armed with loans from the State, enter the market, the value of building sites will rise still further if the owners of the filthiest dens commanding monopoly rents are to be allowed under a compulsory sale to value the profits of their own wrong. The principle of laissez-faire has never been extended to prevent us from prohibiting the sale of noxious food. It cannot be invoked to forbid the valuation of house property according to its value for legal use, and for legal use alone. It remains for the State to define what, looking to the requirements of health and the prevention of crime and immorality, such legal use shall be. Whatever action the State may ultimately take, it is to be hoped that while the duties of the community are enlarged on and pressed, the duties of individuals, and the propriety of enforcing them, may not be neglected.

The general question is obviously too large for treatment on my part to-night, and there is a certain inconvenience in dealing with a topic of such grave importance in an incidental manner; but looking to the interest it excites, and the degree to which the principle of Government interference is sure to be discussed in connection with it, some allusion to it was indispensable.

Let me resume the thread of my argument. I have placed before you the principal causes which I hold to have influenced the judgment of the public in its attitude towards "Laissez-faire." I shall not attempt in the short time still at my disposal to examine, as to each class of the new demands for interference, to what extent they may be based on illusions, or to what ultimate risk compliance with them may expose the community, or in what cases paramount reasons may justify such compliance. But I cannot conclude without asking you to consider some of the general difficulties and dangers which beset the course on which the public is electing to travel, apparently with a light heart, certainly with a confidence which, if justified at all, must be justified by the existence of totally new conditions, and of a much purer and more perfect atmosphere of national life than other ages and other countries have ever enjoyed. For all historic experience tends to show that the very gravest misgivings may reasonably be felt as to the success likely to attend our new departure.

I have spoken of difficulties and dangers. By difficulties I mean impediments likely to prevent the methods proposed from meeting the objects towards which they are directed; by dangers I wish to indicate the risks of evil consequences, even on the assumption that the new methods do effect what they propose.

To what extent can Government be expected to carry out efficiently the constantly increasing work put upon it? To what ultimate powers and influences do you look for the performance of the work? Of what character are the instruments to be employed? Such are some of the first questions which suggest themselves. Is there no fear that the Government may be overworked? Is there experience of any Government having succeeded in giving satisfaction under such conditions? A very robust faith in the working machinery of the Government departments is required to believe in the possibility of such success. And see what happens! As I have explained before, the democratic spirit does not object on principle to the performance of vastly increased duties by the State. On the contrary, it demands it, and it has confidence in the ultimate controlling power, which is the Legislature, – that is to say, itself; but when we come to the execution of the work decided on by the Legislature, the democratic spirit does not feel confidence, – on the contrary, it is exceedingly critical of all acts of the Executive, and we are confronted by the difficulty of an Executive summoned to all-pervading duties, but with agents who receive little popular support. The public demands inspection, but too often denounces the inspectors; the public demands regulations, but chafes at the red tape employed in carrying them out; it legislates for watchfulness on the part of the State over the shortcomings of local authorities, but nothing is more unpopular than the activity of central agents; it demands organisations which require the appointment of vast numbers of clerks, yet the deficiencies of Government clerks, and the expense of their salaries and pensions, furnish endless food for popular declamation. Theoretically, the Executive Government is the all-wise and benevolent agent of the community, with an eye which is everywhere, and an untiring arm. Practically, in its working capacity, it is a body of over-worked, much-criticised gentlemen who are not trusted half as much as they ought to be.

But let us look a little further and consider the Government, not only in its working capacity, but in the widest meaning of the term, as the body which wields the supreme powers of the State.

Consider what conditions are demanded. A central Government free from jobbery, nay, even free from the suspicion of jobbery, absolutely just between class and class, free from bias or leaning, dependent on the will of the people, for that is the first condition of its being trusted with such extraordinary powers, yet steady and regular in the impartial performance of duties deeply affecting the interests of those on whom their continuance in power depends. Let us probe this matter to the bottom. Who is the State? What is the Government? What is the central authority to whose hands such vast interference with natural liberty is to be confided? It is Parliament and its creature, the Government of the day. What is Parliament? – the representative of the majority of a certain year; the expression of the public will at a certain date. And this is the body which, stripped of conventional expressions, is to fix new relations between classes, and give a fresh direction to and control the currents of our lives. See what we are doing! We are distrusting classes separately. We are acting on the assumption that their self-interest imperils social aims which we have at heart that they are not to be trusted even when notified of the demands of the age, but that inspection and regulation and positive enactments are to clog them at every step, to be present at every contract, and to watch over the fulfilment of every duty. But while we thus proceed on the policy of distrust, we are to have unbounded confidence in successive decisions of Parliamentary majorities.

The State is a noble expression. The idea of the social body politic suggests even higher thoughts. But the homely reminder that the active force of society in its ultimate action is nothing more than the result of a heated electoral contest drags us down again to earth. We may doubt whether society as an active force will be so infinitely superior to its component parts; and if a grave mistake should be made, if, when the era of State Socialism is further developed, we should find that the legislative and executive bodies are not infinitely freer from the imperfections and shortcomings of our common nature than history gives us any right to anticipate, the nation may regret having exacted almost superhuman duties and superhuman virtues, from bodies essentially human.

Again, even if we grant an admirable central Government, do we not run a serious risk, in a vast number of cases, of weakening individual responsibility to such a degree that what we gain on the one side we lose on the other? I have spoken of the Merchant Shipping legislation, where an immense effort was made to diminish the loss of sailors' lives by Government control. I regret to say that there is no evidence of success. All concerned have worked heartily to secure it; but I am informed that, so far as the Returns furnish evidence, the result is *nil*, or worse than *nil*. The Returns as to ships laden with coal, grain, and timber, as to which Legislative Committees and Commissions and the Board of Trade have made special rules and provisions after elaborate inquiry, are disheartening in the extreme. We have cut down individual responsibility, and the State has failed to do better. I submit that one of the lessons to be learned from a case such as this is, that we should exhaust every means of enforcing personal responsibility before we substitute public responsibility. Remember they cannot co-exist in equal force. If a ship is passed by an inspector and goes to the bottom, the shipowner if brought to book pleads that he has satisfied the inspector.

Such are some of the difficulties besetting the accomplishment by the State of the purposes for which its aid is invoked. But even if Government action is partially successful, it is absolutely necessary to consider the drawbacks and dangers to which it may lead. Remember, for instance, the question of cost. As Mill says, "there is in almost all forms of Government agency one thing which is compulsory, the provision of pecuniary means. These are derived from taxation, and the objection necessarily attaching to compulsory contributions is almost always aggravated by the expensive precautions and onerous restrictions which are indispensable to prevent an evasion of a compulsory tax."

Gentlemen, it is incredible to what extent this fact is lost sight of. Increased work means increased cost, and the consequent imposition of new taxes or the retention of old ones, which would otherwise be repealed. It is clear as day that as a set-off to the advantages secured, we must weigh the disadvantages which increased expense involves. No sensible man can ignore the fact that an immense proportion of the augmentation in the Civil Service Estimates is simply due to the new duties imposed on the State. Every succeeding Administration is accused of increasing our national expenditure during its term of office. Heavy indictments are launched to and fro, and as a matter of fact it is perfectly true that notwithstanding the sternest resolution to keep the estimates down, every period of five years witnesses a larger demand on the public purse. How can it be otherwise? Regulation and inspection cannot be conducted gratis. New departments of control are organised at considerable cost, and new branches of business are undertaken which may involve loss for a lengthened period. Yet little notice is taken of such items. The gross cost of Government is held up *ad invidiam* whatever party may be in power. Amongst politicians it is the custom of the trade to denounce the aggregate expenditure. Yet the growth of this expenditure does not arrest for one single moment that demand for State action which costs so much. The increase in the burden of the taxpayers does indeed demand most earnest watchfulness but it should be considered when the Government is asked to perform fresh work. The intervention of the State for the purpose of control does not end in the organisation of the necessary staff. Further intervention is required to raise the funds. If the taxes collected are a discouragement to trade and an incubus on capital, if they hamper industry, diminish comfort, handicap the English workman in his competition with foreigners, and compel interference with absolute freedom of trade, let us be rational and just and candid. We pay in such discomfort and disadvantage the price of that Government action which in so many different ways public opinion demands. It is a very expensive luxury when such action is not indispensable. It is a very costly necessary when such action is absolutely unavoidable. Extensive ramifications of State interference mean heavy taxation, with all its attendant evils and abuses. Light financial burdens are incompatible with heavy public work. The good must be weighed against the evil. The good may weigh much heavier than the evil, but the evil is there.

Consider, again, the effect of the conduct by the Government of large industrial undertakings, not only from a purely financial point of view, but from that of consequential additional interference. Monopolies are hostile to inventions and improvements and substitutes. Their success is imperilled when new forces of nature are pressed into the service of man to perform rival functions; but a monopoly is frequently indispensable to protect a Government business against loss. Consequently the dilemma arises, either that a particular business must be protected by monopoly, which is injurious to the development of other promising agencies, or the general taxpayer must be mulcted as a set-off to the benefit derived from that Government monopoly.

Sometimes the public is ready knowingly to risk financial loss for the sake of a cheap and convenient service. I call to mind a late striking instance where it demanded such a service in spite of the protest of the responsible department. Personally I should consider such a course as being questionable as a precedent, but arguments based on the creation of bad precedents are almost as unpopular and out of date as arguments based on the neglect of previous warnings. Such general considerations count for nothing nowadays. Still, the question as to the bearing of State interference generally on our national finance is, I hope, sufficiently practical, present, and pressing to secure grave and constant attention.

Another objection to the extension of Government interference is of a more insidious but not less real character. Every additional transfer of duties to the State saps the belief of the community in the value of natural liberty. For instance, if the protection of one class of individuals is entrusted to a public department, no sooner do difficulties beset another class than similar protection is invoked. Every calamity which occurs, every shortcoming discovered, constitutes a case for fresh interference. The conviction that self-reliance and the conflict of interests are elements of power and success, is weakened at every turn, and public opinion discharges individual responsibility from its duties in one department after another of our social life and industrial business. Then, further, new claims are established. If Government have interfered in favour of one set of interests, other interests will clamour for similar favour at the hands of the State. The reality of such dangers can scarcely be denied, and the risk is heightened by the obvious difficulty of retracing steps taken under such conditions. It is one thing to place a trade or a class under State protection. It is a very different thing to withdraw it, especially if moral considerations have prompted the original act. Trade might long be paralysed, capital expelled, wages lowered, and the national interests generally prejudiced, before it would be possible to repeal a system of Government control, even if condemned as a failure, in favour of the restoration of natural liberty. Once pass a moral condemnation on "Laissez-faire" in any particular case, and its rehabilitation becomes an almost hopeless task.

Consider a further element of risk. Much of the new business imposed on the State relates to what may be called a kind of arbitration between classes. The State is to hold the balance, and to fix a standard for bargains, to provide rules for the conduct of business. It is to check self-interest by the curb of Government control. But, as I have said before, the State resolves itself ultimately into a Parliamentary majority, and it is from this majority that we are to look for that judicial impartiality undisturbed by passion, that superiority to selfish interests, that purer standard, which are to cure the wicked ways of natural liberty.

Once more, permit me to invoke the authority of John Stuart Mill:-

"Experience proves that the depositaries of power, who are mere delegates of the people, that is of a majority, are quite as ready, when they think they can count on popular support, as any organs of oligarchy, to assume arbitrary power and encroach unduly on the liberty of private life. The public collectively is abundantly ready to impose not only its generally narrow views of its interests, but its abstract opinions, and even its tastes, as laws binding upon individuals. And the present civilisation tends so strongly to make the power of persons acting in masses the only substantial power in society, that there never was more necessity for surrounding individual independence of thought, speech, and conduct, with the most powerful defences, in order to maintain that originality of mind and individuality of character which are the only source of any real progress, and of most of the qualities which make the human race much superior to any herd of animals. Hence it is no less important in a democratic than in any other Government that all tendency on the part of public authorities to stretch their interference and assume a power of any sort which can easily be dispensed with, should be regarded with unremitting jealousy."

I know what is thought at the present day of such generalisations. They have lost much of their authority. Indirect benefits are seldom allowed to weigh in the scale against immediate profit. Abstract principles are more and more being abandoned in favour of whatever may at a given moment seem to answer a given purpose, and eternal truths have ceased to command any practical faith. Believe me, there is danger in the excess to which this scepticism is carried; there is danger and folly in neglecting or denying "tendencies." It is all very well to scoff at laws of nature and to degrade the term "common sense" by placing it in opposition to the assertion of principles which, if rightly appreciated, cover the teachings of common sense as well as of scientific law. It is all very well to invoke the aid of common sense to justify men in framing their opinions simply on the temporary circumstances of the moment, to the exclusion of far-sighted considerations of future results. But this habit of mind appears more than ever dangerous at a time when the nation is embarking on new social questions, and when, if ever, we have need of the steady aid of principles and of the knowledge gained in the world's history as to the bearing of certain tendencies on the ultimate shape of events.

One last general remark I should wish to be allowed to make. I have spoken throughout of the Central Government or the State, but the Central Government is not the only agency, nor always the best agency by which the community can give effect to its wish of exercising control. The original powers of control can only be derived from the Central Legislature, but a large proportion of public work is performed by local bodies. So far as the objection to the substitution of public for individual responsibility is held to be valid, it holds good against the action of the community, operating through a local body, as much as against the action of a central authority; but the more work in the way of public interference the country demands to be performed, the greater in my opinion is the necessity of transferring to local authorities as large a proportion as possible of public functions. Such a transfer promises incalculable advantages. It diminishes *pro tanto* that extension of central power and patronage of which I have said little, but which is a most undesirable accompaniment of increased Government action. It reduces the number of the army of men whom the central authority is compelled to employ. Secondly, it eases the work of the Government – a great gain in view of the certainty that if, as is but too probable, the Government is overworked, many of its duties will be ill-discharged. Thirdly, it distributes weight. It imposes public functions on a different class of citizens. It interests an additional stratum of society in public business. And lastly, it provides to some extent a safety-valve against possible overbearing tyranny on the part of an all-powerful class. If the community is in many cases to encroach on the limits of individual independence, it is, at all events, an advantage to split up the community into many fractions in the discharge of its self-imposed obligations. Strong local bodies, firmly rooted in public esteem, are an invaluable bulwark against the dangers arising either from the caprice, or the impatience, or the imperiousness, or the jobbery of a central authority. If the extended demand for Government interference is to be progressively satisfied, it is earnestly to be hoped that we may proceed *pari passu* on the lines of decentralisation.

Gentlemen, I dare not trespass further on your patience. I have endeavoured, as far as lay in my power, to observe an impartial tone in the examination which I have made. I do not wish to be understood to be a blind and unreasonable champion of "Laissez-faire," under all circumstances. "Laissez-faire" has suffered in reputation, because its advocates have often pushed its claims on public favour to extremes. I have wished to avoid that error, and I have not failed to recognise the honest, well-intentioned, and often noble aims which have inspired the accelerated pace of legislation and of opinion towards extended Government interference. The awakening of the public conscience in respect of many deep-rooted evils in trade and society, in the relations between classes and the treatment of individuals, has rendered most signal service in raising the standard of morality, and in showing sounder and safer paths of duty. Whole classes have been roused to the knowledge that their conduct of affairs in certain respects was below what the age demanded of them. Sometimes the paths of duty become overgrown with weeds, and he who passes daily along them does not perceive their gradual growth. But when the outer public are let in and complain that the paths are not properly kept, the owner himself is as keen as the public to uproot the noxious growth. The discovery of evils and abuses demanding a remedy is not always a justification for substituting an entirely new organisation, and for withdrawing responsibility in favour of regulation. When we contemplate with satisfaction the greater care for the security of the employed, the greater solicitude for the mental and moral welfare of children, the anxiety for sanitary improvements, the desire for better house accommodation for the poorest classes, the efforts in the cause of temperance, the sympathy for the suffering of dumb animals, and generally the struggles of the philanthropist and the social reformer for the elevation of the masses in comfort and refinement, we shall not be relieved of the necessity of considering the efficiency of their methods, because their aims are high and pure. We shall ill serve the common cause of increasing the sum of human happiness by ignoring dangers which surround the execution of even lofty purposes. Nor for the sake of quick and palpable reform is it always right to compromise the future. The flattering aspect of an immediate improvement must not blind us to sowing the seeds of future danger. We might sap for ever the self-reliance of a class in order to remove some present abuse which other methods might even more effectually remedy.

The dangers in the road of social reconstruction under Government control are so grave that they can scarcely be exaggerated; dangers arising, not only from the serious chance of inefficiency in the methods chosen, but from the transfer of responsibilities, from the establishment of national law in the place of individual duty, from the withdrawal of confidence in the qualities of men in order to bestow it on the merits of administrations, from the growing tendency to invoke the aid of the State, and the declining belief in individual power. I press these risks on you as citizens as well as economists. We cannot see universal State action enthroned as a new principle of government without grave misgivings. Your ideal will not be that of a time when the whole duty of man would be edited in bulky blue books, and when due preparation for an inspector's visit would represent the discharge of all obligations, and the fulfilment of all claims.

Let us hope that in the State Socialism of the future, to

which some thinkers suggest we are drifting at no slow pace, room will still be left for that self-reliance and independence and natural liberty, which, if history has taught us anything, are the main conditions on which depend the strength of the State, the prosperity of the community, and the greatness of nations.

LIBERTY AND SOCIALISM
Article published by the Central Office of the
Liberty and Property Defence League; also in
the "National Review"
George R. C. Herbert

Interference and non-interference
IN a leading article of the *Times* of February 15, on the
alarming increase in Government expenditure, I read the following sentences:

> "The admirable maxims which a generation ago were the
> watchwords of Liberalism are disappearing with an alarm-
> ing rapidity from the minds of men. Long after the Prime
> Minister entered Parliament, one of the chief notes of
> instructed Liberalism was the dogma that the best govern-
> ment is that which interferes least with social affairs. The
> grandeur of the principle that the free play of individual
> character is the surest guarantee for the well-being of the
> nation was then unquestioned; save by the retrograde and
> disaffected. It required as much courage to deny its uni-
> versal truth and applicability as to doubt the sphericity of
> the earth. Now, it is hardly too much to say that every
> Liberal measure of any consequence involves, directly or
> indirectly, a negation of that principle."

And in another notable article, of later date, apparently by
the same hand:
> "The doctrine of *Laissez faire* is as dead as the worship of
> Osiris."

Coming from such a source, such words possess, I think,
no little significance. The *Times* is not much given to unpro-
voked researches into the deeper strata of political philosophy. Neither, except on those rare occasions when it tries
to ascertain by experiment whether it can still make the
British public think whatever it pleases, as it used to do in
days of old, can it be called a rash print. Its leading articles

are more often characterized by a caution inclining towards generality and vagueness, than by the over-boldness that is born of the desire to be clear and striking. So when we find it making so important and so decisive a statement about the fundamental principles of politics, we may be tolerably certain that the facts on which it is founded are nearly indisputable.

I doubt, moreover, whether any competent person will be found to deny that the statement is in the main correct. The most careless observer of politics cannot fail to be aware that a complete revolution of ideas has taken place upon this subject. A few years ago the doctrine of non-interference seemed to be paramount in English politics, and anyone who ventured to prophesy that there would be a reversal of public opinion before the end of the century was ridiculed as a crotcheteer and an alarmist.

Yet even then it ought not to have been difficult to discern the growth of several factors hostile to its existence; and a slight examination of the grounds on which it was based in the popular mind might have suggested a doubt of its permanence. The number of people who could have defined their belief in it, and justified it by solid and sufficient reason, was at no time very large. With the vast majority it was little more than a feeling, impressed on them by a peculiar concurrence of causes; some, at least, of which were of a merely temporary character.

Amongst these the chief cause, no doubt, was the prestige the doctrine had acquired during the long struggle for commercial freedom. From beginning to end it had always turned out to be right. It came to be regarded with superstitious reverence. When men observe constantly recurring phenomena, they always infer some law – whether Divine or natural – beneath it. They began to suspect that what was true in trade was true in every other department of human affairs. They hoped they had discovered an infallible maxim applicable to every political problem. Now that they have found it is not quite this, there has been a natural, but undue, revulsion of feeling, and a tendency to doubt the truth of it in matters to which it unquestionably applies.

Secondly, the people had just arrived at the end of a similar struggle with the State for more complete personal liberty and self-government. They had not yet had time to forget the advantages of freedom, as nations so often do when they have possessed it a little while; nor had they got out of the old habit of regarding the State as an alien and semi-hostile power. They had not realized that they themselves had become the State, and that in future the exercise of State power would mean the gratification of their own wishes. It was inevitable that when they did realize this, there should ensue a considerable modification of their views upon State interference. Men invariably look upon persecution or dominion with a different eye, according as they are persecutor or victim, ruler or ruled. Of all the honest and eloquent treatises on behalf of slavery and arbitrary government that the world contains, I never heard of one being written by a man who was suffering, or thought himself in danger of suffering, under either. There is always a tacit proviso that the advocate of it is to belong to the dominant faction.

When we further remember that the doctrine of *Laissez faire* seems like a justification of the unequal distribution of wealth from which the majority are suffering, or by which, at any rate, their poverty is made more galling, it ought not to have been difficult to foresee that it would not hold sway for long without a determined challenge, even in those industrial departments in which its value had been most conclusively proved.

In truth, its effects on these very departments constitute one of the most important of the factors that have produced the reaction. As the *Times* points out in the articles from which I have quoted, the *Laissez faire* doctrine has brought into existence a superabundant population of working producers, the monotony of whose existence it is awful to think of, and the squalor[1] of whose lives is inevitably increased by every increase in their numbers beyond a certain point that has long since been passed. It is by their daily growing sufferings and wants that we are being driven, with a pressure that feels irresistible, into expedients that no principle can justify, and of which, I fear, we shall find out the desperate unwisdom when it is too late.

---

[1] I use the word "squalor" advisedly. I do not believe that the increase in our population has as yet caused any increase in the general poverty of the people. The fact that, though the army is a more attractive profession in every way than it has ever been before, it is impossible to get a sufficiency of able-bodied recruits, is worth a bundle of ordinary statistics. – P.

The difficulty of resisting demands for mischievous and futile tinkerings with the distribution of wealth and other matters, is made the more hopeless by the fact that we have lately transferred all the governing power of the nation into the hands of this very class. By this I do not mean merely that they may be expected to use their power selfishly. A really wise regard to their own permanent interests, even if they considered nothing else, would be of no danger to the State, and of very little to any other class. It is their ignorance and want of experience in the business of government that are dangerous.

Complexity of human affairs
The old governing classes, if they had little scientific understanding of the matter, had at least found out by long experience that human affairs are extremely complex; that it is not nearly so easy to obtain a desired end by legislation as it looks; that, on the contrary, new laws very often not only fail to produce the desired effect, but are followed by indirect consequences which no one ever expected; and that false steps in legislation are most difficult to retrace, and generally gave birth to an interminable chain of evil results, growing at once more intolerable and more difficult to get rid of with every succeeding link.[2] But to the new constituencies, who now command our law makers[3] to an extent that was unknown before, these things are as a lesson that has yet to be learnt, and which must and will be learnt, partly, I hope, by the

---

[2] The Poor Laws are a trite but striking instance. – P.
[3] Professor Huxley seems rather to have forgotten this in his article on "Administrative Nihilism" ("Critiques and Addresses," p. 13), when, in minimizing the dangers of State interference, he remarks: "So far as my experience of those who carry on the business of government goes, I must say that I find them far less eager to interfere with the people than the people are to be interfered with. And the reason is obvious. The people are keenly sensible of particular evils, and, like one suffering from pain, desire an instant remedy. The statesman, on the other hand, is like the physician who knows that he can stop the pain at once by an opiate, but who also knows that the opiate may do more harm than good in the long-run." Very true; but who determines what legislation shall take place in these days – the people or the statesmen? Sometimes the latter, no doubt, but very often the former. It is an open secret that measures are often passed of which the authors and supporters really disapprove; though they consider them necessary on account of the strength of the popular demand for them. – P.

infusion of a more scientific and thorough spirit into the study of politics, chiefly, I fear, by the bitter teaching of experience. Nothing seems easier and simpler to many of our new citizens at present than to put a stop to what they do not like by passing a law against it; and even the wiser among them are loath to believe that their passionate wants and grievances cannot be in some measure relieved by Acts of Parliament of the proper sort.

Amongst other things that helped to bring about the reaction, was the fact that it had been an era of continual political reform. Laws and institutions that the nation had outgrown had to be removed; restrictions that our wiser knowledge had shown us the folly of had to be swept away. One would hardly have supposed that this process could have been favourable to a belief in the efficacy of interference. But, however strange and unreasonable, it is undeniably true that in many minds this purely liberative and destructive course of legislation has given rise to the notion that perpetual meddling by Act of Parliament is necessary to prevent stagnation; that unless our legislators keep stirring things up, progress will stop; that what is called on platforms "beneficial legislation" is a kind of stimulating manure indispensable to the national growth. To those who hold this profoundly foolish, but by no means uncommon view, the very name *Laissez faire* implies dereliction of duty, and thereby stands condemned.

I have no doubt that the exaggerations in which the preachers of the doctrine of non-interference have often, no doubt quite honestly, indulged, have had a like tendency. In their enthusiasm for self-help they laid down unlimited principles that would really condemn all laws whatever, and replace them by the more primitive and invigorating methods of boycotting, lynching, and private vendetta. They invested the State with an almost supernatural power of doing wrong and idiotic things. They proved their denunciation of it by vast catalogues of its mistakes and failures, forgetting, apparently, that by such a method it would be equally easy to condemn the practice of medicine or surgery; and these failures (often selected, by the way, from undertakings to effect which private enterprise would be completely powerless) they compared, not with the failures, but with the successes of private enterprise. Sanitary, Adulteration, and

Factory Acts they condemned off-hand, without a hearing, as infractions of the sacred principle.

Public opinion has revolted instinctively against such an overpressing of the case. The Government, it is felt, is nothing but a picked body of men carefully selected for the service of the nation, and, in England at any rate, a very high class both as to intellect and character; and as to its mistakes and failures, what would private enterprise look like if its mistakes and failures were collected and pilloried in a similar manner? Law is nothing but public opinion organized and equipped with force, however grave the questions affecting such organization and equipment may be; and so far from law being always a worse thing than private action, the difference between them is in many cases simply the difference between civilization and barbarism. So long as you employ or permit a policeman to arrest a burglar, instead of leaving the injured householder to catch him himself, and to learn in a wholesome way the folly of not having iron shutters and a blunderbuss by his bedside, it is absurd to contend that Factory or Sanitary or Adulteration Acts can be disposed of by a mere appeal to the virtues of self-help and the mischief of State protection.

Where State interference is necessary.
In the first place, we must consider whether the evils which these Acts are intended to meet are ever likely to be modified without the aid of that organization and equipment of public opinion that we call law. It is a law of human nature that when an evil is impossible to remove except at a very great cost of time and trouble, men and women will prefer to endure it for ever, even at the cost of health, and even life; and, as a fact, it is practically impossible for poor men to protect themselves against such evils as adulteration or bad drains. In such cases it is absurd to claim that private enterprise would be more "effective" than State regulation. Should the fanatical non-interventionist rejoin that even so it would be better to let Nature take its course, as by protective legislation we should be simply producing a survival of the unfittest, to the injury of future generations, it may be answered, not only that such an argument logically carried out would forbid the removal of any causes detrimental to health, and

all social ameliorations whatever;[4] but that female labour in mines and undue child labour in factories, and bad food, and unsanitary dwellings, also tend to lower the physical and moral type of the race; and so, as Dame Nature has not the smallest scruple about either deteriorating or exterminating even Englishmen (a fact that those who are for leaving everything to her care seem sometimes curiously forgetful of), there is nothing for it but to choose the least of the two sets of evils involved.

And here we touch upon the more reasonable causes of the general defection from the creed which the thinking politicians of the last generation believed and practised so stoutly. Paradoxical as it may sound, I think that there can be no doubt that the present chaos of opinion as to the proper province and principles of government has been brought about in no small degree by new and truer perceptions of the nature of human affairs; and that if it is the case that an ignorant idea of their simplicity has tended towards the discarding of the old doctrine of thorough-going non-interference, it is no less true that a sounder idea of their complexity has worked somewhat in the same direction.

Antagonism of principles.
It is the progress of natural science that has effected this change of ideas. Science is in the very air we breathe nowadays, and colours all our thoughts, often without our knowing it. Consciously or unconsciously, we are learning to take a scientific view of social communities; to believe more thoroughly that their affairs are governed by natural laws, and to suspect that such laws, when found, will prove, up to a certain point, analogous to those which have been discovered in other departments of the universe. And observation and experience are confirming the suspicion.

All through the natural universe we see a constant, never-ending strife between opposing and contradictory forces, and evolution proceeding by the balance that is the result of their antagonism. All through animate Nature we see life carried on by a continual balancing of hostile and irreconcilable considerations, all true, and all involving some punishment for their neglect, between which every living creature has

[4] "Introduction to the Study of Sociology," by H. Spencer, p. 338. – P.

constantly to choose, with a remorseless penalty hanging over him should he choose wrongly and incur the greater sacrifice.

In the lives of men and nations we see the same mysterious process equally at work. Social progress is carried on by the conflict of antagonistic forces, such as Egoism and Altruism, Conservatism and Progress, Peace and War,[5] Liberty and Socialism, each necessary and true in spite of their absolute opposition to each other; making, therefore, no course that we can take in life wholly right (in the sense of being without evil consequence), but only the least wrong.

What can be more irreconcilable than the principles of Egoism and Altriusm? It is quite contradictory to say, "You ought to care for your own interests more than your neighbours', and also you ought to care for your neighbours' interests more than your own." Yet both principles must be regarded in life. We cannot adopt the one and repudiate the other. If every man thought only of his own interests and nothing of his neighbours', society would break up. If, on the other hand, every man cared for his neighbours' interests and neglected his own, a state of confusion would ensue that no one but the gifted author of the "Pirates of Penzance" could adequately depict. Every day we have to balance (whether we do so consciously or not) the considerations which support the one against those that are involved with the other, and decide according to our lights and the circumstances of the particular case to which we should give the preference, which sacrifice it is least harmful to incur.

So it is with the forces with which we are here more particularly concerned. The complete antagonism between individual liberty and Socialism is generally, though not invariably, recognized; but it is not infrequently forgotten that, contradictory as they may be, both are indispensable. One hears often enough of proposals to eradicate altogether the elements of Socialism from our civilization, and to carry the principles of individual liberty to their complete and logical end; and no doubt in other circles one might hear the converse of these doctrines. I hope and believe that in the future political science will give us a far wider and more

---

[5] On the way in which these two hostile forces evolve progress, see some very interesting remarks in the "Introduction to the Study of Sociology," by H. Spencer, p. 191. – P.

definite knowledge than we possess at present, of the particular departments of social life in which each of these principles
is generally or invariably to be preferred to the other. But to
talk of eliminating either is surely nonsense.[6] To subordinate
individual liberty entirely to State control would at once stop
the growth of the healthiest nation in existence, and probably
kill it almost immediately; while to carry the principle of
individual liberty to its logical end would be to bring about
its instant dissolution. Professor Huxley tersely sums up the
question in these words:[7] "If individuality has no play, society
does not advance. If individuality breaks out of all bounds,
society perishes." The truth of these remarks is proved by the
whole history of the world; and they seem to me to contain
one of the keys to the great mystery of the rise and decay of
civilizations.

Compromise

We must make up our minds, then, that we cannot get rid of
either, and that, inharmonious as they may be, we must find
a compromise between them. And as in this, so in other
matters. Everywhere we find a clashing of true considerations, and a necessity for arriving at an illogical compromise
between them. There is hardly one of what are commonly
called political principles that will not lead to ruin and
absurdity if carried to its logical end, and which must not,
therefore, be met at some point, and limited by its opposite.
There are no plain ways to absolute truth and wisdom in
human affairs, no simple principles by adhering to which we
can make sure of always being right. I only wish there were.

It is pretty obvious that if these views are common, it
cannot be their pleasantness that has made them so. The
moderation they enjoin must be distasteful to many an ardent
nature; the atmosphere of doubt and difficulty that they cast
over every political problem, and their pessimist reminder
that all we can do at best is to choose the lesser evil, must
be painful to all; the very idea that there should be, in any
sense, a want of harmony between things that are true feels

---

[6] I am aware that such language as the above is sometimes used with a
meaning that could not be fairly so characterized, but I can only say that
when it is so used I think it is very misleading. – P.
[7] Essay on "Administrative Nihilism" in "Critiques and Addresses." – P.

to some at first like an outrage on human nature. It is the stern logic of facts that has, I believe, driven them, or something like them, into many a man's head; and to them must be attributed in no small degree the unsettling of the articles of political faith that a few years ago promised to become as firm as rocks.

For it is evident that no one who holds these views can be content with the principles that so amply satisfied the last generation on the subject of liberty and State interference. It is not that he doubts the truth of those principles; it is that he feels they are only a portion of the truth, and that the question of their applicability must depend upon whether they are the larger or the smaller portion. The old-fashioned Radical who believed that freedom was the one and only requisite for the attainment of moral and material perfection; the Cobdenite who believed that non-interference would always turn out to be right, however much facts might seem to be against it, and that Factory, Adulteration and Sanitary Acts were mere concessions to ignorance and folly – seem to him about as wise as a man who, having mastered the principle of gravitation, insists that a small stone placed on the roof of a house will find its way to the ground. If I may borrow a sentence from Mr. Justice Stephen, it seems to him "that the *erreur mère* of their speculations on political subjects lies in the fact that they are advocates of one out of many forces, which, as they act in different directions, must and do come into collision, and produce a resultant according to the direction of which life is prosperous or otherwise."

But such opinions, it will be said, are not of a sort likely to lead to over-confident legislation, or rash attacks upon liberty; they are really a justification of that moderate and compromising spirit in politics that is so often derided as though it were based upon a mere deficiency in the logical faculty. This is certainly true. But the doubts they have cast upon the broad and simple maxims about non-interference have afforded men of strong equalizing, or socialistic, predilections a good excuse for following their political inclinations at the expense of considerations of liberty, and of the due limits of State action; and this, I believe, is the chief explanation of the strange spectacle we witnessed in '81, when the successors of Cobden and the political economists figured as the chief supporters of an Act that undertook (amongst other things) to prescribe the rent a farmer should charge to the labourers of whose weekly wages he was left free to decide the amount.

Moreover, these opinions have this great inherent weakness, when it is attempted to use them for purposes of defence, that it is impossible to get up the slightest enthusiasm for them. No one can feel enthusiastic about moderation or compromise. The ideas that move the world are always extremes. The man who makes the crowd follow him is never a preacher of wise compromise, but one who takes a single one-sided principle, and makes it so luminous in the eyes of mankind that they fancy they can see in it a solution of all their doubt and difficulties, and a satisfaction of their desires. If Sakya-Muni had declared that the principle of self-conquest must be compromised with a rational enjoyment of what life can give, he would have been nearer to the truth than he was, but I doubt if we should ever have heard of Buddhism.

So much for the reasons that have caused the change of popular opinion in the past. Let us now turn to the future, and inquire whether any, and if so, what, position can be taken up on the basis of the new ideas for the defence of the proper province of individual liberty and private enterprise against unwise and improper aggressions by the State.[8]

If the view here laid down is correct – if it is true that Socialism and Individuality are of the nature of two antagonistic but indispensable forces evolving social progress by their continual collision – it is evident that whenever they are thus opposed, their claims must be weighed against each other, and that element disregarded, the neglect of which, in the particular case, will be least harmful to the permanent welfare of the nation. Of course, I do not mean that this process is to be gone through in every case – less cumbrous rules for guidance can no doubt be found; but whatever secondary rules or classifications we may make use of, this is the fundamental principle that must underlie them all. Nor does it, of course, imply that in every case there must be doubt as to

[8] On this point see a remarkable passage by Kant, quoted by Professor Huxley in his article on "Administrative Nihilism," "Critiques and Addresses," p. 22. The work from which it is taken is called "A Conception of Universal History in Relation to Universal Citizenship," and was translated by De Quincey. – P.

whether the claims of Individuality or Socialism should prevail. In many classes of cases there is no doubt whatever. Experience has proved, and common-sense shows us, that the considerations on the one side always largely outweigh those on the other.

To glance at the analogous forces of Egoism and Altruism, no man doubts that he has a right to keep his wife's affections, and that he is not bound to forego them for the benefit of others; and, on the other hand, there is (*pace* the Fenians) no question that a man may not blow up his neighbour's house to gratify his taste for pyrotechnic display. Nor, in the same way, does anyone question the right of the State to restrain crime, or to control the organization of the army; nor, on the other hand, of the individual to choose his own boots, or go into trade. But between such extremes as are represented by these examples are cases in which the proportions which the claims on either side bear to each other vary in an infinite gradation till something like equality is reached, and when this is the case, I do not see how we are to decide between them, except by weighing them carefully against each other with the aid of every kind of light that can be brought to bear upon the case.

For the sake of simplicity, I have spoken here as though the claims of the two great elements of Individuality and Society were the only considerations that we have got to put into the scales. But this is rarely, if ever, the case, and to argue as if it were would be to commit the very blunder which I borrowed Mr. Justice Stephen's words to condemn – namely, that of considering only two out of the various forces engaged. On an earlier page of this article, I showed briefly the diversity of considerations that are involved in such matters as Factory, Sanitary, and Adulteration Acts. The fact is that, though the two great considerations are nearly always present in any question of State action, whether it be directed towards the undertaking of certain functions or to the actual restraining of individuals, they are by no means usually the only ones, or even always – in seeming, at any rate – the most important.

When we are considering whether the State ought or ought not to undertake the railways of the country, the question whether it will manage them better or worse than private enterprise seems quite as important as the more general question, whether it is good for a country in the long-run that such things as railways should be managed by the State. And when we are considering whether certain forms of wickedness should be restrained by the State, it is not enough to balance the claims of Individuality against those of Socialism[9] to decide that it may do so; we must have regard to more immediate considerations arising from the nature of law as an instrument, and its consequent fitness for the purpose of repressing them. In short, when we are trying the legitimacy of a State action, we have not merely to weigh against each other the two fundamental considerations, but to add to one or both of them a quantity of others.

But, it is said, this method of deciding such questions by weighing and balancing the considerations is an impossible one. No man that ever lived could possess a complete and accurate knowledge of all the factors, past, present, and future, involved in each case. Is there no simple principle to be found limiting the rights of Society against the individual, and of the individual against Society? – a principle which, if it cannot, owing to the limitations of human knowledge, completely solve all difficulties, will at least prove a true guide in all cases in which we can see correctly how to apply it?

Difficulty of finding the exact limitation of individual rights as against those of society.

Though the argument as to impossibility is not quite so conclusive as it may appear, since in all the walks of life we have to act upon merely probable and often utterly insufficient evidence, no one can be more alive than I am to the desirability of discovering such a principle. But I cannot conceive it to be possible. I can no more imagine a principle that would tell us in every case the limits of individual and State rights than one that would tell us in every case whether the dictates of Egoism or Altruism were to be obeyed. Principles, in the sense of sound rules based upon accurate observation of men and societies, their functions and their circumstances, may be found, and prove of great value, no one doubts; but not a single simple principle in the sense here intended, that shall be at once of universal application and of practical use

---

[9] I am very hard driven, all through, for a word to express my meaning. "Socialism" is unsatisfactory; "Society" or "Sociality" would be still more likely to mislead. – P.

in defining the wise limit of State interference. The dual or manifold aspect of all actions, whether of the State or of the individual, and the number and variety of the considerations by which they are affected, seem to me entirely to forbid it. And even if we put aside all alien and secondary considerations, and regard State action as a matter in which the direct interests of Individuality and Socialism only are concerned, I think we shall find that it still is impossible.

[10]If these two great elements in human society really stand towards each other in the relation I have attributed to them, it is evident that there must always be some sort of compromise or compact existing between the individual and the society, and that compact must contain the principle, if such a principle there be. But if we inquire what the terms of this silent treaty are in the various races of the world, in the several stages of their development, we find that they are never the same. Men themselves, the societies of which they are units, and the external circumstances by which those societies are surrounded, are not only all extremely diverse at any given moment, but they are all in a state of continual modification; and at every step in the dual transformation of the man and his society the bargain between them will be, in some degree, a different one. The demands of the individual on the one side, and of the State on the other, alter according to the alterations that have taken place in the nature of each; and the change is probably further increased by variations in the external circumstances of the society, or in its forms of government, which have placed the one party or the other in a better position for driving a bargain.[11]

In an early stage of civilization, for example, the individual probably demands little more than some protection to life and liberty, some certainty of sufficient food, and freedom to marry and bring up children; while his nature is such that

---

[10] See Professor Huxley's treatment of this identical problem, "Administrative Nihilism," p. 23, "Critiques and Addresses." I wish I could afford the space to quote it at length. – P.

[11] When the form of government is democratic, society and the individual will be commonly united in the same person; and this ensures the freedom and fairness of the contract between them, even though the individual has little or no choice about joining or leaving the society. When the form of government is aristocratic or autocratic, this is not the case in the majority of instances, and the bargain will therefore be commonly a very one-sided one. – P.

Society, to avoid dissolution, and to make any progress, is obliged to require of him, in return, a large surrender of his personal liberty, in the form of submissive obedience. But, as man becomes more civilized, the things he requires from Society become more numerous and less simple. In addition to those primary needs enumerated above, the object for which he is ready to barter some portion of his liberty is the opportunity of more fully exercising his faculties in various directions than is possible in a state of solitude: the desire to trade, to interchange ideas, to pursue art, to acquire wealth, power, or fame – all those things that make man more a man. (And here we get a hint of the importance to mankind of a variety of type in his society.) At the same time, his nature having become more rational and intelligent, his instincts more comfortable and more disciplined, and his knowledge of how to do things and his desire to do them having both greatly increased, it is no longer either wise or necessary for Society to do so much for him or to exact of him so great a sacrifice of his liberty as before; except, of course, in so far as the external circumstances of the State may necessitate at times his complete submission for purposes of national defence.

Thus we see a tendency on the part of the State, as civilization advances, to leave more to private enterprise, and to relax its restraints upon individual speech and action; and it seems not impossible that in the immediate future the untoward circumstance of a too rapidly increasing population, causing as it does both a deterioration of the moral type and an insufficiency of material wealth, may bring about a temporary alteration of the compact in a retrograde direction. Until we have learnt how to control or deal with it, Society may consider itself forced to demand temporarily some contradiction of individual liberty in more branches than one. However this may be, it is quite clear that the compact between the individual and his society that we are enjoying in England in the nineteenth century is not only different from that which existed in the feudal ages, but would have brought about general dissolution if it had been applied to those times; and there is no reason for believing that it will not prove just as unsuitable in one direction or the other to the civilization that will be in existence five centuries hence.

Now, what principle can we find, common to all these varied compacts, which would be of the slightest use to us in determining the proper limits of Government interference at the present day? The school that is represented by Mr. Spencer and Von Humboldt would probably reply that the common feature that is to be observed in all these bargains is that what man barters some portion of his freedom for is always more freedom – freedom to use his faculties; and they would deduce from this that the principle of Government should be "Absolute freedom for each, limited only by the like freedom for others." I do not feel satisfied with this deduction[12]; for one reason, because it seems to me to be only arrived at by an undue straining of language. What man barters some portion of his freedom for seems to me to be: first, some security for life and liberty; secondly, *opportunity* rather than freedom to exercise his faculties. But, allowing it to pass as correct, of what use is it for our purpose?

If by any effort of ingenuity it be stretched wide enough to be made the true rule in all known stages of human progress, it is evident that its width of interpretation would make it quite useless as a practical guide to us. If, on the other hand, it is admitted that it could not apply as a wise practical rule to all these phases, or even to any one of them that has yet been known – and it is only claimed that it is an ideal principle towards which progress is constantly tending, and which may become of universal application when men are very different from what they are now – its equal uselessness to us in the present day as practical guide or test is no less plain.

I would ask those who hold that, whatever may be the case with the past, the time has now come in which it may be safely treated as an infallible guide, to consider how, by way of an instance, they propose to deal with the law of marriage. Are they prepared to abrogate this greatest of all interferences with freedom of contract, and do they hold that such a reform would bring a preponderance of benefit in our present state of civilization? If, on the other hand, they declare that the principle of "Absolute freedom for each, limited only by

---

[12] I think it is an instance of the usual futile endeavour to discover in human affairs a simplicity and unity that never exist. If man requires of Society opportunity to exercise his faculties, he also requires of it the very contrary benefit – that is, to be saved the trouble of using them – and no theory that leaves this out of sight can be a true one. – P.

the like freedom of all," does not condemn such a law, I am puzzled to guess what form of State regulation it is capable of defending us against. We must not loosen or tighten its interpretation to suit our convenience.

I do not think, then, that it is possible to find any single principle of any practical use that will prescribe for us the proper limits of State action, and I think if we carefully study the argument of the greatest of living philosophers, who has certainly gone nearer than anyone else to the establishment of such a principle, that we shall not fail to find indications of its impossibility, and fresh grounds for suspecting that the debateable land between the State and the individual is still a very wide one, and likely to remain so for some time to come.

The principle he lays down is this: That, excepting for purposes of external defence, such as the army and navy, the action of the State should be always negatively regulative, never positively regulative; that it should restrain, but never stimulate nor direct; and that it should always be directed to the securing of freedom. He illustrates the meaning of the terms in the following manner:

"If a man has land, and I either cultivate it for him, partially or wholly, or dictate any or all of his modes of cultivation, my action is positively regulative; but if, leaving him absolutely unhelped and unregulated in his farming, I simply prevent him from taking his neighbour's crops, or making approach roads across his neighbour's land, or depositing rubbish upon it, my action is negatively regulative. There is a tolerably sharp distinction between the act of securing a citizen's ends for him and the act of checking him when he interferes with another citizen in the pursuit of his end."[13]

This conclusion is supported by a mass of arguments that I cannot attempt even to catalogue here, drawn from an exhaustive study of the nature and functions of every sort and kind of human society, either in the present or the past, of which knowledge is attainable, assisted by such lights as can be thrown upon the subject by the working of natural laws in other departments of science. I must content myself here with touching – and that only imperfectly – on what I think may fairly be considered the culminating confirmation

[13] "Specialized Administration," "Essays," vol. iii., pp. 145, 146. – P.

of his argument: the marvellous analogy that he has discovered between the facts of biology and those of sociology.

After pointing out a most curious series of similarities between the body physiological and the body politic, from the lowest to the highest types of each that are known to us, he brings us to this: that, as in the former there are certain external functions, such as movements of the limbs, which are under the direct control of the brain and nerves, and certain internal and nutritive functions that are carried on automatically by the nutritive organs without any such control; so in the latter there are certain external functions, such as the defence of the State, which are necessarily and properly dependent on the governing power, and certain internal industrial and social functions that can and ought to be carried on without the intervention of that power. He calls our attention to the marvellous elaborateness and perfection of these internal structures of Society, such as trade or language, that have grown up from the smallest and rudest beginning to what we see them now, not only without the assistance or direction of Government, but without conscious organization on the part of anyone whatever.

He instances the feeding of a great city like London, and bids us consider the difficulties of the task:

"Difficulties caused by the inconstancy in the arrival of supplies; by the perishable nature of many of the commodities; by the fluctuating numbers of consumers; by the heterogeneity of their demands; by variations in the stocks, immediate and remote, and the need for adjusting the rate of consumption; and by the complexity in the process of distribution, required to bring due quantities of these many commodities to the houses of all citizens."

It may safely be said that the cleverest body of officials in the world, if they were set to organize such a work with every appliance at their command, could not carry it on through its daily varying vicissitudes without constant alternations of waste and shortness of supply. As it is, there is hardly an atom of waste, and scarcely even a household misses its milk in the morning. And this extraordinary work is executed, not only without State organization, but without any conscious organization whatever. To quote Archbishop Whately,[14] from whose work the illustration is taken:

"This object is accomplished far better than it could be by any effort of human wisdom, through the agency of men who think each of nothing beyond his own immediate interest, who, with that object only in view, perform their respective parts with cheerful zeal, and combine unconsciously to employ the wisest means for effecting an object, the vastness of which it would bewilder them even to contemplate."

And Mr. Spencer further points out to us that not only is the State unable to assist these internal functions of which the above is an instance, by positive regulation, but that it has been repeatedly shown that attempts to do so prove uniformly mischievous. All that the State can do, and what it must do for such functions, is to maintain law and order, and to enforce contracts.

Mr. Herbert Spencer's analogy between the body politic and the human body.
"Just in the same way that a bodily organ that performs function, but is not adequately repaid in blood, must dwindle, and the organism as a whole eventually suffer, so an industrial centre which has made and sent out a special commodity, but does not get adequately repaid in other commodities, must decay. And when we ask what is requisite in the body politic to prevent this local innutrition and decay, we find the requisites to be that agreements shall be carried out, the goods paid for at stipulated prices, that justice shall be administered."[15]

But if the correctness of the analogy be admitted, if it be granted that the industrial functions of the State are self-working, and not to be meddled with without mischief; even if it be admitted further – and I own I find it difficult to resist the conviction – that we are dealing here "not with a figurative resemblance, but a fundamental parallelism"[16] of deep significance, the difficulty of defining the precise limits of State action does not seem to me to be got over. We have set apart certain classes of acts as unfit for State regulation,

[14] Introduction to "Lectures on Political Economy." – P.
[15] "Specialized Administration," p. 141. – P.
[16] "Introduction to the Study of Sociology," p. 328. – P.

but that is all. Of course I do not mean that it is of little importance. Protective fallacies are not yet dead, and it is something to be able to set them aside with confidence. It suggests the uselessness and mischief of the wanton interferences with contract that we seem to be so given to in the present era. Its bearing on the Socialist schemes that are so fast becoming popular is of the greatest moment, and it tends to correct the absurd, but extremely widespread, delusion that the material and other progress of a country will necessarily stagnate if its institutions and trades are not continually meddled with by legislation.

But it will be observed that the social functions in which the accuracy and completeness of the analogy are most perfect are precisely those about which there is least dispute. Only a few people contend that Government regulation of trade is desirable; and the wildest politician has never yet proposed the institution of a Minister of Language. If the industrial functions are regarded from the point of view adopted in this article, it will be noticed that they are matters in which there is very little clashing of the interests of Society and the individual; very little sacrifice on either side, therefore, necessary to effect a compromise between them, and the minimum of doubt as to their respective rights. The right of the individual to trade at a profit is unquestionable, since he benefits Society as well as himself by so doing, and the right of Society to prevent his making use of criminal methods is no less indisputable.

The analogy not absolutely perfect.
Moreover, the functions about which there is most dispute are precisely those in which the analogy helps us very little, if at all. They present few, if any, of the similarities to the nutritive functions of the body that are so striking in the case of trade, or the supplying of a great city. No examination of their working will show that they can be trusted to carry themselves on with the utmost completeness and perfection without organization or assistance, under every variety of circumstance. When we examine a social function like the feeding of a great city, we are readily convinced that State interference would be both mischievous and unnecessary, because we perceive that the simple motive of self-interest suffices to carry it on as perfectly as we can conceive possible.

Reasons for compulsory sanitation and compulsory education.

Can we say the same of sewage organization, for instance, or National Education? How much do we see in these social functions of "that curious and admirable arrangement by which each man secures his needs by ministering to those of others"? As regards the former, which Mr. Spencer adduces as an instance of the way that State regulation prevents the introduction of new and improved methods, it is notorious that in our huge towns private enterprise is quite incapable of dealing with it, strong as the promptings of self-interest are, and that State regulation is necessary to prevent disastrous results.[17] The same insufficiency of internal motive power presents itself in the case of National Education. Mr. Spencer complains that the laws of supply and demand are hardly ever recognized as applying to it. No doubt they are not sufficiently recognized, but ought not this very fact to suggest the probability of a difference in the cases? To what *extent* do they apply to it? They will ensure that where there is a demand for authors and engineers, authors and engineers shall be forthcoming. But will they ensure that every household that wants education will get it with the same regularity that they ensure that every household shall receive its milk in the morning?

The cause of its failure to do so lies, I suppose, in the fact that self-interest, which seems to be as necessary to the working of self-acting functions as steam to a boiler, is very often directly opposed to education. It is, or seems to be, of very little importance to factory-owners, or farmers, that their workmen should be educated, while the loss of child-labour is a serious draw-back; and the same remark applies to parents.

[17] Mr. Spencer would probably reply that the State should interfere, but only negatively, by forbidding nuisances under heavy penalties, while leaving everyone free to dispose of his sewage as he thought fit. This is the same principle that Mr. Mill laid down about education. He thought that it should be compulsory, but not provided by the State ("On Liberty," 189). I have no doubt that such a course would be preferable in either case if it were practicable. But it is not. The State could not enforce compulsory education without providing school accommodation, or punish the inhabitants of crowded towns for nuisances without finding them means for disposing of sewage. This is not a bad instance of the way in which a principle that seems undeniable theoretically fails to cope with the complexity of realities. – P.

But whatever the cause, there can be no doubt of the fact. No one can contend that National, in the sense of Universal Education, is possible in the England of our day without State agency. Private enterprise, whether prompted by egoistic or altruistic motives, will not effect it. Mr. Spencer, perhaps, would say that it is not an end that we should determine to attain, because the price we shall have to pay for it in the loss of variety and the habit of self-help is out of all proportion too great. I do not wish to be understood as disputing Mr. Spencer's conclusion on this point. It is a problem about which I have never arrived at any feeling of certainty. I merely wish to show that National Education cannot be defended from State regulation on grounds that are sufficient for the defence of industrial processes, that it cannot be accurately classified with functions which discharge themselves with the greatest conceivable perfection without external assistance from the State, without even any conscious organization on the part of the individuals by whose actions they work.[18] It seems as if it might be rather an instance – perhaps not the best that could be chosen – of social functions of a hybrid character, partially self-working, partially (under certain circumstances) in need of external regulation.

Would not the analogy from Biology, if followed out, lead us to expect such cases? Are there not in the body physiological functions that lie between those that are purely self-working, and those that are always directed by the brain and nerves – belonging partly to one class, partly to the other – sometimes working automatically, sometimes by external

[18] The rough line that is usually drawn between State regulation and private enterprise seems to me very unsatisfactory and unscientific. Many private organizations possess in varying degrees the defects that are commonly held to distinguish State organization. Large Joint Stock Companies, such as Railway and Water Companies, that are necessarily to some extent in possession of monopolies, are actuated by the same reasons for a sluggish regard to the public interest as any body of State officials (in addition to some peculiar to themselves), and private educational endowments exhibit the same disinclination to grow and develop that we observe in public institutions. The one feature that usually distinguishes private from State organizations is that the former are stimulated by self-interest in its strongest and most direct form, while the latter are not. But even this is not invariably the case, as we may see by private endowments on the one hand and local government on the other. But perhaps it will be said that local government should be classed under the other heading. – P.

control, functions with which *the brain and nerves may be said to interfere, or not, according to the circumstances of the particular case?*[19]

I think, therefore, that even if we admit to the full the accuracy of the analogy between the body and the State, it will fail to show us the limits of legitimate Government action.

Furthermore, if we attempt to apply the maxim, that in all internal affairs the action of the State should be only negatively regulative, as a practical rule of scientific truth by which we may determine those limits in every case in which we can see how to make use of it, I think we shall be assailed by the same doubts of its infallibility that beset us in considering the principle of "Absolute freedom, limited only by the like freedom for all," from which it is to some extent a deduction. Let us take the same example as before, and ask how it would apply to the law of marriage. It seems to me that it would unmistakably condemn it. For the doctrine of negative regulation I understand to be this: 1. That the State should only forbid, never direct or prescribe. 2. That the sole and direct object of its action should be to secure the free working of the function affected. Now, surely the law of marriage infringes both these canons. It is the clearest case of positive regulation; and it is not aimed directly at the securing of freedom. The State does not content itself with enforcing such contracts as men and women are pleased to make. It prescribes the contract. I think we have a right to ask those who tell us this is an infallible practical rule, whether they are prepared to adhere to it in this instance. If they answer in the affirmative, as Von Humboldt did,[20] most people will have a strong opinion about the soundness and wisdom of the principle; if they admit that we have hit on an exception, there is an end of its infallibility and trustworthiness.

But perhaps it will be said that I have given the principle a narrower interpretation than would be sanctioned by its great expounder – that under it the State need not be confined to action directly and immediately aiming at freedom, that it

---

[19] I should not have ventured upon this suggestion if I had not found some confirmation of such an idea in Professor Huxley's article already quoted. – P.

[20] P. 34. Humboldt's "Ideen," etc. – P.

would be justified in considering the more remote consequences of men's actions and their effects upon freedom, and
that, understood in this way, the principle would not condemn the law of marriage. I do not believe that I am guilty
of any misinterpretation,[21] or that Mr. Spencer would endorse
such a construction; but the answer to it seems to me to be
twofold.

In the first place, it does not in the least get over the
objection as to the positiveness of the regulation; secondly, if
it is to be construed in this way, I do not see how it is to be
any sort of bulwark against State aggression. If the State
may interfere with a man's liberty on the ground that the
secondary and possible consequences of his free action may
be prejudicial to the liberty of others, I cannot see that there
is any limit (in principle) to what the State might do with
him. All the worst interferences with liberty the world has
seen have been excused on the ground that, when the remote
consequences of the action interfered with were considered,
they really protected freedom, in this world or the next, and
it is against this doctrine that every defence of liberty has
been directed.

Lest, from my having selected it twice, it should be thought
that there is any unique peculiarity about the marriage law
that has led me into a misconception, I would point out that
the infallibility of the principle of negative regulation can be
equally well tested by so simple and familiar an example as
the prescription of cab fares. This is a glaring and unmistak-
able infraction of the principle. Yet will anyone contend that
its abolition would be an improvement? that cabmen should
be allowed to make what bargains they please, Government
contenting themselves with enforcing the contracts? Think
what extortions would be practised on the nervous, and

---

[21] I am not quite free from doubt, however. I am not always able to follow
the distinction which Mr. Spencer draws between positive and negative
regulation. For instance, he seems to put Building Acts in one class and
Merchant Shipping Acts in the other. I should have thought that their
principle was identical, and that they were both positively regulative.
Adulteration Acts he calls negatively regulative on the ground that adulteration is a breach of contract and an injurious fraud, but I am not sure
that the Contagious Diseases Acts, which he unreservedly condemns,
might not be justified on the same ground, if anyone cared to undertake
so odious a task. – P.

everyone who was obviously anxious to catch a train or keep an appointment!

The argument that was made use of in testing the value of the maxim of "Absolute freedom, limited only by the like freedom of all," will not apply to the very similar principle enunciated by Mr. Mill. And for this reason. Mr. Mill deliberately limited it to comparatively modern times. By so doing he deprived it of a good deal of authority. When we are told that a principle would have been generally inapplicable in the time of Charlemagne, we cannot help suspecting that there may be cases in which it is inapplicable in the present day. But a principle so limited escapes the destructive criticism that can be levelled against one that professes to be an eternal law inherent in the nature of man. But this is of little practical moment, as the slightest examination will show that as a defence against Government aggression it is wholly insufficient.

"The principle is," to use Mr. Mill's own words, "that the sole end for which mankind are warranted, individually or collectively, in interfering with the liberty of action of any of their number, is self-protection; that the only purpose for which power can be rightfully exercised over any member of a civilized community against his will is to prevent harm to others. His own good, either physical or moral, is not a sufficient warrant. He cannot rightfully be compelled to do or forbear because it will be better for him to do so; because it will make him happier; because, in the opinion of others, to do so would be wise, or even right. These are good reasons for remonstrating with him, or reasoning with him, or persuading him, or entreating him, but not for compelling him, or visiting him with any evil in case he do otherwise. To justify that, the conduct from which it is desired to deter him must be calculated to produce evil to someone else. The only part of the conduct of anyone for which he is amenable to Society is that which concerns others. In the part which merely concerns himself, his independence is, of right, absolute. Over himself, over his own body and mind, the individual is sovereign."[22]

I do not think this dictum can be considered indisputable, even though its application be restricted, as Mr. Mill restricts

[22] "On Liberty," pp. 21, 22. – P.

it, to civilized times and nations, and adult men and women. Those who, like Mr. Huxley and Mr. Justice Stephen, hold that societies are governed and guided by a minority of the wise and good, will generally, I think, meet it with a direct negative. Personally, I have no wish to run atilt against it. On the broad ground of the widest expediency on which it professes to be based, and with which its imperious tone sounds perhaps a trifle inconsistent, I think its wisdom as a practical rule of government can generally be justified; and that limited, as Mr. Mill has limited it, it would seldom lead us into serious mischief, and would keep us out of a good deal. But, regarded as a rampart against improper interference with liberty, it seems to me perfectly useless.

All that it really lays down is that Society can have no business to interfere with acts that are purely self-regarding. But how far does this take us? The very kernel of our difficulty is the fact that hardly any actions are purely self-regarding. The greater part of them bear a double aspect – one which concerns self, another which concerns others – and Mr. Mill admits that, "as soon as any part of a person's conduct affects prejudicially the interest of others, Society has jurisdiction over it[23] ... that whenever there is a definite damage, or a definite risk of damage, either to an individual or to the public, the case is taken out of the province of liberty, and placed in that of morality or law."[24] It is true that he qualifies this by excepting "merely contingent or constructive injury to Society," on the grounds that "the inconvenience is one that Society can well afford to bear, for the sake of the greater good of human freedom"; but what is this really but a weighing of the considerations on the one side against those on the other, and an expression of Mr. Mill's opinion that in certain cases the benefit to Individualism will outweigh the injury inflicted on Society? The fact is, that hardly any acts are purely self-regarding, and Mr. Mill could only establish the claims of liberty to the provinces he wished to assign to it, partly by dubbing certain classes of acts self-regarding that are only occasionally or usually so, partly by leaving his principle behind him occasionally, and fighting with the weapons that some of his followers characterize as useless.

---

[23] "On Liberty," p. 135. – P.
[24] *Ibid.*, p. 147. – P.

Mill's argument for complete liberty for individuals sketched too widely.

He executed this surprising change of front with the utmost frankness. For instance, after claiming under his principle "complete liberty of conscience, thought, and feeling, absolute freedom of opinion and sentiment on all subjects, practical or speculative, scientific, moral, or theological," he goes on to say "the liberty of expressing or publishing opinions may seem to fall under a different principle, since it belongs to that part of the conduct of an individual that concerns other people; but being almost of as much importance as the liberty of thought itself, and resting in great part on the same reasons, is practically inseparable from it."[25] In other words, or almost the same words transposed, "Liberty of speech and writing is almost as important as liberty of thought itself, rests in great part upon the same reasons, and is practically inseparable from it. But it cannot be brought under the simple principle by which liberty is to be defended, because it is not a self-regarding action" (as we hardly need to be reminded at a time when a statesman whose liberality is unquestionable has solemnly declared, without possibility of contradiction, that "articles and speeches may be just as much a part of the machinery of murder as sword-canes and pistols"). Therefore Mr. Mill leaves his principle to take care of itself, and goes forth to do battle on behalf of free speech and a free press without it.

Indeed, when it is applied to any practical question, such as the sale of intoxicating liquors, its futility becomes at once apparent. Mr. Mill dealt with this question himself,[26] and demolished a temperance secretary who wanted to put a stop to the drink traffic on the ground that it invaded his social rights. I think Mr. Mill's arguments against such interference overwhelming, but, for the life of me, I cannot see how his principle condemns it. Is drunkenness purely self-regarding? Does it not injure others? Is it not notoriously accompanied by poverty, crime, and consequent taxation, and do not others have to bear the burden of such things? We may argue if we like, with Mill, that all these evils are less than those that are inflicted on national character by a Maine liquor law, and

[25] "On Liberty," p. 26. – P.
[26] "On Liberty," p. 159. – P.

declare, with an eloquent prelate, that we would rather see England free than England sober, if it were necessary to choose between the two; but this is to throw the principle overboard, and argue the question on its merits.

The more we examine it, the more clearly shall we perceive that it is quite insufficient for our purpose. When we are considering whether, in a particular case, the claims of the Individual or of the Social elements should be considered paramount, how often is it of any use to remind ourselves that Society may only coerce a man to prevent harm to others? What we generally want to know is the limit to this right of Society's, which the principle admits; and of that it will tell us nothing.

I think, therefore, that we must make up our minds to give up the idea of discovering any single principle that will enable us in all cases to set the proper boundaries to State action and protect the province of individual freedom. It is not without great reluctance that I have come to this conclusion. It would be difficult to exaggerate the value that such a principle would possess to mankind. Equivalent to a law of nature, it would constitute a valuable confirmation, even where proof from expediency was clearest, and an infallible guide when proof from expediency was impossible. Especially valuable would it be at a moment like the present, when the temptation to ignore the importance of Individualism is so peculiarly great. If anything could certainly save us from the undue leaning towards Socialism that marks the present day, and the disastrous consequences that must, I believe, inevitably ensue from it, it would be the discovery of some such simple principle, easy to comprehend, believe, and apply. I can well understand, therefore, the almost passionate reluctance of those who believe they are in possession of such a touchstone to admit that it has yet to be discovered.

But a searching analysis of the problem has shown us the *primâ facie* impossibility of finding such a principle; and we have seen that the test of practical application throws a grave doubt upon the validity of all the maxims that make any claim to such a character. And if a true principle would be invaluable, a faulty one is worse than worthless; for when it is discovered to be fallible, and, therefore, useless as a universal rule, all the truth it contains is apt to suffer with it. It has been found false in one case; it is forgotten how true it is in many others. The genuine considerations on which it is based are discredited and discarded along with it. Common men will not draw fine distinctions between a principle, and the contentions on which it is based, and the arguments by which they are justified, separate and distinct though the three may really be. I cannot but think that Mr. Mill's magnificent pleas for freedom of thought and discussion, and for the necessity of individual variety as an element of well-being, have suffered somewhat in their influence on public opinion from being (apparently) bound up to stand or fall with a principle that has been felt insufficient to justify them.

But if it is the case that any such principle is out of our reach, the task set the present generation is to discover how the just claims of individualism are to be maintained without it; whether it is not possible, on the view of the nature of human affairs described in this article, to make an adequate defence of the proper province of individual liberty and enterprise by means of experience and observation (in the widest meanings of those words), and such rules and generalizations as we are able legitimately to base upon them.

I am aware that most of the champions of liberty are given to expressing little hope of such an enterprise. They answer usually that it means deciding all cases by a balance of narrow expediencies; that proof from expediency is impossible, because it is impossible to obtain possession of all the data involved in such questions; and that if there is no definite principle to appeal to, there is no commanding reason why Government should not decree the shape of our hats, and the shops we should buy them at, to-morrow, or anything else that is mischievous and absurd. To which I should like to give the following general answers:

In the first place, if the view we have taken of human affairs be admitted, there is a principle to appeal to, none the less real because we are unable to define it exactly. If Individualism is admitted to be an essential element in social progress, the action of Government must always be restrained by a due consideration for it. There is no greater fallacy than to think that men will pay no regard to considerations which they know to be real, because they are unable to define them precisely.

And why "narrow" expediencies? Why not the widest

expediencies, such as those on which Mr. Mill based the principle he attempted to establish? Whatever may be the case with that principle (and I have already said that, when not unduly stretched, it seemed to me to be a sound one), there was nothing in his method of arriving at it in the least inconsistent with the view here adopted. He recognized the antagonism of social and individual considerations. He set himself to prove that in certain classes of cases the evils of interference with liberty always exceeded the benefits, and that interference, therefore, was, in such cases, invariably inexpedient; and on the base of these contentions he attempted to frame a general rule for the guidance of mankind. It cannot, therefore, necessarily land us in chaos to have to decide such questions by considerations of expediency, unless we are willing to admit that Mr. Mill's rule was founded upon chaos. The method on which we have to rely for ascertaining whether, in certain cases, the State ought or ought not to interfere, is simply the method that he relied on for the same purpose, and the work that he did is the work that we have to go on doing.

Moreover, I deny that proof is so hopeless of attainment as it is sometimes made out to be. The reasons why the State should not do certain things, should not interfere with certain actions, are often obvious enough, and, when they are not, experience in the shape of history frequently steps in and gives us the required guidance. Doubtless there are many cases in which it seems impossible to arrive at certainty by such means. But it is the merest rhetorical trick to speak of this uncertainty as though it were peculiar to this subject. The old myth of the Sphinx applies for ever, not to one, but to every kind of human action. It is not merely in politics, but in every department of our life, that we have to act constantly on evidence of the merest probability, and that even when the direst penalties in case of mistake are hanging over our heads.

Nor will it be the least necessary to decide every case on its merits, as if nothing of the sort had ever happened before. Experience and observation will enable us to frame rules and principles that will become wider and more general with the advance of political science; and if in this science the first principles should be the last things to be discovered, we should remember that it will prove no exception to the general rule.[27]

Lastly, those who speak so strongly about the impossibility of deciding such matters by a balance of expediencies should recollect that, even if they were in possession of a perfect general principle, its truth would have to be proved in that very manner if they wished to convert the world to a belief in it. It could only gain general acceptance by repeated and continual appeals to facts for its confirmation. Not only are most men incapable of appreciating the cogency of deductions from a principle, but they are rightly quite as sceptical about a man's infallibility in arriving at truth by this process as of his arriving at what is expedient by calculating the practical consequences of actions; and they feel besides that, while it is comparatively easy to check the accuracy of the latter process, as all its mistakes are exposed by the course of events, errors in the former may pass undetected for an indefinite period. It might even be added that human nature is so weak that men will often go wrong on points about which they really have no doubt, unless the practical consequences of their action are kept steadily before them. Not even the religious can afford to dispense with this kind of proof from expediency. On all these grounds, it is evident that, even were we in possession of a general principle that would determine for us the true provinces of Individuality and State regulation, we should be compelled to justify the boundary-line by demonstrations from expediency as well.

To those who have already set their hands to the defence of freedom by joining the Liberty and Property Defence League, I venture specially to commend the considerations which this article contains. For, in the first place, such a body, though it cannot hope to be unanimous, and though it may wisely abstain from any profession of faith, must, in practice, make up its mind as to the broad grounds on which it will fight.

Secondly, to have any hope of success, it is necessary that it should be, to a certain extent, in sympathy with current ideas and beliefs. It is not merely that it is impossible to

---

[27] I believe this is true of all the sciences, including even mathematics. We all know that it is true of morality, the first principles of which are as obstinately disputed now as they were 2,000 years ago. – P.

refute what is not fully understood: it is that it is impossible to convert anyone unless there can be found some common premises to start from. If the League wishes to convert the world in general, it must find somewhere premises on the subject to which the world will not be unready to assent. It is not of the slightest use for it to content itself with a mere repetition of the maxims loss of faith in which has been the cause of its being called into existence. Of course what was true in the old formulas is true still, but it must be presented in a form suited to the wider knowledge and the altered feelings of the present day. For instance, there may be good reasons for opposing measures akin to the Factory or Sanitary Acts; but to denounce them on the *sole* ground that they are infractions of a sacred principle would have, in my opinion, no effect but to put the League hopelessly out of court. Unless it remembers this, as I trust it will, it must fail to obtain any real influence in the country; and it will tend to become nothing but an obstructive Society for the protection of vested interests, and the preservation of ideas that are out of date.

In the present article I have attempted, first, to delineate the view of human affairs that I believe to be both approximately true, and to some extent in harmony with the current ideas of the majority, or at least a large portion, of thinking humanity; secondly, to point out what I think should be the nature of the defence of individual liberty and enterprise that we should strive to base upon it.

Space forbids me to go farther at this moment, but in a future article I hope to show conclusively the urgent practical necessity for framing such a defence at the present time, and to enumerate a few of the points which I think it should not neglect.

ECONOMIC SOCIALISM
Henry Sidgwick

OBSERVERS of the current drift of political thought and practice, however widely they may diverge in their judgments of its tendencies, appear to be generally agreed upon one point – viz., that all Socialism is flowing in upon us with a full tide. Whether, like M. de Laveleye, they regard this phenomenon complacently as a "good time coming," or whether, with Mr. Spencer, they hold that what is coming is "slavery," they seem to have no doubt that the political signs are pointing to a great extension of governmental interference in the affairs of private members of the community. And a second point on which they appear to agree is that this socialistic movement – as it is often called – is altogether opposed to "orthodox political economy"; that the orthodox political economist teaches us to restrict the intervention of Government on all the lines on which the socialistic movement aims at extending it. The object of the present paper is not to argue directly for or against any proposed governmental interference, but to reduce to its proper limits the supposed opposition between orthodox political economy and what is vaguely called socialistic, or semi-socialistic, legislation. I admit that the opposition really exists to some extent; and, so far as it exists, I am – for the most part – on the side of orthodox political economy; but I think that the opposition has been dangerously and misleadingly exaggerated for want of a proper distinction of the different grounds on which different kinds of governmental interference are reasonably based.

I will begin by stating briefly the general argument by which orthodox political economy seeks to show that wealth tends to be produced most amply and economically in a society where Government leaves industry alone; – that is, where Government confines itself to the protection of person, property, and reputation, and the enforcement of contracts not obtained by force or fraud, leaving individuals free to produce and transfer to others whatever utilities they may choose, on any terms that may be freely arranged. The argument is briefly that – assuming that the conduct of individuals is generally characterized by a fairly intelligent and alert pursuit of their private interests – regard for self-interest on the part of consumers will lead to the effectual demand for the commodities that are most useful to society, and regard for self-interest on the part of producers will lead to the production of such commodities at the least cost. If any material part of the ordinary supply of any commodity A were generally estimated as less adapted for the satisfaction of social needs than the quantity of another commodity B that could be produced at the same cost, the demand of consumers would be diverted from A to B, so that A would fall in market value and B rise; and this change in values would cause a diversion of the efforts of producers from A to B to the extent required. On the other hand, the self-interest of producers will tend to the production of everything at the least possible cost; because the self-interest of employers will lead them to purchase services most cheaply, taking account of quality, and the self-interest of labourers will make them endeavour to supply the best paid – and therefore most useful – services for which they are adapted. Thus the only thing required of Government is to secure that every one shall be really free to buy the utility he most wants, and to sell what he can best furnish.

If the actual results of the mainly spontaneous organization by which the vast fabric of modern industry has been constructed do not altogether realize the economic ideal above delineated, they at any rate exhibit, on the whole, a very impressive approximation to it. The motive of self-interest does, I hold, work powerfully and continually in the complex manner above described; and I am convinced that no adequate substitute for it, either as an impulsive or as a regulating force, has as yet been found by any socialistic reformer. Still, the universal practice of modern civilized societies has admitted numerous exceptions to the broad rule of *laisser faire* with which the argument above given concludes; and it seems worth while to classify these exceptions, distinguishing as clearly as possible the principles on which they are based, in order that, in any novel or doubtful case, we may at least apply the appropriate general considerations for determining the legitimacy of the exception, and not be misled by false analogies.

Let us begin by marking off a class of exceptions with which political economy, as I conceive it, is only indirectly or partially concerned; – exceptions which are due to the manifest limitations under which abstract economic theory is necessarily applied in the art of government. Thus, in the first place, the human beings with whom economic science is primarily concerned, – who, in the general argument for *laisser faire*, are assumed to be capable of a sufficiently alert and careful regard for their private interests, – are independent adults. The extremest advocate of *laisser faire* does not extend this assumption to children; hence the need of governmental interference to regulate the education and employment of children has to be discussed on principles essentially different from those on which we determine the propriety of interfering with the industry of adults. It is, no doubt, a very tenable proposition that parents are the best guardians of their children's interests, but it is quite a different proposition from that on which the general economic argument for industrial non-interference is based – viz., that every one is the best guardian of his own interests; and the limitations within which experience leads us to restrict the practical application of the two principles respectively differ to an important extent.

But secondly, what the political economist is primarily concerned with is the effect on the *wealth*[1] of the community caused by interference or non-interference; but we all agree that from the statesman's point of view considerations of wealth are not decisive; they are to be subordinated to conditions of physical or moral well-being. If we regard a man merely as a means of producing wealth, it might pay to allow a needle-grinder to work himself to death in a dozen years, as it was said to pay some American sugar-planters to work their slaves to death in six or eight; but a civilized community cannot take this view of its members; and the fact that a man will deliberately choose to work himself to death in a dozen years for an extra dozen shillings a week is not a decisive

---

[1] I use the term wealth for brevity; but I should include along with wealth all purchased utilities – whether "embodied in matter" or not – so far as they are estimated merely at their value in the market.

reason for allowing him to make the sacrifice unchecked. In this and similar cases we interfere on other than economic grounds: and it is by such extra-economic considerations that we justify the whole mass of sanitary regulations; restrictions on the sale of opium, brandy, and other intoxicants; prohibitions of lotteries, regulation of places of amusement; and similar measures. It is, no doubt, the business of the political economist to investigate the effects of such interference; and, if he finds it in any case excessively costly, or likely to be frustrated by a tenacious and evasive pursuit of private interest on the part of persons whose industry or trade is interfered with, he must direct attention to these drawbacks: but the principles on which the interference is based carry him beyond the scope of his special method of reasoning, which is concerned primarily with effects on wealth.

This last phrase, however, suggests another fundamental distinction to which attention must be drawn. We have to distinguish effects in the *production* of wealth from effects on its *distribution*. The argument for *laisser faire*, as given above, dealt solely with its tendency to promote the most economical and effective production of wealth: it did not aim at showing that the wealth so produced tends to be distributed among the different classes that have co-operated in producing it in strict accordance with their respective deserts. On this latter point there has, I think, always been a marked difference between the general tone of English political economists and the general tone of leading continental advocates of *laisser faire*, of whom Bastiat may be taken as a type. Bastiat and his school do boldly attempt to show that the existing distribution of wealth – or rather that which would exist if Government would only keep its hands off – is "conformable to that which ought to be"; and that every worker tends to get what he deserves under the economic order of unmodified competition. But the English disciples of Adam Smith have rarely ventured on these daring flights of optimistic demonstration: when (*e.g.*) Ricardo talked of "natural wages," he had no intention of stamping the share of produce so designated as divinely ordered and therefore just; on the contrary, a market-price of labour above the natural price is characteristic, in Ricardo's view, of an "improving society." And, generally speaking, English political economists, however "orthodox," have never thought of denying that the remuneration of workers tends to be very largely determined by causes independent of their deserts – *e.g.,* by fluctuations in supply and demand, from the effects of which they are quite unable to protect themselves. If our economists have opposed – as they doubtless have always opposed – any suggestion that Government should interfere directly to redress such inequalities in distribution, their argument has not been that the inequalities were merited; they have rather urged that any good such interference might do in the way of more equitable distribution would be more than out-weighed by the harm it would do to production, through impairing the motives to energetic self-help; since no Government could discriminate adequately between losses altogether inevitable and losses that might be at least largely reduced either by foresight or by promptitude and energy in meeting unforeseen changes. If, however, we can find a mode of intervention which will reduce inequalities of distribution without materially diminishing motives to self-help, this kind of intervention is not, I conceive, essentially opposed to the teaching even of orthodox political economy – according to the English standard of orthodoxy; for orthodox economy is quite ready to admit that the poverty and depression of any industrial class is liable to render its members less productive from want of physical vigour and restricted industrial opportunities. Now, an important part of the recent, and the proposed, enlargement of governmental functions, which is vaguely attacked as socialistic, certainly aims at benefiting the poor in such a way as to make them more self-helpful instead of less so, and thus seeks to mitigate inequalities in distribution without giving offence to the orthodox economist. This is the case (*e.g.*) with the main part of governmental provision for education, and the provision of instruments of knowledge, by libraries, &c., for adults. I do not say that all the money spent in this way is well spent; but merely that the principle on which a great part of it is spent is one defensible even in the court of old-fashioned political economy; so far as it aims at equalizing, not the advantages that should be earned by labour, but the opportunities of earning them.

At this point it will probably be objected that the means of equalizing opportunities in the way proposed can only be raised by taxation, and that it cannot be economically sound to tax one class for the benefit of another. If, however, the result sought is really beneficial to the production of the community as a whole, it may, I conceive, be argued – on the premises of the most orthodox political economy – that the expense of it may be legitimately thrown on the community as a whole – *i.e.*, may be raised by taxation equitably distributed. In order to make this plain, it will be convenient to pass to the general consideration of a kind of exceptions to *laisser faire* differing fundamentally in principle from those which we have so far considered; cases in which it may be shown *à priori* that *laisser faire* would not tend to the most economic production of wealth or other utilities, even in a community whose members were as intelligent and alert in seeking and guarding their private interests as any human beings can reasonably be expected to be. I do not argue that in all such cases Government ought to interfere: in human affairs we have often only a choice of evils, and even where private industry fails to bring about a satisfactory result, it is possible that governmental interference might on the whole make matters worse. All I here maintain is that in such cases the general economic presumption in favour of leaving social needs to be supplied by private enterprise is absent, or is balanced by strictly economic considerations on the opposite side.

To give a complete systematic account of these exceptional cases would carry me beyond the limits of an article: my present object is merely to illustrate the general conception of them by a few leading examples, in choosing which I shall try as far as possible to avoid matters of practical controversy.

We may begin by noticing that there are certain kinds of utility – which are or may be economically very important to individuals – which government, in a well-organized modern community, is peculiarly adapted to provide. Complete security for savings is one of these. I do not of course claim that it is an attribute of governments, always and everywhere, that they are less likely to go bankrupt, or defraud their creditors, than private individuals or companies. History would at once refute the daring pretension. I merely mean that this is likely to be an attribute of governments in the ideal society that orthodox political economy contemplates. Of this we may find evidence in the fact that even now, though loaded with war debts and in danger of increasing the load, the English Government can borrow more cheaply than the most prosperous private company. We may say, therefore, that government is theoretically fit to be the keeper of savings for which special security is required. So again – without entering dangerously into the burning question of currency – we may at least say that if *stability* in the value of the medium of exchange can be attained at all, without sacrifices and risks outweighing its advantages, it must be by the intervention of government: a voluntary combination powerful enough to produce the result is practically out of the question.

In other cases, again, where *uniformity* of action or abstinence on the part of a whole class of producers is required for the most economical production of a certain utility, the intervention of government is likely to be the most effective way of attaining the result. It should be observed that it is not the mere need of an extensive combination of producers which establishes an exception to the rule of *laisser faire*, for such need can often be adequately met by voluntary association: the case for governmental interference arises when the utility at which the combination aims will be lost or seriously impaired if even one or two of the persons concerned stand aloof from the combination. Certain cases of protection of land below the sea-level against floods, and the protection of useful animals and plants against infectious diseases, exemplify this condition. In a perfectly ideal community, indeed, we might perhaps assume that all the persons concerned would take the requisite precautions; but in any community of human beings that we can expect to see, the most that we can hope is that the great majority of any industrial class will be adequately enlightened, vigilant, and careful in protecting their own interest; and in the cases just mentioned, the efforts and sacrifices of a great majority might easily be rendered almost useless by the neglect of one or two individuals.

But the case for governmental interference is still stronger where the very fact of a combination among the great majority of a certain industrial class to attain a certain result materially increases the inducement for individuals to stand aloof from the combination. Take, for instance, the case of certain fisheries, where it is clearly for the general interest that the fish should not be caught at certain times, or in certain places, or with certain instruments; because the increase of actual supply obtained by such captures is much over-balanced by the detriment it causes to prospective supply. We may fairly assume that the great majority of possible fishermen would enter into a voluntary agreement to observe the required rules of abstinence; but it is obvious that the larger the number that thus voluntarily abstain, the stronger inducement is offered to the remaining few to pursue their fishing in the objectionable times, places, and ways, so long as they are under no legal coercion to abstain.

So far I have spoken of cases where it is difficult to render a voluntary association as complete as the common interest requires. But we have also to consider cases where such a combination may be too complete for the public interest, since it may give the combiners a monopoly of the article in which they deal. This is, perhaps, the most important of all the theoretical exceptions to the general rule of *laisser faire*. It is sometimes overlooked in the general argument for leaving private enterprise unfettered, through a tacit assumption that enlightened self-interest will lead to open competition; but abstract reasoning and experience equally show that under certain circumstances enlightened self-interest may prompt to a close combination of the dealers in any commodity: and that the private interest of such a combination, so far as it is able to secure a monopoly of the commodity, may be opposed to the general interest. Observe that my objection to monopoly – whether resulting from combination or otherwise – is not that the monopolist may make too large a profit: that is a question of distribution with which I am not now concerned. My objection is that a monopolist may often increase his profit, or make an equal profit more easily, by giving a smaller supply at higher prices of the commodity in which he deals rather than a larger supply at lower prices, and so rendering less service to the community in return for his profit. Wherever, from technical or other reasons, the whole of any industry or trade in a certain district tends to fall under the condition of monopoly, I do not say that there ought to be governmental interference, but at any rate the chief economic objection to such interference is absent.

A familiar instance of this is the provision of lighting and water in towns. Experience has amply shown – what might have been inferred *à priori* – that in cases such as these it is impossible to obtain the ordinary advantages from competition.   Competition invariably involves an uneconomical outlay on works, for which the consumers have ultimately to pay when the competing companies – necessarily few – have seen their way to combination.

And it is to be observed that the same progress of civilization which tends to make competition more real and effective, when the circumstances of industry favour competition, also increase the facilities and tendencies to combination when the circumstances favour combination.

But again, *laisser faire* may fail to furnish an adequate supply of some important utility for a reason opposite to that just considered, not because the possible producer has too much control over his product, but because he has too little. I mean that a particular employment of labour or capital may be most useful to the community, and yet the conditions of its employment may be such that the labourer or capitalist cannot remunerate himself in the ordinary way, by free exchange of his commodity, because he cannot appropriate his beneficial results sufficiently to sell them profitably. Contrast, for instance, the case of docks and lighthouses. In an enlightened community, the making of docks might be left to private industry, because the ships that use them could always be made to pay for them; but the remuneration for the service rendered by a lighthouse cannot be similarly secured. Or, to take a very different instance, contrast scientific discoveries and technical inventions. A technical invention may be patented; but, though a scientific discovery may be the source of many new inventions, you cannot remunerate that by a patent; it cannot be made a marketable article. In other cases, again, where it is quite possible to remunerate labour by selling its product, experience shows that the process of sale is uneconomical from the cost and waste of trouble involved. This, for instance, is why an advanced industrial community gets rid of tolls on roads and bridges.

It is under this last head that a portion at least of the expenditure of government on education, and the provision of the means of knowledge for adults, may, I think, be defended in accordance with the general assumptions on which "orthodox political economy" proceeds; so far as this outlay tends to increase the productive efficiency of the persons who profit by it to an extent that more than repays the outlay. For it will not be denied (1) that the poverty of large classes of the community, if left without aid, would practically prevent them from obtaining this increment of productive efficiency; and (2) that even when it is clearly worth paying for, from the point of view of the community, the business of providing it could not be remuneratively undertaken by private enterprise. So far, therefore, there is a *primâ facie* case for governmental interference on strictly economic grounds.

I do not, however, contend that this defence is applicable to the whole of the expenditure of the funds actually raised, by compulsory taxation, for educational purposes; still less that it is applicable to the whole of the expense that eager educational reformers are urging upon us. Nor do I mean to suggest that the economic reason just given is that which actually weighs most with such reformers. I should rather suppose that their strongest motive usually is a desire to enable the mass of the community to partake effectively in that culture, which – though not perhaps the most generally valued advantage which the rich obtain from their wealth – is at any rate the advantage to which the impartial philanthropist sincerely attaches most importance. Is this desire, then, one that may legitimately be gratified through the agency of government? "No," say Mr. Spencer and his disciples; "let the philanthropist diffuse knowledge at his own expense as much as he likes; to provide for its diffusion out of the taxes is a palpable infringement of the natural rights of the taxpayers." "Yes," say the semi-Socialists – if I may so call them – taking the same ground of natural right, "the equalization of opportunities by education, the free communication of culture, are simple acts of reparative justice which society owes to the classes that lie crushed at the base of our great industrial pyramid."

Now this whole discussion of natural rights is one from which, as a mere empirical utilitarian, I should prefer to stand aloof. But when it is asserted that the prevalent semi-socialistic movement implies at once a revolt from orthodox political economy, and a rejection of Kant's and Mr. Spencer's fundamental political principle, that the coercive action of government should simply aim at securing equal freedom to all, I feel impelled to suggest a very different interpretation of the movement. I think that it may be more truly conceived as an attempt to realize natural justice as taught by Mr.

Spencer, under the established conditions of society, with as much conformity as possible to the teachings of orthodox English[2] political economy. For what, according to Mr. Spencer, is the foundation of the right of property? It rests on the natural right of a man to the free exercise of his faculties, and therefore to the results of his labour; but this can clearly give no right to exclude others from the use of the bounties of Nature: hence the obvious inference is that the price which – as Ricardo and his disciples teach – is increasingly paid, as society progresses, for the use of the "natural and original powers of the soil," must belong, by natural right, to the human community as a whole; it can only be through usurpation that it has fallen into the hands of private individuals. Mr. Spencer himself, in his "Social Statics," has drawn this conclusion in the most emphatic terms. That "equity does not admit property in land;" that "the right of mankind at large to the earth's surface is still valid, all deeds, customs, and laws notwithstanding;" that "the right of private possession of the soil is no right at all;" that "no amount of labour bestowed by an individual upon a part of the earth's surface can nullify the title of society to that part;" that, finally, "to deprive others of their rights to the use of the earth is a crime inferior only in wickedness to the crime of taking away their lives or personal liberties;" – these conclusions are enforced by Mr. Spencer with an emphasis that makes Mr. Henry George appear a plagiarist. Perhaps it will be replied that this argument only affects land: that it doubtless leads us to confiscate land "with as little injury to the landed class as may be" – giving them, I suppose, the same sort of compensation that was given to slave-owners when we abolished slavery – but that it cannot justify taxation of capitalists. But a little reflection will show that this distinction between owners of land and owners of other property cannot be maintained. In the first place, on Mr. Spencer's principles, the rights of both classes to the actual things they now legally own are equally invalid. For, obviously, the original and indefeasible right of all men to the free exercise of their faculties on their material

---

[2] I say "English" because Bastiat and other continental writers have partly, I think, been led to reject the Ricardian theory of rent by their desire to avoid the obvious inference that the payment of rent was opposed to natural justice.

environment must – if valid at all – extend to the whole of the environment; property in the raw material of moveables must be as much a usurpation as property in land. As Mr. Spencer says, "the reasoning used to prove that no amount of labour bestowed by an individual upon a part of the earth's surface can nullify the title of society to that part," might be similarly employed to show that no one can, "by the labour he expends in catching or gathering," supersede "the just claims of other men" to "the thing caught or gathered." If it be replied that technically this is true, but that substantially the value of what the capitalist owns is derived from labour, whereas the value of what the landlord owns is largely not so derived, the answer is that this can only affect the respective claims of the two classes to receive compensation when the rest of the community enforce their indefeasible rights to the free use of their material environment; and that, in fact, these different claims have now got inextricably mixed up by the complicated series of exchanges between land and movables that has taken place since the original appropriation of the former. To quote Mr. Spencer again, "most of our present landowners are men who have, either mediately or immediately, given for their estates equivalents of honestly earned wealth" – at least as honestly earned as any other wealth – so that if they are to be expropriated in order to restore the free use of the land to the human race, the loss entailed on them must be equitably distributed among all other owners of wealth.

But is the expropriation of landlords a measure economically sound? We turn to the orthodox economists, who answer, almost unanimously,[3] that it is not: that, not to speak of the financial difficulty of arranging compensation, the business of owning and letting land is, on various grounds; not adapted for governmental management; and that a decidedly greater quantum of utility is likely to be obtained from the land, under the stimulus given by complete ownership, than could be obtained under a system of leasehold tenure. What then is to be done? The only way that is left of reconciling the Spencerian doctrine of natural right with the teachings of orthodox political economy, seems to be just that "doctrine

[3] J. S. Mill is, so far as I know, the only important exception; and his orthodoxy on questions of this kind is somewhat dubious.

of ransom" which the semi-socialists have more or less explicitly put forward. Let the rich, landowners and capitalists alike, keep their property, but let them ransom the flaw in their titles by compensating the other human beings residing in their country for that free use of their material environment which has been withdrawn from them; only let this compensation be given in such a way as not to impair the mainsprings of energetic and self-helpful industry. We cannot restore to the poor their original share in the spontaneous bounties of Nature; but we can give them instead a fuller share than they could acquire unaided of the more communicable advantages of social progress, and a fairer start in the inevitable race for the less communicable advantages; and "reparative justice" demands that we should give them this much.

That it is not an easy matter to manage this compensation with due regard to the interests of all concerned, I readily grant; and also that the details of the legislation which this semi-socialistic movement has prompted, and is prompting, are often justly open to criticism, both from the point of view of Mr. Spencer and from that of orthodox economists; but, when these authorities combine to attack its general drift, it seems worth while to point out how deeply their combined doctrines are concerned in its parentage.

At this point the reader may perhaps wonder where I find the real indisputable opposition, which I began by admitting, between orthodox political economy and the prevalent movement in our legislation. The most obvious example of it is to be found in the kind of governmental interference, against which, the request for *laisser faire* was originally directed, and which is perhaps more appropriately called "paternal" than "socialistic": legislation which aims at regulating the business arrangements of any industrial class, not on account of any apprehended conflict between the private interests, properly understood, of the persons concerned, and the public interest, but on account of their supposed incapacity to take due care of their own business interests. The most noteworthy recent instance of this in England is the interference in contracts between (English) agricultural tenants and their landlords in respect of "compensation for improvements;" since no attempt, so far as I know, was made by those who urged this interference to show that the properly understood interests of landlords and tenants combined would not lead them to arrange for such treatment of the land as was under their existing circumstances economically best.

A more important species of unorthodox legislation consists of measures that attempt to determine directly, by some method other than free competition, the share of the appropriated product of industry allotted to some particular industrial class. The old legal restrictions on interest, old and new popular demands for "fair" wages, recent Irish legislation to secure "fair" rents, all come under this head. Any such legislation is an attempt to introduce into a social order constructed on a competitive basis a fundamentally incompatible principle; the attempt in most cases fails from its inevitable incompleteness, and where it succeeds, its success inevitably removes or weakens the normal motives to industry and thrift. You can make it illegal for a man to pay more than a certain price for the use of money, but you cannot thus secure him the use of the money he wants at the legal rate; so that, if his wants are urgent, he will pay the usurer more than he would otherwise have done to compensate him for the risk of the unlawful loan. Similarly, you can make it illegal to employ a man under a certain rate of wages, but you cannot secure his employment at that rate, unless the community will undertake to provide for an indefinite number of claimants work remunerated at more than its market value; in which case its action will tend to remove, to a continually increasing extent, the ordinary motives to vigorous and efficient labour. So again, you can ensure that a tenant does not pay the full competition rent to his landlord, but – unless you prohibit the sale of the rights that you have thus given him in the produce of the land – you cannot ensure that his successor in title shall not pay the full competitive price for the use of the land in rent *plus* interest on the cost of the tenant-right; and, in any case, if you try by a "fair rent" to secure to the tenant a share of produce on which he can "live and thrive," you inevitably deprive him of the ordinary motives – both attractive and deterrent – prompting to energetic self-help and self-improvement. I do not say dogmatically that no measures of this kind ought ever, under any circumstances, to be adopted, but merely that a heavy burden of proof is thrown on any one who advocates them, by the valid objections of orthodox political economy; and that, in the arguments used in support of recent legislation of this kind, this burden does not appear to me to have been adequately taken up.

Section 3

The Critics of Individualism

THE DIFFICULTIES OF INDIVIDUALISM[1]
Sidney Webb

OF all the intellectual difficulties of Individualism, the greatest, perhaps, is that which is presented by the constant flux of things. Whatever may be the advantages and conveniences of the present state of society, we are, at any rate, all of us, now sure of one thing – that it cannot last.

The Constant Evolution of Society.
We have learnt to think of social institutions and economic relations as being as much the subjects of constant change and evolution as any biological organism. The main outlines of social organization, based upon the exact sphere of private ownership in England to-day, did not "come down from the Mount."

The very last century has seen an almost complete upsetting of every economic and industrial relation in the country, and it is irrational to assume that the existing social order, thus new-created, is destined inevitably to endure in its main features unchanged and unchangeable. History did not stop with the last great convulsion of the Industrial Revolution, and Time did not then suddenly cease to be the Great Innovator. Nor do the Socialists offer us a statical heaven to be substituted for an equally statical world here present. English students of the last generation were accustomed to think of Socialism as a mere Utopia, spun from the humanity-intoxicated brains of various Frenchmen of the beginning of this century. Down to the present generation every aspirant after social reform, whether Socialist or Individualist, naturally embodied his ideas in a detailed plan of a new social order, from which all contemporary evils were eliminated. Bellamy is but a belated Cabet, Babœuf, or Campanella. But modern Socialists have learnt the lesson of evolution better than their opponents, and it cannot be too often repeated

---

[1] Reprinted, with minor changes, from the *Economic Journal* for June 1891.

that Socialism, to Socialists, is not a Utopia which they have invented, but a principle of social organization which they assert to have been discovered by the patient investigators into sociology whose labors have distinguished the present century. That principle, whether true or false, has, during a whole generation, met with an ever-increasing, though often unconscious, acceptance by political administrators.

Thus, it is the constant flux of things which underlies all the "difficulties" of Individualism. Whatever we may think of the existing social order, one thing is certain – namely, that it will undergo modification in the future as certainly and steadily as in the past. Those modifications will be partly the result of forces not consciously initiated or directed by human will. Partly, however, the modifications will be the results, either intended or unintended, of deliberate attempts to readjust the social environment to suit man's real or fancied needs. It is therefore not a question of *whether* the existing social order shall be changed, but of *how* this inevitable change shall be made.

"Social Problems."
In the present phase of acute social compunction, the mal-adjustments which occasion these modifications appear to us in the guise of "social problems." But whether or not they are the subjects of conscious thought or conscious action, their influence is perpetually at work, silently or obtrusively modifying the distribution of social pressure, and altering the weft of that social tissue of which our life is made. The characteristic feature of our own age is not this constant evolution itself – for that, of course, is of all time – but our increasing consciousness of it. Instead of unconscious factors we become deliberate agents, either to aid or resist the developments coming to our notice. Human selection accordingly becomes the main form of natural selection, and functional adaptation replaces the struggle for existence as the main factor in social progress. Man becomes the midwife of the great womb of Time, and necessarily undertakes the responsibility for the new economic relations which he brings into existence.

Hence the growing value of correct principles of social action, of valid ideals for social aspiration. Hence, therefore, the importance, for weal or for woe, of the change in social ideals and principles which marks off the present generation of Socialists from the surviving economists and statesmen brought up in the "Manchester school." We may, of course, prefer not to accept the watchwords or shibboleths of either party; we may carefully guard ourselves against "the false-hood of extremes"; we may believe that we can really steer a middle course. This comforting reflection of the practical man is, however, an unphilosophical delusion. As each diffi-culty of the present day comes up for solution, our action or inaction must, for all our caution, necessarily incline to one side or the other. We may help to modify the social organism either in the direction of a more general Collectivism or in that of a more perfect Individualism; it will be hard, even by doing nothing, to leave the balance just as it was. It becomes, accordingly, of vital importance to examine not only our practical policy but also our ideals and principles of action, even if we do not intend to follow these out to their logical conclusion.

Individualism and Collectivism.

It is not easy, at the present day, to be quite fair to the opinions of the little knot of noble-minded enthusiasts who broke for us the chains of the oligarchic tyranny of the eight-eenth century. Their work was essentially destructive, and this is not the place in which to estimate how ably they carried on their statical analysis, or how completely they mis-understood the social results of the industrial revolution which was falsifying all their predictions almost before they were uttered. But we may, perhaps, not unfairly sum up as follows the principles which guided them in dealing with the difficulties of social life: that the best government is that which governs least; that the utmost possible scope should be allowed to untrammelled individual enterprise; that open competition and complete freedom from legal restrictions furnish the best guarantees of a healthy industrial community; that the desired end of "equality of opportunity" can be ultimately reached by allowing to each person the complete ownership of any riches he may become possessed of; and that the best possible social state will result from each individual pursuing his own interest in the way he thinks best.

Fifty years' further social experience have destroyed the faith of the world in the validity of these principles as the basis of even a decent social order, and Mr. John Morley himself has told us[2] that "the answer of modern statesmanship is that unfettered individual competition is not a principle to which the regulation of industry may be intrusted."

"It is indeed certain," sums up Dr. Ingram, at the end of his comprehensive survey of all the economic tendencies, "that industrial society will not permanently remain without a systematic organization. The mere conflict of private interests will never produce a well-ordered commonwealth of labor."[3]

Modern Socialism is, accordingly, not a faith in an artificial Utopia, but a rapidly-spreading conviction, as yet only partly conscious of itself, that social health and consequently human happiness is something apart from and above the separate interests of individuals, requiring to be consciously pursued as an end in itself; that the lesson of evolution in social development is the substitution of consciously regulated coordination among the units of each organism for their internecine competition;[4] that the production and distribution of wealth, like any other public function, cannot safely be intrusted to the unfettered freedom of individuals, but needs to be organized and controlled for the benefit of the whole community; that this can be imperfectly done by means of legislative restriction and taxation, but is eventually more advantageously accomplished through the collective enterprise of the appropriate administrative unit in each case; and that the best government is accordingly that which can safely and successfully administer most.

The New Pressure for Social Reform.
But although the principles of Individualism have long been tacitly abandoned by our public men, they have remained, until quite recently, enshrined in the imagination of the middle class citizen and the journalist. Their rapid supersession in these days, by principles essentially Socialist, is due to the prominence now given to "social problems," and to the failure of Individualism to offer any practicable solution of these. The problems are not in themselves new; they are not even

[2] *Life of Cobden*, vol. i., ch. xiii., pp. 298, 303.
[3] Article "Political Economy," in *Ency. Britt.*, ninth edition, vol. xix., 1886, p. 382; republished as *History of Political Economy*.
[4] See Professor Huxley's pregnant declaration to this effect in the *Nineteenth Century*, February, 1888. Compare D. G. Ritchie's *Darwinism and Politics*.

more acute or pressing than of yore; but the present generation is less disposed than its predecessors to acquiesce in their insolubility. This increasing social compunction in the presence of industrial disease and social misery is the inevitable result of the advent of political democracy. The power to initiate reforms is now rapidly passing into the hands of those who themselves directly suffer from the evils to be removed; and it is therefore not to be wondered at that social re-organization is a subject of much more vital interest to the proletarian politicians of to-day than it can ever have been to the University professors or Whig proprietors of the past.

Now the main "difficulties" of the existing social order, with which Individualist principles fail to deal, are those immediately connected with the administration of industry and the distribution of wealth. To summarize these difficulties before examining them, we may say that the Socialist asserts that the system of private property in the means of production permits and even promotes an extreme inequality in the distribution of the annual product of the united labors of the community. This distribution results in excess in the hands of a small class, balanced by positive privation at the other end of the social scale. An inevitable corollary of this unequal distribution is wrong production, both of commodities and of human beings; the preparation of senseless luxuries whilst there is need for more bread, and the breeding of degenerate hordes of a demoralized "residuum" unfit for social life. This evil inequality and disastrous malproduction are enabled to continue through the individual ownership of the instruments of industry, one inevitable accompaniment of which is the continuance, in the commercial world, of that personal rule which is rapidly being expelled from political administration. The increasing integration of the Great Industry is, indeed, creating – except in so far as it is counteracted by the adoption of Socialist principles – a kind of new feudalism, based upon tenure, not of land, but of capital employed in the world-commerce, a financial autocracy against which the democracy sullenly revolts. In the interests of this oligarchy, the real interests of each community tend to be ignored, to the detriment of its capacity to hold its own in the race struggle – that competition between communities rather than between individuals in a community which is perhaps now becoming the main field of natural selection.

In examining each of these difficulties in greater detail, it will be fair to consider, not only how far they can be solved by the existing order and in what way they are actually being dealt with by the application of Socialist principles, but also what hope might, on the other hand, be found in the greatest possible development of Individualism. For to-day it is the Individualist who is offering us, as a solution of social difficulties, an untried and nebulous Utopia; whilst the Socialist occupies the superior position of calling only for the conscious and explicit adoption and extension of principles of social organization to which the stern logic of facts has already driven the practical man. History and experiment have indeed changed sides, and rank now among the allies of the practical Socialist reformer. Factory Acts and municipal gas-works we know, but the voice of Mr. Auberon Herbert, advocating "voluntary taxation," is as the voice of one crying in the wilderness.

Inequality of Income.

Inequality in wealth distribution is, of course, no new thing, and it is unnecessary to contend that the inequality of the present age is more flagrant than that of its predecessors. The extreme depth of poverty of those who actually die of starvation is, indeed, obviously no less than before; and when 30 per cent. of the five million inhabitants of London are found to be inadequately supplied with the bare necessaries of life, and probably a fourth of the entire community become paupers at 65, it would profit us little to enquire whether this percentage is greater or less than that during the Middle Ages. On the other hand, the wealth production of the community advances by leaps and bounds, being now far greater than ever it was, and greater than that of any other country of the Old World. The riches of a comparatively small number of the owners of our land and capital are colossal and increasing.

Nor is there any doubt or dispute as to the causes of this inequality. The supersession of the Small by the Great Industry has given the main fruits of invention and the new power over Nature to a comparatively small proprietary class, upon whom the mass of the people are dependent for leave to earn their living. When it suits any person having the use of land and capital to employ the worker, this is only done on condition that two important deductions, rent and interest, can be made from his product, for the benefit of two, in this capacity, absolutely unproductive classes – those exercising the bare ownership of land and capital. The reward of labor being thus reduced, on an average, by about one-third, the remaining eightpence out of the shilling is then shared between the various classes who *have* co-operated in the production – including the inventor, the managing employer, and the mere wage-worker – but shared in the competitive struggle in such a way that at least fourpence goes to a favored set of educated workers, numbering less than one-fifth of the whole, leaving four-fifths to divide less than fourpence out of the shilling between them. The consequence is the social condition we see around us. A fortunate few, owing to their legal power over the instruments of wealth-production, command the services of thousands of industrial slaves whose faces they have never seen, without rendering any service to them or to society in exchange. A larger body of persons contribute some labor, but are able, from their cultivated ability or special education, to choose occupations for which the competition wage is still high, owing to the small number of possible competitors. These two classes together number only one-fifth of the whole. On the other hand is the great mass of the people, the weekly wage-earners, four out of five of the whole population, toiling perpetually for less than a third of the aggregate product of labor, at an annual wage averaging at most £40 per adult, hurried into unnecessarily early graves by the severity of their lives, and dying, as regards at least one-third of them, destitute or actually in receipt of poor-law relief.

Few can doubt the fundamental causes of this inequality of condition. The abstraction from the total of over one-third of the product necessarily makes a serious inroad in that which the "niggardliness of Nature" allows us, and the distribution of the remaining two-thirds is, of course, itself fatally affected by the secondary results of the division into "two nations" which the private appropriation of rent and interest creates.

Can we Dodge the Law of Rent?
Individualists may tell us of the good things that the worker
could get for himself by thrift and sobriety, prudence and
saving, but no economist will for a moment suggest that
any conceivable advance in these virtues would remove the
fundamental inequality arising from the phenomenon of rent.
The mere worker, *quà* worker, is necessarily working, as far
as its own remuneration is concerned, on the very worst
land in economic use, with the very minimum advantage
of industrial capital.   Every development towards a freer
Individualism must, indeed, inevitably emphasize the power
of the owner of the superior instruments of wealth-production to obtain for himself all the advantages of their
superiority.   Individualists may prefer to blink this fact, and
to leave it to be implied that, somehow or other, the virtuous
artizan can dodge the law of rent.   But against this complacent
delusion of the philanthropist political economy emphatically
protests.   So long as the instruments of production are in
unrestrained private ownership, so long must the tribute of
the workers to the drones continue: so long will the toilers'
reward inevitably be reduced by their exactions.   No tinkering
with the land laws can abolish or even diminish economic
rent, however much it may result in the redistribution of this
tribute.   The *whole* equivalent of every source of fertility or
advantage of all land over and above the worst in economic
use is under free competition necessarily abstracted from the
mere worker on it.   So long as Lady Matheson can "own"
the island of Lewis, and (as she says) do what she likes with
her own – so long as the Earls of Derby can appropriate at
their ease the unearned increment of Bootle or Bury – it is
the very emphatic teaching of political economy that the earth
may be the Lord's, but the fulness thereof must inevitably be
the landlord's.

There is an interesting episode in English history among
James I.'s disputes with the Corporation of London, then the
protector of popular liberties.   James, in his wrath, threatened
to remove the Court to Oxford.   "Provided only your Majesty
leave us the Thames," cleverly replied the Lord Mayor.   But
economic dominion is more subtle than kingcraft – our landlords steal from us even the Thames.   No Londoner who is
not a landlord could, under completely free Individualism,
obtain one farthing's worth of economic benefit from the

existence of London's ocean highway; the whole equivalent of its industrial advantage would necessarily go to swell the compulsory tribute of London's annual rental.

It has often been vaguely hoped that this iron law was true only of land, and that, in some unexplained way, the worker did get the advantage of other forms of industrial capital. But further economic analysis shows, as Whately long ago hinted, that rent is a genus of which land rent is only one species. The worker in the factory is now seen to work no shorter hours or gain no higher wages merely because the product of his labor is multiplied a hundred-fold by machinery which he does not own.

Whatever may be the effect of invention on the wages of one generation as compared with the last, it has now become more than doubtful to economists whether the worker can count on getting any more of the product of the machine, in a state of "complete personal liberty," than his colleagne contemporaneously laboring at the very margin of cultivation with the very minimum of capital. The artizan producing boots by the hundred in the modern machine works of South-wark or Northampton gets no higher wages than the surviving hand cobbler in the by-street. The whole differential advantage of all but the worst industrial capital, like the whole differential advantage of all but the worst land, necessarily goes to him who legally owns it. The mere worker can have none of them. "The remuneration of labor, as such," wrote Cairnes in 1874,[5] "skilled or unskilled, can never rise much above its present level."

The "Population Question."
Neither can we say that it is the increase of population which effects this result. During the present century, indeed, in spite of an unparalleled increase in numbers, the wealth annually produced in England *per head* has nearly doubled.[6] If population became stationary to-morrow, and complete personal

---

[5] *Some Leading Principles*, p. 348.
[6] Hence the remarkable suppression of "Malthusianism" in all recent economic literature, notably the hand-books of Symes, Cannan, Ely, and Gonner; and its significantly narrow subordination in Prof. Marshall's *Principles of Economics*. The birth-rate of Great Britain is now apparently lower than it has ever been during the whole of the past century, and it seems tending steadily downwards.

liberty prevailed, with any amount of temperance, prudence, and sympathy, the present rent and interest would not be affected; our numbers determine, indeed, how bad the margin of cultivation will be, and this is of serious import enough; but, increase or no increase, the private ownership of land and capital necessarily involves the complete exclusion of the mere worker, as such, from all the economic advantages of the fertile soil on which he is born, and of the buildings, machinery, and railways he finds around him.

The "Wickedness" of Making any Change
Few Individualists, however, now attempt to deny the economic conclusion that the private ownership of land and capital necessarily involves a serious *permanent* inequality in the distribution of the annual product of the community; and that this inequality bears no relation to the relative industry or abstinence of the persons concerned. They regard it, however, as impossible to dispossess equitably those who now levy the tribute of rent and interest, and they are therefore driven silently to drop their original ideal of equality of opportunity, and to acquiesce in the *perpetual* continuance of the inequality which they vainly deplore. It is immoral, we are told, to take any step, by taxation or otherwise, which would diminish even by a trifle the income of the present owners of the soil and their descendants for ever and ever. This cannot be done without sheer confiscation, which would be none the less confiscation because carried out gradually and under the guise of taxation.

The problem has, however, to be faced. Either we must submit for ever to hand over at least one-third of our annual product to those who do us the favor to own our country, without the obligation of rendering any service to the community, and to see this tribute augment with every advance in our industry and numbers, or else we must take steps, as considerately as may be possible, to put an end to this state of things. Nor does equity yield any such conclusive objection to the latter course. Even if the infant children of our proprietors have come into the world booted and spurred, it can scarcely be contended that whole generations of their descendants yet unborn have a vested interest to ride on the backs of whole generations of unborn workers. Few persons will believe that this globe must spin round the sun for ever charged with the colossal mortgage implied by private owner-ship of the ground-rents of great cities, merely because a few generations of mankind, over a small part of its area, could at first devise no better plan of appropriating its surface.

There is, indeed, much to be said in favor of the liberal treatment of the present generation of proprietors, and even of their children. But against the permanent welfare of the community the unborn have no rights; and not even a living proprietor can possess a vested interest in the existing system of taxation. The democracy may be trusted to find, in dealing with the landlord, that the resources of civilization are not exhausted. An increase in the death duties, the steady rise of local rates, the special taxation of urban ground values, the graduation and differentiation of the income-tax, the simple appropriation of the unearned increment, and the gradual acquirement of land and other monopolies by public authori-ties, will in due course suffice to "collectivize" the bulk of the tribute of rent and interest in a way which the democracy will regard as sufficiently equitable even if it does not satisfy the conscience of the proprietary class itself. This growth of collective ownership it is, and not any vain sharing out of property, which is to achieve the practical equality of opportunity at which democracy aims.

Why Inequality is Bad.

Individualists have been driven, in their straits, to argue that inequality in wealth is in itself a good thing, and that the objection to it arises from the vain worship of a logical abstraction. But Socialists (who on this point are but taking up the old Radical position) base their indictment against inequality, not on any metaphysical grounds, but on the plain facts of its effect upon social life. The inequality of income at the present time obviously results in a flagrant "wrong production" of commodities. The unequal value of money to our paupers and our millionaires deprives the test of "effective demand" of all value as an index to social requirements, or even to the production of individual happiness. The last glass of wine at a plutocratic orgy, which may be deemed not even to satisfy any desire, is economically as urgently "demanded" as the whole day's maintenance of the dock laborer for which its cost would suffice. Whether London shall be provided with an Italian Opera, or with two Italian Operas, whilst a million of its citizens are without the means of decent life, is now determined, not with any reference to the genuine social needs of the capital of the world, or even by any comparison between the competing desires of its inhabitants, but by the chance vagaries of a few hundred wealthy families. It will be hard for the democracy to believe that the conscious public appropriation of municipalized rent would not result in a better adjustment of resources to needs, or, at any rate, in a more general satisfaction of individual desires, than this Individualist appropriation of personal tribute on the labors of others.

The Degradation of Character.

A more serious result of the inequality of income caused by the private ownership of land and capital is its evil effect on human character and the multiplication of the race. It is not easy to compute the loss to the world's progress, the degradation of the world's art and literature, caused by the demoralization of excessive wealth. Equally difficult would it be to reckon up how many potential geniuses are crushed out of existence by lack of opportunity of training and scope. But a graver evil is the positive "wrong-population" which is the result of extreme poverty and its accompanying insensibility to all but the lowest side of human life. In a condition of society in which the *average* family income is but a little over £3 per week, the deduction of rent and interest for the benefit of a small class necessarily implies a vast majority of the population below the level of decent existence. The slums at the East End of London are the corollary of the mansions at the West End. The depression of the worker to the product of the margin of cultivation often leaves him nothing but the barest livelihood. No prudential considerations appeal to such a class. One consequence is the breeding in the slums of our great cities, and the overcrowded hovels of the rural poor, of a horde of semi-barbarians, whose unskilled labor is neither required in our present complex industrial organism, nor capable of earning a maintenance there. It was largely the recognition that it was hopeless to expect to spread a Malthusian prudence among this residuum that turned John Stuart Mill into a Socialist; and if this solution be rejected, the slums remain to the Individualist as the problem of the Sphinx, which his civilization must solve or perish.

The Loss of Freedom.

It is less easy to secure adequate recognition of the next, and in many respects the most serious "difficulty" of Individualism – namely, its inconsistency with democratic self-government. The Industrial Revolution with its splendid conquests over Nature, opened up a new avenue of personal power for the middle class, and for every one who could force his way into the ranks either of the proprietors of the new machines, or of the captains of industry whom they necessitated.   The enormous increase in personal power thus gained by a comparatively small number of persons, they and the economists not unnaturally mistook for a growth in general freedom. Nor was this opinion wholly incorrect.   The industrial changes were, in a sense, themselves the result of progress in political liberty.   The feudal restrictions and aristocratic tyranny of the eighteenth century gave way before the industrial spirit, and the politically free laborer came into existence. But the economic servitude of the worker did not disappear with his political bondage.   With the chains of innate status there dropped off also its economic privileges, and the free laborer found himself in a community where the old common rights over the soil were being gradually but effectually extinguished.   He became a landless stranger in his own country. The development of competitive production for sale in the world market, and the supremacy of the machine industry, involved moreover, in order to live, not merely access to the land, but the use, in addition, of increasingly large masses of capital – at first in agriculture, then foreign trade, then in manufacture, and finally now also in distributive industries. The mere worker became steadily less and less industrially independent as his political freedom increased.   From a self-governing producing unit, he passed into a mere item in a vast industrial army over the organization and direction of which he had no control.   He was free, but free only to choose to which master he would sell his labor – free only to decide from which proprietor he would beg that access to the new instruments of production without which he could not exist.

In an age of the Small Industry there was much to be said

for the view that the greatest possible personal freedom was to be obtained by the least possible collective rule. The peasant on his own farm, the blacksmith at his own forge, needed only to be let alone to be allowed to follow their own individual desires as to the manner and duration of their work. But the organization of workers into huge armies, the directing of the factory and the warehouse by skilled generals and captains, which is the inevitable outcome of the machine industry and the world-commerce, have necessarily deprived the average workman of the direction of his own life or the management of his own work. The middle class student, over whose occupation the Juggernaut Car of the Industrial Revolution has not passed, finds it difficult to realize how sullenly the workman resents his exclusion from all share in the direction of the industrial world. This feeling is part of the real inwardness of the demand for an Eight Hours Bill.

The ordinary journalist or member of Parliament still says: "I don't consult any one except my doctor as to my hours of labor. That is a matter which each grown man must settle for himself." We never hear such a remark from a working man belonging to any trade more highly organized than chimney-sweeping. The modern artisan has learnt that he can no more fix for himself the time at which he shall begin and end his work than he can fix the sunrise or the tides. When the carrier drove his own cart and the weaver sat at his own loom they began and left off work at the hours that each preferred. Now the railway worker or the power-loom weaver knows that he must work the same hours as his mates.

It was this industrial autocracy that the Christian Socialists of 1850 sought to remedy by re-establishing the "self-governing workshop" of associated craftsmen; and a similar purpose still pervades the whole field of industrial philanthropy. Sometimes it takes the specious name of "industrial partnership"; sometimes the less pretentious form of a joint-stock company with one-pound shares. In the country it inspires the zeal for the creation of peasant proprietorships, or the restoration of "village industries," and behind it stalk those bogus middle class "reforms" known as "free land" and "leasehold enfranchisement." But it can scarcely be hidden from the eyes of any serious student of economic evolution that all these well-meant endeavors to set back the industrial clock are, as regards any widespread result, foredoomed to failure.

The growth of capital has been so vast, and is so rapidly increasing, that any hope of the great mass of the workers ever owning under any conceivable Individualist arrangements the instruments of production with which they work can only be deemed chimerical.[7]

Hence it is that irresponsible personal authority over the actions of others – expelled from the throne, the castle, and the altar – still reigns, almost unchecked, in the factory and the mine. The "captains of industry," like the kings of yore, are indeed honestly unable to imagine how the business of the world can ever go on without the continuance of their existing rights and powers. And truly, upon any possible development of Individualistic principles, it is not easy to see how the worker can ever escape from their "beneficent" rule.

The Growth of Collective Action

But representative government has taught the people how to gain collectively that power which they could never again individually possess. The present century has accordingly witnessed a growing demand for the legal regulation of the conditions of industry which represents a marked advance on previous conceptions of the sphere of legislation. It has also seen a progress in the public management of industrial undertakings which represents an equal advance in the field of government administration. Such an extension of collective action is, it may safely be asserted, an inevitable result of political democracy. When the Commons of England had secured the right to vote supplies, it must have seemed an unwarrantable extension that they should claim also to redress grievances. When they passed from legislation to the exercise of control over the executive, the constitutional jur-

---

[7] The estimated value of the wealth of the United Kingdom to-day is 10,000 millions sterling, or over £1,100 per family. The co-operative movement controls about 13 millions sterling. The total possessions of the 31 millions of the wage-earning class are less than 250 millions sterling, or not £7 capital per family. The eight millions of the population who do not belong to the wage-earning class own all the rest; the death duty returns show, indeed, that one-half of the entire total is in the hands of about 25,000 families. For references to the authorities for these and other statistics quoted, see Fabian Tract No. 5, *Facts for Socialists*.

ists were aghast at the presumption. The attempt of Parliament to seize the command of the military forces led to a civil war. Its control over foreign policy is scarcely two hundred years old. Every one of these developments of the collective authority of the nation over the conditions of its own life was denounced as an illegitimate usurpation foredoomed to failure. Every one of them is still being resisted in countries less advanced in political development. In England, where all these rights are admitted, each of them inconsistent with the "complete personal liberty" of the minority, the Individualists of to-day deny the competence of the people to regulate, through their representative committees, national or local, the conditions under which they work and live. Although the tyranny which keeps the tramcar conductor away from his home for seventeen hours a day is not the tyranny of king or priest or noble, he feels that it is tyranny all the same, and seeks to curb it in the way his fathers took.

The captains of war have been reduced to the position of salaried officers acting for public ends under public control; and the art of war has not decayed. In a similar way the captains of industry are gradually being deposed from their independent commands, and turned into salaried servants of the public. Nearly all the railways of the world, outside of America and the United Kingdom, are managed in this way. The Belgian Government works its own line of passenger steamers. The Paris Municipal Council opens public-bakeries. The Glasgow Town Council runs its own common lodging houses, Plymouth its own tramways. Everywhere, schools, water works, gas-works, dwellings for the people, and many other forms of capital, are passing from individual into collective control. And there is no contrary movement. No community which has once "municipalized" any public service ever retraces its steps or reverses its action.

Such is the answer that is actually being given to this difficulty of Individualism. Everywhere the workman is coming to understand that it is practically hopeless for him, either individually or co-operatively, to own the constantly growing mass of capital by the use of which he lives. Either we must, under what is called "complete personal freedom," acquiesce in the personal rule of the capitalist, tempered only by enlightened self-interest and the "gift of sympathy," or we must substitute for it, as we did for the royal authority, the collective rule of the whole community. The decision is scarcely doubtful. And hence we have on all sides, what to the Individualist is the most incomprehensible of phenomena, the expansion of the sphere of government in the interests of liberty itself. Socialism is, indeed, nothing but the extension of democratic self-government from the political to the industrial world, and it is hard to resist the conclusion that it is an inevitable outcome of the joint effects of the economic and political revolutions of the past century.

Competition

Individualists often take refuge in a faith that the extension of the proprietary class, and the competition of its members, will always furnish an adequate safeguard against the tyranny of any one of them. But the monopoly of which the democracy is here impatient is not that of any single individual, but that of the class itself. What the workers are objecting to is, not the rise of any industrial Buonaparte financially domineering the whole earth – though American experience makes even this less improbable than it once was – but the creation of a new feudal system of industry, the domination of the mass of ordinary workers by a hierarchy of property owners, who compete, it is true, among themselves, but who are nevertheless able, as a class, to preserve a very real control over the lives of those who depend upon their own daily labor.

Moroeover, competition, where it still exists, is in itself one of the Individualist's difficulties, resulting, under a system of unequal incomes, not merely in the production, as we have seen, of the wrong commodities, but also of their production in the wrong way and for the wrong ends. The whole range of the present competitive Individualism manifestly tends, indeed, to the glorification, not of honest personal service, but of the pursuit of personal gain – not the production of wealth, but the obtaining of riches. The inevitable outcome is the apotheosis, not of social service, but of successful financial speculation, which is already the special bane of the American civilization. With it comes inevitably a demoralization of personal character, a coarsening of moral fibre, and a hideous lack of taste.

The Lesson of Evolution

This, indeed, is the lesson which economics brings to ethics. The "fittest to survive" is not necessarily the best, but much more probably he who takes the fullest possible advantage of the conditions of the struggle, heedless of the result to his rivals. Indeed, the social consequences of complete personal liberty in the struggle for existence have been so appalling that the principle has had necessarily to be abandoned. It is now generally admitted to be a primary duty of government to prescribe the plane on which it will allow the struggle for existence to be fought out, and so to determine which kind of fitness shall survive. We have long ruled out of the conflict the appeal to brute force, thereby depriving the stronger man of his natural advantage over his weaker brother. We stop as fast as we can every development of fraud and chicanery, and so limit the natural right of the cunning to overreach their neighbors. We prohibit the weapon of deceptive labels and trade marks. In spite of John Bright's protest, we rule that adulteration is not a permissible form of competition. We forbid slavery: with Mill's consent, we even refuse to enforce a lifelong contract of service. We condemn long hours of labor for women and children, and now even for adult men, and insanitary conditions of labor for all workers.

The whole history of social progress is, indeed, one long series of definitions and limitations of the conditions of the struggle, in order to raise the quality of the fittest who survive. This service can be performed only by the government. No individual competitor can lay down the rules of the combat. No individual can safely choose the higher plane so long as his opponent is at liberty to fight on the lower. In the face of this experience, the Individualist proposal to rely on complete personal liberty and free competition is not calculated to gain much acceptance. A social system devised to encourage "the art of establishing the maximum inequality over our neighbors" – as Ruskin puts it – appears destined to be replaced, wherever this is possible, by one based on salaried public service, with the stimulus of duty and esteem, instead of that of fortune-making.

The Struggle for Existence between Nations

But perhaps the most serious difficulty presented by the present concentration of energy upon personal gain is its effect upon the position of the community in the race struggle. The lesson of evolution seems to be that interracial competition is really more momentous in its consequences than the struggle between individuals. It is of comparatively little importance, in the long run, that individuals should develop to the utmost, if the life of the community in which they live is not thereby served. Two generations ago it would have been assumed, as a matter of course, that the most efficient life for each community was to be secured by each individual in it being left complete personal freedom. But that crude vision has long since been demolished. Fifty years' social experience have convinced every statesman that, although there is no common sensorium, a society is something more than the sum of its members; that a social organism has a life and health distinguishable from those of its individual atoms. Hence it is that we have had Lord Shaftesbury warning us that without Factory Acts we should lose our textile trade; Matthew Arnold, that without national education we were steering straight into national decay; and finally even Professor Huxley taking up the parable that, unless we see to the training of our residuum, France and Germany and the United States will take our place in the world's workshop. This "difficulty" of Individualism can be met, indeed, like the rest, only by the application of what are essentially Socialist principles.

Argument and Class Bias

These "difficulties" will appeal more strongly to some persons than to others. The evils of inequality of wealth will come home more forcibly to the three millions of the submerged tenth in want of the bare necessaries of life than they will to the small class provided with every luxury at the cost of the rest. The ethical objection to any diminution in the incomes of those who own our land will vary in strength according, in the main, to our economic or political prepossessions. The indiscriminate multiplication of the unfit, like the drunkenness of the masses, will appear as a cause or an effect of social inequality according to our actual information about the poor, and our disposition towards them. The luxury of the rich may strike us as a sign either of national wealth or of national maladjustment of resources to needs. The autocratic administration of industry will appear either as the beneficent direction of the appropriate captains of industry, or as the tyranny of a proprietary class over those who have no alternative but to become its wage-slaves. The struggle of the slaves among themselves, of the proprietors among themselves, and of each class with the other, may be to us "the beneficient private war which makes one man strive to climb on the shoulders of another, and remain there;"[8] or it may loom to us, out of the blood and tears and misery of the strife, as a horrible remnant of the barbarism from which man has half risen since

> "We dined, as a rule, on each other:
> What matter? the toughest survived."

That survival from an obsolescent form or the struggle for existence may seem the best guarantee for the continuance of the community and the race; or it may, on the other hand, appear a suicidal internecine conflict, as fatal as that between the belly and the members. All through the tale two views are possible, and we shall take the one or the other according to our knowledge and temperament.

This power of prepossession and unconscious bias constitutes, indeed, the special difficulty of the Individualists of today. Aristotle found it easy to convince himself and his friends that slavery was absolutely necessary to civilization. The Liberty and Property Defence League has the more difficult task of convincing, not the proprietary class, but our modern slaves, who are electors and into whose control the executive power of the community is more and more falling. And in this task the Individualists receive ever less and less help from the chief executive officers of the nation. Those who have forced directly upon their notice the larger aspects of the problem, those who are directly responsible for the collective interests of the community, can now hardly avoid, whether they like it or not, taking the Socialist view. Each Minister of State protests against Socialism in the abstract, but every decision that he gives in his own department leans more and more away from the Individualist side.

---

[8] Sir Henry Maine, *Popular Government*, pp. 49, 50.

Socialism and Liberty.

Some persons may object that this gradual expansion of the collective administration of the nation's life cannot fairly be styled a Socialistic development, and that the name ought to be refused to everything but a complete system of society on a Communist basis. But whatever Socialism may have meant in the past its real significance now is the steady expansion of representative self-government into the industrial sphere. This industrial democracy it is, and not any ingenious Utopia, with which Individualists, if they desire to make any effectual resistance to the substitution of collective for individual will, must attempt to deal. Most political students are, indeed, now prepared to agree with the Socialist that our restrictive laws and municipal Socialism, so far as these have yet gone, do, as a matter of fact, secure a greater well-being and general freedom than that system of complete personal liberty, of which the "sins of legislators" have deprived us. The sacred name of liberty is invoked, by both parties, and the question at issue is merely one of method. As each "difficulty" of the present social order presents itself for solution, the Socialist points to the experience of all advanced industrial countries, and urges that personal freedom can be obtained by the great mass of the people only by their substituting democratic self-government in the industrial world for that personal power which the Industrial Revolution has placed in the hands of the proprietary class. His opponents regard individual liberty as inconsistent with collective control, and accordingly resist any extension of this "higher freedom" of collective life. Their main difficulty is the advance of democracy, ever more and more claiming to extend itself into the field of industry. To all objections, fears, doubts, and difficulties, as to the practicability of doing in the industrial what has already been done in the political world, the democratic answer is "*solvitur ambulando*;" only that is done at any time which is proved to be then and there practicable; only such advance is made as the progress in the sense of public duty permits. But that progress is both our hope and our real aim: the development of individual character is the Socialist's "odd trick" for the sake of which he seeks to win all others.

Industrial democracy must therefore necessarily be gradual in its development; and cannot for long ages be absolutely complete. The time may never arrive, even as regards material things, when individual is entirely merged in collective ownership or control, but it is matter of common observation that every attempt to grapple with the "difficulties" of our existing civilization brings us nearer to that goal.

THE MORAL FUNCTION OF THE STATE
David G. Ritchie

"WHY need we take an interest in politics? Are not politics a despicable tangle of personal ambitions, party prejudices, unworthy compromises and dishonourable intrigues, deliberate exaggerations and wilful misstatements, unreasoning admiration and intemperate abuse? Is it not wiser for those, who are anxious to do their duty in the world and to lead a life that may be considered well-pleasing to God, to withdraw from the temptations and degrading influences of political activity? After all, can even the best laws and the best institutions – suppose we could secure them – avail to remedy the corruption of the human heart? Does not each of us need all his energies to struggle with his proper enemies, the passions within his own soul, and if we can do anything to help others than ourselves, have we not our obvious duties towards our own families and those with whom we are brought into contact in the ordinary course of life? There is 'the daily round, the common task' – is not that sufficient and more than sufficient? And if we still wish to attempt something further, is not personal help given to the poor, the sick, the sorrowing, infinitely better than anything that can be done through acts of parliament? Let us lead quiet and peaceable lives and keep ourselves, if we can, unspotted from the world, leaving the dirty work of politics to those whom God has set in authority over us." (Apparently, it does not matter that they should be soiled.)

These are the sort of arguments that we very often hear: and there is obviously a great degree of truth in them. We know exactly the kind of politician, whom people speaking thus have in their minds, the man who, while professing to work for the noblest ends, seems only to be loudly advertising himself and to care for nothing beyond the mere machinery of politics. An overwhelming majority at an election, a triumphant division in the House, the overthrow of the party to which he does not belong and the elevation to high office of the leader with whom he has thrown in his lot, seem the ultimate aims and objects of his life's labour. And, in contrast with such an one, is suggested the image of some unobtrusive individual, a hard-working clergyman who is not heard of outside his own parish or a district visitor, probably a self-sacrificing woman, whose presence brings hope and light to the dark abodes of poverty, suffering and sin. The contrast is impressive; but it is fallacious, if we assume that it correctly expresses the relation between politics and individual duty. There are many current opinions and many current phrases which help to countenance this assumption. Thus, it is supposed that there is a complete severance between morals and politics: we frequently hear it accounted one of the advantages of modern over ancient moral philosophy that this severance has been effectually and finally made. And if morals are distinct from politics, does not religion seem to be much more distinct? There is the view of those who are apt to claim exclusive possession of "Evangelical" Christianity, according to which, religion is entirely an affair of the individual soul: and, intimately connected with this view in logic and in history, there is the doctrine that Government has nothing to do with morality, that it is merely a mechanism for the better protection of individual rights, and that consequently a government is good in direct proportion to the narrowness of its sphere. Individualism in politics and religion is a good deal on the wane: and these opinions are not now quite so prevalent as they were; but they are prevalent enough to influence seriously the practice, both of those who openly accept them and of those who hold them unawares – nay, even of those who do not hold them, but live in an atmosphere that has been permeated by them. They arise, like all other widely accepted opinions that contain a mixture of truth and error, from the habit people have of looking at a part only of the phenomena with which they are concerned. On the one hand, it is said, "You cannot make men moral by act of parliament:" on the other, "No one can shake off his individual responsibility for the use he makes of his life." These are undoubted truths. But to estimate the effect, and consequently the importance of government-action, we must consider indirect, as well as direct results: and to understand the meaning of individual responsibility we must not treat individuals as isolated and similar agents,

equally free and equally capable of goodness. There have
been many protests against the immorality of the doctrine of
Predestination: but I question very much if it has been the
cause of so much practical mischief as the doctrine of
the Freedom of the Will – in the crude form in which that is
accepted by popular philosophy. "What is the good" it is said,
"of improving the condition of the poor? What is the good of
more wages, better houses, better schools, of baths, public
parks, picture galleries and so on? People won't be a whit
better, unless there is a moral change, a change in the heart
and character." Doubtless the armchair Christian moralist,
who talks in this fashion, does not want better wages and
better housing – he has probably a good house of his own
and a good income derived from investments in the funds:
he does not want rate-supported schools – he probably has
no craving for more education and rather prefers that such
education as he has should be a monopoly of himself and his
class: he does not want a public park – he has his own garden:
he signs petitions against the Sunday opening of picture galleries – he does not want to go there; and he has no temptation to spend his time or his money in the public house –
he has his club and a round of highly genteel dinner parties.
Has he ever considered how very much, how almost entirely,
his respectability, which he dignifies with the name of morality, is the product of his circumstances? When the pious
clergyman – John Newton, I think it was, though it may quite
well have been somebody else – pointing to a criminal going
to the gallows, said, "There, but for the Grace of God, goes
John Newton," he expressed a perfectly true sentiment,
though his way of understanding "the Grace of God" probably took too little account of the modifiable human agencies
through which individuals are influenced for good and for
evil. There are heroic souls that even in the most adverse
surroundings keep on struggling towards noble ideals – they
are the salt of the earth; but most human beings are not
heroic. The society in which we live, by its organization and
the opinions to which that organization gives rise, produces
its regular crop of narrow-minded respectable persons rooted
to existing institutions, of wealthy idlers wasting their own
lives and the lives of others, of weary toilers dulled into
apathy by drudgery or liable to be thrown out of work by
the caprices of the labour-market, of helpless women driven

by starvation and social pressure to sell themselves for a living, of drunkards, thieves, swindlers and other habitual criminals, transmitting their evil tendencies to coming generations. And for all this we are responsible as a community.

In the middle ages, when governments were weak and administered too often in the interests of a family or a ruling caste, the only means of endeavouring to stem the tide of oppression and misery were private charity and private beneficence organized by ecclesiastical agencies. St. Francis might almost be called the renovator of Christianity, because he turned the religious enthusiasm of his age into the channel of active service to the poor and the sick. We know, alas! only too well, what becomes of charitable endowments – how there grow up wealthy and indolent corporations, surrounded by a pauperised and demoralised population, so that one is tempted to say of charity, in this sense of alms-giving: "It is twice cursed: it curseth him that gives and him that takes." It deadens the intelligence and conscience of the giver: it degrades the character and will of the recipient. This is a hard saying, and it sounds a harsh one. The giving of alms is a venerable duty: it has been enjoined in all religions; it satisfies, at the moment, the feelings of both giver and receiver; it seems, though generally in a fictitious way, to bring about a personal relation between human beings which is lacking in more indirect methods of attempting to remedy suffering. In those ages, places and respects, in which the State is so little developed as to be unavailable as a means of relieving or preventing want, there alms-giving is a duty, just as indiscriminate hospitality was a duty as well as a convenience in the days of few travellers and no-inns. But, if in changed circumstances we cling to ancient forms of beneficence, we are sacrificing human welfare to a prejudice in favour of the picturesque. The gracious figure of the lady of the manor, dispensing blankets and soup to the curtseying dames of the village, must not blind our eyes to the less pleasing features of the English system of land tenure, which, along with the growth of the large capitalist, are accountable for a great part of the squalor of our overgrown towns. The game-keeper's cottage looks very pretty at the park-gate: and there are perhaps a few model dwellings on the estate. But what of the rest of the rural population? The most fortunate are no longer in England. What has become of those that have not escaped from their native land? And, meanwhile, the Landlord sits in the House of Land-lords, obstructing all changes: nor should we blame him very much, for "'tis his nature to." But he is probably a liberal subscriber to all the local charities. It is not charity, in the wretched sense in which the word has come to be used, it is justice that is wanted by a free people. You give the crumbs to Lazarus; but why is there a Lazarus there? Charity is only a temporary remedy. We must face the evil conditions which are the source of misery and try to remedy them.

"For all this we are responsible as a community." When we have traced an evil back to *Society*, we have no right to quiet our consciences by the phrase. By the denial of individualism and of the supposed arbitrary and absolute freedom of the individual will, it must not be imagined that our responsibility is diminished: it is enormously increased. Because of the *solidarité* of mankind, no man can escape from being "his brother's keeper." For the miseries of our age and for everything that tends to mitigate these miseries we are indebted to those who have gone before us: and every one of us, by act and by word and even by thought, is contributing something of good or evil to those who are to come after us.

That society is an organism and that its history is a history of continuous growth – these have become the truisms of popular science. But we are very much misled, if we think the truths involved in them justify any fatalistic acceptance of things as they are and any refusal to endeavour to remedy evils of which we have become acutely conscious. In our *consciousness* of the process that is going on and of the society of which we find ourselves members tis to be found what differentiates the social organism from the natural organisms which are studied by the biologist. In this consciousness, also, is to be found the secret of what is so often incorrectly represented as a non-natural and mysterious power of volition. The merely vegetable or animal organisms are engaged in a struggle for existence and those which prove themselves most capable of surviving do survive, (the "survival of the fittest" means nothing more than that). But *we* can think about the end towards which we find ourselves moving, and we can pronounce it good or bad and can endeavour, accordingly, to accelerate the movement or to prevent it, or at least, to diminish the accompanying suffering.

The wise statesman is he who can foresee the inevitable in politics – who knows in which direction the current is moving and does not blindly try to thrust it back, but to direct it in safe channels, making its force beneficent instead of destructive.

It is as a State, *i.e.* as an ordered political society, that a social organism becomes most distinctly conscious of its existence as an organism and consequently most capable of regulating the tendencies, which if left to themselves, would make its history a merely natural process. I do not say that the State is the only organization in which human beings feel their community with one another and their capacity for influencing one another's lot. By no means. The family and the various associations into which men group themselves, more or less consciously, come nearer to the life of each individual and seem more obviously to touch and influence it and at a greater number of points. Religious organizations affect more readily the highest motives, call forth greater enthusiasm and may extend beyond the limits of national existence; but the State has the greatest *force* to compel at least outward obedience in the majority of persons and its working is the most open, and the most capable of being observed and criticised.

There are those who hold that States cannot affect the natural processes going on in Society and there are those who hold that they ought not to attempt this, if they could. It is curious how some who are fond of protesting against the belief in the State, with a large S, are so ready to throw themselves into the arms of Nature, with a very large N. If Nature be taken in so wide a sense as to include *all* human thought and effort, then the State is one of the manifestations of Nature which must be allowed its own capacities to struggle with the other natural forces. But if so, it is not logically justifiable to draw arguments from Nature against the State. If, on the other hand, the State be expressly excluded as artificial from our conception of Nature, what becomes of the advance we are supposed to have made from the "mechanical" to the "organic" way of regarding human institutions?

To clear the way, we must first mark off a sense in which the State *cannot* make men moral. No moral act, strictly so-called, can be commanded by Law. If an act which we call a right act, because outwardly resembling acts which are the outcome of a good character, be done solely in obedience to an external command and through fear of penalties, that act is not a morally right act at all. Only if the agent accepts the external command as reasonable and brings his will into inward accordance with it, only then has he acted in a morally right manner. This truth agrees with the principle, which is generally admitted in theory, that Laws are ultimately ineffectual unless they are in accordance with the opinion of at least a great part of the community. But another and connected principle is not always so readily recognised, – viz., that public opinion gradually (often, indeed, very rapidly) comes to adapt itself to a Law which may at first have been strongly approved only by a small number, if that Law be really such as to promote the social health and well-being of the community. Marvellous is the power of accomplished facts. A long, long struggle was needed to abolish slavery. How many defenders has that institution now? Catholic Emancipation, the Abolition of Tests, Extensions of the Franchise afford other, though less conspicuous, instances in which what was once fanatically opposed has very soon after come to be calmly accepted. Most people are wanting in imagination and they find a difficulty in figuring to themselves society existing and flourishing in any different forms from those to which they are accustomed. Only let the change once be made, and if it be a wise and successful one, these same persons or their representatives will have difficulty in believing that they could ever have held other opinions than those which result from the changed set of circumstances.

Laws and institutions cannot directly produce morality, but they may produce those opinions and sentiments which go to the furtherance of morality.

Even if the function of Government be limited to the mere police duties of arresting wrong-doers and punishing them, the State cannot escape its moral responsibility. For has it not determined, in at least certain matters, what is to be considered right and what is to be considered wrong? If the State aims only at protecting individual rights of person and property (as the phrase goes) has it not determined what these rights are? These rights are just what they have been made by Society; and if the State leaves them alone and maintains them, it thereby gives them its sanction and becomes responsible for them.

Can any thinking person be deceived by the programme of the "Liberty and Property Defence League?" Do we not know that it means a defence at all hazards of the *status quo*? It is a league for the defence of the strong and for prohibiting the protection of the defenceless. Its motto ought to be "To him that hath shall be given" – in a material and not a spiritual sense.

Again, the imposition of punishments involves a very serious and very difficult moral responsibility. What will be the effect of various penalties on the characters of the persons punished and on those of other persons? If the State prohibits murder and imposes the penalty of death, is it not doing what it can to produce a certain sentiment of respect for human life? And when there were no Factory Acts, was not the State by its neutrality diminishing the checks to the reckless sacrifice of children on the altars of Mammon? We may be afraid of making mistakes by interfering, but we do not escape responsibility by washing our hands and doing nothing.

Legislation would be a very easy matter if there were some definite sphere of individual right which could be known *à priori* and within which no state-action must come. But human beings are not atoms moving in the void without contact. The rights of the individual are exactly those which society gives him, no more and no less. Can we then lay down no rule at all by which to test any proposed measure of state-action? "Natural rights" will not help us; for the phrase is meaningless or mischievous, unless it signifies just those rights which a well-organized society *ought* to secure to its members: and what these are is the very question to which we seek an answer. We have said already that the State cannot directly command morality (commanded morality being a contradiction in terms): but what the State can do, and what it ought to do, is to provide all its members so far as possible with such an environment as will enable them to live as good lives as possible – good in every sense of the term. "Compulsion," "interference," "liberty," are ambiguous words and give us little help in determining such matters. There is no evil in compulsion and interference *per se*: there, is no good in liberty in the mere negative sense of "being left alone." The more the mischievous forces in society can be compelled and interfered with, the better for the only liberty that is worth having – the liberty to make the best of our lives that the limitation of our physical nature allows of. Opposition to compulsory education and compulsory sanitation means advocacy of permissive ignorance and permissive disease. Absolute liberty of contract means the slavery of the weak.   In the sense in which alone Liberty may be regarded as an *end*, there is no inconsistency between Liberty and Law.

But cannot a great deal be done by voluntary effort? Is it not the special honour of Englishmen, as it certainly is their favourite boast, that they do not at every grievance call out (like those foreigners) for the help of the State, but put their own shoulders to the wheel and so escape from giving too much power to governments? Undoubtedly very great things have been done and can be done by voluntary association: and, wherever and so long as political power is chiefly in the hands of those who have not very lofty ideals as to their use of it, the most important thing to be done is often to secure and maintain the liberty of association. But history makes it unfortunately too clear that associations are very apt to become close and narrow as they grow old and to acquire a good deal of the selfishness of individuals, without being equally accessible to new ideas.   The history of monastic orders, of trade-guilds, of universities, of trades-unions, of co-operative societies, of philanthropic and charitable institutions shews a tendency in associations formed by voluntary contract to stiffen into rigid bodies, whereas the State, however some of its organs may become inefficient, is always in the last resort the outward expression of the national spirit and, where there is any spirit in a people, must grow and live with the life of that spirit. Thus voluntary associations are mainly useful *to lead the way in social experiments*, to shew in what modes individuals can best receive help from an organized body of their fellow men. But, as time goes on, they have to be modified and controlled by the State, or absorbed in it. I know that this is a statement which would be contradicted by the large majority of Englishmen; but I think that the recent history of Europe points pretty clearly to its truth. The growing activity of the State on behalf of the well-being of the community will still leave abundant fields open for the energy of individuals and of voluntary associations. When one set of evils is remedied, another will certainly enough be noticed. There are many things which we consider evils now and which we attempt to remedy, that were not noticed at all, or were accepted as a matter of course, in ruder conditions of society. There are many respects in which the world is becoming, not worse, but more sensitive to its remediable miseries. Again, new conditions produce new evils to be coped with. Slavery is abolished; but the evils which came from the industrial revolution have grown up in the meantime. The worst thing that can happen to a community is to be contented with its efforts in the past – to go on building the sepulchres of the old prophets whilst it slays the new ones.

The demand for increased recognition of the moral function of the State is constantly met by the objection that States, as we know them, are little deserving of trust and that it would be dangerous to give governments more power. It is easy to draw up a long list of the blunders, the follies, the crimes and the cruelties, which rulers have committed in times past: it is easy to point out the defects in the best governments that now exist. The State whose activity we demand is undoubtedly an ideal State. Those who are perfectly contented with things as they are, would like it to remain an ideal, to be realized only in an infinitely remote future, or in another world. They may profess to believe in a divine kingdom of justice and brotherhood – only a few persons are cynical and candid and pagan enough to deny this – but they seem to have no real wish or anxiety that the will of God should be done *in earth* as in heaven. They tell us that Christianity has abolished the distinctions of race, of caste, of sex; but, with a false idealism, they are very much afraid of "turning the spirit into flesh."

This type of objection, which we have just been considering, calls our attention to the importance of what those interested in moral and spiritual progress are apt to despise and dislike, viz. the machinery of politics. "Why glory in representative government? Why care for mere political reforms? Why excite ourselves about the organization of representative bodies? Why make a fuss about the franchise? Why wish to multiply little parliaments, with all their idle talk, up and down the country by schemes of local government?" All these things may seem to matter very little; but they do matter very much to the well-being of every man, woman and child. In themselves they are merely *means to the means to the end* that we really care for. And sometimes one set of means may be equally good with another. But they *are* means: and no end can be reached without means. It matters very much that the political machine should be in good order and capable of turning out good work; or, to use a more adequate image, that the constitution of a country in its every fibre should be such an organism as to give a genuine and healthy expression to the "general will" or spirit of the community. How can a people realize what is best in them, if their government is corrupt, selfish, incompetent, or, while nominally free, is really controlled by long purses and narrow minds? Hence it is a symptom of disease when a large number of intelligent and educated and kindhearted persons in a country profess to be indifferent to politics. To refer to one matter only, it were well if the giving of votes at elections were regarded always as a public duty and its neglect punished with a fine, like the non-attendance of jurymen when summoned – not that the reluctantly given votes or the voting papers spoilt in bad temper would be of much value to the community, but in order to impress every one with the opinion that the suffrage is a duty to one's fellow beings, not a privilege to boast about, a source of occasional excitement, or, worst of all, an opportunity of immoral gain. "Yes," it will be said "we should take an interest in politics, if it were not for the division into *parties*. Are not the best men in a community wise in holding aloof from the wretched contests of rival factions?" Certainly, some individuals may be placed in positions where a strongly partizan attitude at elections would seriously impair their general usefulness: there are many cases where an honest man may conscientiously feel himself obliged to remain neutral: and there are persons of refined instincts and gentle temperament, who are repelled by the coarser and less scrupulous natures which political struggles are apt to bring into prominence. But one may be excused for having less sympathy with these Pococurantes of culture, than with the law of Solon, which disgraced the citizen who took no part in civil dissension, and the indignation of Dante, who did not hesitate to put a saintly Pope in the vestibule of Hell,

because he made the great refusal and decided neither for
God nor for his enemies.

This matter of parties raises some very difficult questions
of political casuistry, through which it is not easy to steer
one's way. It is obvious that where parties exist, the practical
man, the man who is anxious to help others by political
agencies, must work with them. There are certain extreme
cases in which any compromise is dishonourable, but in most
instances we may go upon the homely maxim, that half a
loaf is better than no bread – provided always that our getting
half a loaf to-day does not put an obstacle in the way of our
ever getting a whole loaf afterwards. We must work on the
whole with those whose policy, however inadequate it may
seem, we honestly consider most likely in the end to bring
about those changes which we consider necessary. It is better
to shove a party on from behind than to turn round and slap
it in the face, through impatience at the short-sightedness and
half-heartedness of those who after all are moving, however
slowly and blindly, in our direction. To give way to such
impatience is only to play into the hands of our enemies.
That, in any very near future, we are likely to find any of the
great countries of the world with popular government and
yet without party government one can hardly venture to hope.
It is very distressing, that in the United States of America,
where the constitution, making the executive independent of
the legislative body, might seem to promise, as well as to
imply, a government without parties, some of the very worst
evils of party government have at various times been experienced. For the worst and most demoralising kinds of parties
are those not based on difference about great principles, but
merely on a contest between "ins" and "outs." Accepting
parties, in the meantime at all events, as a necessary evil for
ourselves, we must distinguish between the unavoidable use
of, and co-operation with, parties, which represent real differences in principle or in method such as may occur between
perfectly sincere and well intentioned men, and the deplorable
habit of regarding politics as a gigantic game in which the
sporting proclivities, that are the curse of English life, find
opportunity of gratification as an agreeable variety from the
turf and the stock-exchange. If politics are a game, it must
not be forgotten that the pieces played with are human bodies
and human souls. It rests with everyone who has any sense

of public duty to aid in the formation of a saner public opinion on the subject. Not by disdaining and disregarding political movements, but by considering them always in the light of their bearing on the moral elevation of human beings, can we hope to spiritualize, or, let me say, to Christianize the State.

Corresponding to, if not identical with this endeavour, is the endeavour to socialize Christianity,[1] to get rid of the narrowness and selfishness of much that is popularly considered religion and to shake indolent souls out of their trust in conventional formulas and their unreal way of apprehending the spiritual principles they profess to believe. This I understand to be one of the objects of your Guild: and so far I am most heartily with you. I must ask your toleration, if I have less confident hopes than you have, of the possibility of animating existing ecclesiastical organizations with this large and practical spirit. If it can be done, so much the better: reform without revolution means a great saving of energy. You at least "have not despaired of your republic." We often look back with envy or with pride on some of the great churchmen of the middle ages who stood forth as tribunes of the people and who, in defence of the oppressed, regarded not the anger of king and noble; but it is to little purpose, if we only dream of them as picturesque figures in a dim historic background and make no attempt to renew their spirit amid the prosaic details of modern politics. It is to equally little purpose that we praise Reformers who protested against the corruptions of the mediæval Church, if we have forgotten the intellectual and moral fearlessness, which is the worthiest part of the example they have left us.

This paper has probably dwelt too exclusively in vague generalities to be of much direct practical service to anyone. But it is occasionally worth while to go back on some fundamental questions: and political and social problems will be better studied, if we do not shirk an enquiry into the nature and ends of society and the State. The foregoing statement,

---

[1] Of course this statement implies a view about "the essence of Christianity" which many persons would repudiate. But such persons ought not then to be astonished that many of those who are most zealous for social reform have so little sympathy with *their* Christianity. If we really thought that the essence of Christianity was a combination of intellectual suicide with selfish "other-worldliness," we should not care about retaining the name.

being brief, is necessarily very inadequate, and many remarks would need much illustration and elucidation to give them their fair claim to acceptance. I have said nothing about the relation between Church and State. But what I have said is consistent either with the view that Church and State are identical, *i.e.* that they are the same body of persons under different aspects, or with the view that the Church is a distinct organization extending beyond the limits of States and essentially independent. (These two views are perhaps not ultimately so incompatible as may at first appear.) What I have said is inconsistent only with the view that the State is in no sense a spiritual power, a view which, though maintained by very able men, seems to me hardly capable of defence; for, as I have tried to show, even if the function of the State be limited in the most extreme manner, it is still *indirectly* a moral function, and the moral interests of the community *must* be considered by its legislators.

I have said nothing about that part of the function of the State which is usually most debated, viz. its relation to economic matters. That question is so large that it has to be taken by itself. I would only now point out that, even if it be held that in purely economic matters the State ought not to interfere at all (as the phrase goes), *purely* economic matters form a very limited class indeed, if such a class exists at all. About the "laws" of political economy much nonsense is talked, even by those who ought to know better. What are called economic laws are not precepts for conduct; at best they are generalisations of facts, usually they are only deductions from supposed facts. Abstract economics are farther removed from practical politics than abstract dynamics from practical engineering. Dynamics, supplemented by practical knowledge of the materials he has to work with, will tell the engineer how best to construct a bridge; but the authorities, who determine whether a bridge is to be constructed in a particular place or not, must be guided by the requirements of human beings. The physician rightly studies the *law* of a disease, but is not thereby absolved from the duty of trying to cure the patient. And so, economic study may show that under certain conditions certain effects will follow; but, if the effects are detrimental to human well-being, our duty as practical persons is, not to acquiesce in the sacred name of Political Economy, but to endeavour to alter the conditions. There is indeed a sense in which we have to recognise inevitable tendencies in human societies; but these tendencies are something deeper and stronger than the economic laws, which so far as they are true, are true only of a particular stage of social evolution and yet are proclaimed by the organs of the money-market as if they were immutable laws of nature or, through a strange confusion of ideas, as eternal principles of morality. We may feel great doubts as to how far the State – meaning thereby any one State as now existing – can engage directly in economic production except in regard to those matters which are necessarily monopolies. It may be a long time before any State can take upon itself as an acknowledged function the organization of industry and the distribution of its products – a function at present discharged by competing individuals or groups of individuals, blindly, anarchically and irresponsibly. But we need therefore have no doubts about the advisability of immediate State-action to secure the health and the intelligence of the community and a fair chance for its moral progress.

These two subjects, religion and economics, have more connection than might at first appear. One of the main difficulties in the way of a State engaging directly in economic undertakings, is the fear that it might thereby put itself at a disadvantage in comparison with other States. Even as it is, we know how restrictions on the selfishness and recklessness of employers of labour are met by the outcry that they are put at a disadvantage in their competition with producers in other countries where such restrictions do not exist. The movement for industrial emancipation must in the long run be an international one: and the way for it must be prepared by the spread of an enlightened public opinion and public sentiment. Now, a religious body which professes to be Christian and Catholic, *i.e.* Universal, is false to its profession, if it remains an organization of members of one nation only: still more so, if it consists mainly of one social caste in that nation. The Christian Church must be really democratic in its sentiments and it must be supra-national in its aims: else it is false to its professed belief in the brotherhood of all mankind. If in any way the spiritual teachers of the race can be the bridgemakers to unite those divided by self-interest and prejudice, they are earning the blessing of the peacemaker and are preparing the way for the better society of the future. The materialist may consistently disbelieve in the possibility of putting an end to the competition between nations, which we call war, and the often not less cruel competition between individuals, which we disguise under the name of commercial enterprise. Those who profess to be Christians have no excuse for such hopelessness. Many of the reforms, which we look for, cannot soon take place; but none the less, rather all the more, must we keep before us the ideal towards which we are moving, in order to stimulate our interest and direct our conduct in the practical politics of the present. It is easy to scoff at those who are thinking always of the day-after-to-morrow; but perhaps the work of each day will not be done in a less worthy manner, because some of us are not satisfied with merely that. Not the hope of the Promised Land, but the memory of the flesh pots of Egyptian bondage made Israel disobedient in their wandering through the wilderness. And *we* are more likely to lead unprofitable lives by longing with a sickly sentimentalism for the good old days of contentment and subjection, than by cherishing an aspiration after an ideal commonwealth, that is to say, by really meaning the petition that all Christendom repeats: "Adveniat regnum tuum; fiat voluntas tuan, sicut in coelo, *et in terra.*" "Thy kingdom come: Thy will be done *in earth* as it is in Heaven."

THE ANTITHESIS BETWEEN
INDIVIDUALISM AND SOCIALISM
PHILOSOPHICALLY CONSIDERED[1]

THE purpose which I have set before myself this evening is a
very humble and limited one. I have not come here to instruct
skilled economists and statisticians in political economy and
the use of statistics; I have not come here to attempt an
analysis of the probable working of Economic Socialism. I
am not going to deny, so far as I am aware, any of the
fundamental principles which are really involved in the
Socialist contention. What I want to be allowed to attempt
is simply to state a question, to emphasise a distinction. And
the good which I should hope to effect, if I had the power to
effect it, would be to help in refocussing the Socialist picture
of social phenomena, not obliterating its details, but perhaps
taking in a little more at both sides, and altering the light
and shade, and putting some things in the foreground that
are now in the background, and *vice versâ*. Or, to change
the metaphor, the Socialist express seems to me to be at
present approaching a junction. I do not want it to shut off
steam, but I wish I could be pointsman when it comes up;
for I think that one line of rails will take it to a very barren
country, and the other to a very fruitful country.

I think it only fair to myself to say that I suppose I was
asked to come here on purpose to try and criticise, and I
mean to do so. But if I had before me an audience of
plutocratic sympathies, then I should have the pleasure of
speaking much more than I shall to-night in the language
of the Fabian Essays.

(α) Individualism and Socialism may be considered as
names which designate different conditions or organisations
of the productive and distributive work of society: Individual-

[1] A paper read by invitation at a meeting of the Fabian Society on February
21, 1890, by Bernard Bosanquet.

ism meaning a competitive system based on private property, such as under certain limitations exists to-day in Europe; and Socialism meaning a collective organisation of these same functions. Simply for the sake of clearness I shall call these systems and the advocacy of them by the names of Economic Individualism and Economic Socialism respectively.

But (β) the two generic names in question carry with them associations belonging to pregnant views of life as a whole; and Individualism at least may be used to represent a recognised philosophical doctrine of human relations analogous to the theory of matter indicated by the equivalent Greek term Atomism. And by opposition to this pregnant use of Individualism, and also in virtue of its own obvious derivation, the term Socialism is acquiring, if it did not at first possess, a deeper meaning as a name for a human tendency or aspiration that is operative throughout history, in contrast, we have been told, with "Unsocialism." To distinguish this more human signification of the words we are discussing from their purely economic usage, I shall specify them when thus employed as Moral Individualism and Moral Socialism respectively, everything being moral, in the philosophical sense, which deals with the value of life as a whole.

Moral Individualism, then, is the materialistic or Epicurean view of life (which when reasonably interpreted has a good deal to be said for it: see Professor Wallace's "Epicurus," a beautiful book); and moral Socialism is the opposite view to this, the view which makes Society the moral essence of the Individual. And I may say at once that for practical purposes of discussion I shall assume this second view to be the right view. In strict philosophy neither of them is right, but only a rational conception which satisfies the demands of both. But there is this great difference between them, that the individual or atomic animal man has a visible body, and therefore we are already quite certain not to deny *his* reality, and we need not further insist upon it by help of a theory; while the moral being of man as a centre of social functions and relations is not visible to the bodily eye, and therefore we do need a theory to insist upon *it*. This shows the ground of philosophical connection between Materialism and Moral Individualism in the tendency to start from what you can most easily see.

For convenience of antithesis, then, I shall speak of Moral

Individualism in the sense of actual or theoretical egoism, and Moral Socialism (though this latter is not an accepted expression) in the sense of actual or theoretical recognition that man's moral being lies in his social being. I do not assume that Moral Socialism is the view of morality entertained by Economic Socialists. My object this evening is rather to put the question whether it is so either most naturally, or as a matter of fact. Therefore, what I wish to discuss is the relation between two antitheses: between the antithesis of Economic Individualism to Economic Socialism, and the antithesis of Moral Individualism to Moral Socialism.

There is, I think, a widespread tendency simply to confuse these two distinctions with one another. The mere name of Socialism evokes an enthusiasm and devotion which show that it is not felt to be merely one system of property-holding. Though it is seldom distinctly announced to be anything more; and still less is the question raised, which I am trying to raise just now, *what* more it is. Mr. Kirkup, in the article "Socialism" of the "Encyclopædia Britannica," has a curiously suggestive passage. He says, "Most of the prevailing Socialism of to-day is based on the frankest and most outspoken revolutionary materialism." Well! Materialism going along with Moral Individualism, this is to say that the two antitheses which we are discussing are *cross-connected*, or at least that Economic Socialism is based on Moral Individualism. But then he continues, "The ethics of Socialism are closely akin to the ethics of Christianity, if not identical with them." This, again, is to say that the two antitheses which I am discussing correspond term for term, or at least that Economic Socialism is based on Moral Socialism. But the question is not pursued after this very suggestive contradiction, which might, one would have thought, have led up to an inquiry how there comes to be this very decided right and left wing in Socialist morality. Even in the Fabian Essays I cannot think that the distinction between Economic and Moral Socialism, with the questions that arise out of it, is quite plainly faced. The sentence on page 148, "The system of property-holding which we call Socialism is not in itself such a life, &c., is therefore refreshing to a philosopher, who has found himself a little bewildered by an implied assumption that two things are the same, about which he wants to know whether they have any connection at all, and if so, what. The "moral ideas appropriate to Socialism," or "Socialism" as an[2] object of moral judgment,[3] are in another paper rather assumed to be of the nature of what I call Moral Socialism, than shown to be so; nor do I feel absolutely sure that the author of this paper has made a final choice between the ethical right and left wing. We all see, indeed, that more general comfort would give morality a better chance, and that industrial co-operation is a good ethical training; but the statement of these two points hardly amounts to a recognition and treatment of the distinction and connection between Economic Socialism and Moral Socialism. The pages of this volume, with which, speaking as an ethical student, I feel most at home, are the concluding page and a half of the Essay on Industry under Socialism.[4] And I do not at all maintain that the connection between economic and moral Socialism, which is there indicated, need be visionary. Even if I am betrayed into a little polemic, illustrative of what I consider the risks of a false perspective, it is not my object to make an attack. My object is to get the question recognised in its full difficulty and importance. I begin, therefore, by stating the *prima facie* case against a connection between Moral and Economic Socialism.[5]

Morality consists in the presence of some element of the social purpose as a moving idea before the individual mind; that is, in short, in the social constitution of the individual will. This has been the recognised morality of the Western nations for more than two thousand years, without any essential or fundamental change whatever, the deepening of the individual spirit and intelligence, which has sometimes seemed to tear society apart, having been in every case the germination of a membership in a new social order, sometimes, by illusion, taken for a time to be invisible as well as visible. Able writers (Mr. Belfort Bax and Mr. Mackay)

[2] p. 127
[3] p. 104
[4] pp. 168–9.
[5] The Author of the paper on The Moral Basis of Socialism says there is no special Socialistic view of the basis of morals. This may be so, but then I hardly think you could speak of moral ideas appropriate to Socialism. At least, you would have to *make* the connection.

have absolutely and utterly misunderstood this phenomenon, which they take for a growth of Individualism.

Now, why should Economic Socialism not be favourable to a developed morality of this kind? Stated in the abstract, the reason is that it is the same thing in a quite different form, and the general rule is that different forms of the same thing are hostile. A regular Gallio has no objection to a State Church. Like Mr. M. Arnold, he thinks that it saves people from becoming too religious. But a man who thinks that the State is itself spiritual is apt to be fanatically opposed to an Establishment. The one form is always seeming to claim the functions of the other, and two different things cannot occupy the same place. It may be answered that all is well so long as they do not claim to occupy the same place, but simply to assist one another as distinct means to the same end. That may be, but then the distinction and the mode of assistance must be very precisely defined.

Morality, as I said, consists in the social purpose working by its own force on the individual will. Economic Socialism is an arrangement for getting the social purpose carried out just not by its own force, but by the force of those compulsory motives or sanctions which are at the command of the public power.

Therefore, *primâ facie*, the normal relation of the two antitheses of which I spoke would be that of cross-correspondence. Economic Individualism would go with Moral Socialism, and Moral Individualism (or Egoism) with Economic Socialism. If you want to treat your social units as bricks in a wall or wheels in a machine, you cannot also and at the same time treat them as elements in an organism. Or, it is truer to say, if you can treat them in these two ways at once, you have solved an exceedingly difficult problem. *Primâ facie*, machinery and morality are quite different things, and if you are trying to model your machinery directly upon your morality, it is long odds that you are guided simply by a confusion. Economic Socialism need not presuppose the social organism. It is, in appearance, a *substitute for* the life of that organism, intended to operate on the egoistic motives of individuals for the good of the whole, which cannot, it is assumed, be attained by the moral power of the social purpose. In this point of view at least it naturally rests on Moral Individualism. All compulsion through the material necessities of individuals is morally individualistic. But Economic Individualism does presuppose the social organism, and without it would be the dissolution of society. It is often alleged that the time of the factory development 100 years ago was a time of unmixed Economic Individualism. But this is not so; perhaps the worst evils of that time arose directly from the intentionally lax or "socialistic" Poor Law. It was the public institutions that for the most part supplied the children who were ill treated. Owen's life shows us that by sheer competitive attraction you could *not* get the respectable country people to work under factory conditions. This suggests a different moral. Economic Individualism assumes that the moral purpose has power to take care of itself throughout the general life of society, and only embodies that purpose in acts of the public power when such acts appear definitely necessary on specific grounds for the support of the private moral will. The Economic Individualist, indeed, who thinks the State to be unconcerned with morality, and to be unjustified in any interference on moral grounds, is a fanatic and doctrinaire, and is the precise counterpart of the Economic Socialist who assumes straight away that collectivism in property naturally implies socialisation of the will. Each of these doctrinaires imagines that the economic and the moral forms of his principle are necessarily coherent with each other, whereas it is much more natural that they should be antagonistic.

If I am asked, "Does this apparent antagonism between Moral and Economic Socialism represent what I believe to be the fact?" I reply, "It represents to me the reality of certain conditions, and my own judgment of any existing or proposed economical machinery would depend upon the degree in which, at the time of its proposal, it should satisfy those conditions." And these conditions, in accordance with what has been said, may be summed up as the necessity of avoiding the confusion of machinery with morality, on the ground that the moment this confusion begins your Moral Socialism turns automatically into Moral Individualism.

It is therefore the second antithesis – the moral antithesis – and not the first – the economical antithesis – that dominates the question. Our joint purpose is, as I understand, to find a machinery which will assist morality and not be confounded with it. To my own mind the great requisite is to acknowledge that all these problems are matters of contrivance and matters of degree. I was electrified, but also edified, not long ago, to find an able writer of the extreme school of doctrinaire Individualists talking about devising new tenures of private property, and about an admirable *substitute for* private property. (He was speaking of Insurance.) This latter phrase is one with which I do not think an Economic Socialist need quarrel. It is perfectly plain and undeniable, I think, that liberty and regulation are increasing side by side as the whole range of life becomes larger, and that what is important is not the relative amount of regulation and of liberty, but the adaptation of both with delicacy and flexibility to the shape and growth of life.

Thus the question assumes the form, not of choosing between two ready-made economic systems, but of developing a specific system to suit the necessities of our life.

From this point of view it is plain that the spirit in which we go to work, the focussing of our picture, the precise line of rail on which we progress, will be simply decisive of the all-important question which I am trying to put before you: "Does Economic Socialism carry with it Moral Socialism or Moral Individualism?" In the former case it is heaven, and in the latter case it is hell. What I now propose to attempt is to insist further, by help of details both of opinion and of practice, upon the dangerous conditions which I have endeavoured to set out in the above abstract deduction – upon the danger, that is, which lies in the facility of connection between Economic Socialism and Moral Individualism. I want to show, if I can, at how important a parting of the ways Modern Socialism is about to arrive.

1. I quoted from Mr. Kirkup to the effect that there is a great deal of materialism – which means Moral Individualism – in modern Socialism. Much of this is inherited, no doubt, though not from Robert Owen, and may be passing away. But much remains, and is inherent – as a *tendency* is inherent – in Economic Socialism.

Take the case in which Economic Socialism frequently appeals to moral considerations; the polemic against private property.

As a matter of the history of opinion, to begin with, this cuts off Economic Socialism at once from the two greatest expounders of the social organism that the world has ever seen – I mean Aristotle[6] and Hegel. I do not mention this as if their authority was decisive on practical questions of to-day, because the nature of property has changed and is continually changing. But it is important, when Economic Socialists begin to speak about the social organism, as I am glad to see that they are beginning to, to bear in mind that a radical and fundamental polemic against private property is quite incompatible with any legitimate affiliation to those who gave us this spiritual principle. What about Plato? it may be asked. Well! Aristotle's complaint against him, reduced to modern terms, is that Plato had needlessly destroyed the social organism by trusting to machinery instead of morality. On the other hand, private property, as Aristotle would have it, is a different thing from ours. Now, with reference to Hegel, one notices at times a tendency in Economic Socialism to be a little proud of a somewhat doubtful affiliation to him. It is quite true that Karl Marx used the forms of the dialectic with extraordinary ingenuity, and one hopes that the deeper spiritual ideas of Hegel's teaching are passing, and will pass, more and more into the temper of nineteenth-century reformers. It is, moreover, true that Hegel denounced as a blunder the idea which I have stigmatised as characteristic of doctrinaire Individualism: the idea that the public recognition of moral purposes is necessarily fatal to individual moral freedom. So far, an Economic Socialist can count upon Hegel as against a doctrinaire Individualist. But when you read Hegel's treatment of private property, and realise the depth and complexity of the moral problem to which he regards it as the answer, and then pass from that treatment to the view which regards it as the embodiment of individual cupidity and indolence, I think everyone must be aware that one has passed to another and not a higher moral atmosphere. I hope I shall not weary you too much if I quote a characteristic page from Hegel's "Philosophy of Right"[7]:

"As, in property, my will is made real for me as a personal will – that is, as the will of an individual – property is characteristically *private* property; while common property, such as in its nature can be severally possessed, bears the

---

[6] Newman, Introd. to Pol. 164 and 178.
[7] Rechtsphil, p. 81.

character of a dissoluble combination, in which I can choose or not choose to leave my share.

"The use of the elements" [I suppose he means air and water – he might have meant land but for the next sentence] "is incapable of being made a private possession. The agrarian laws at Rome contain a conflict between collectivism and private property in land; the latter necessarily gained the day, as the more reasonable factor in the social system, although at the expense of other rights. Family trust property contains a factor which is opposed to the right of personality, and therefore to that of private property. But the rules which deal with private property may be subordinated to higher spheres of right, to a corporation or to the State, as in the case when ownership is vested in a so-called moral person – property in mortmain. However, such exceptions must not be founded in caprice or private interest, but only in the rational organisation of the State.

"The idea of Plato's Republic contains as a general principle the injustice against the person of making him incapable of holding private property. The idea of a pious or friendly or even compulsory fraternity of human beings with community of goods, and the banishment of the principle of private property, may easily occur to a habit of thought which mistakes the nature of spiritual freedom and of right, and does not apprehend them in their definite factors. As for the moral or religious point of view, Epicurus deterred his friends from organising such a community of goods, when they thought of doing so, precisely on the ground that to do so would indicate mistrust, and that people who mistrust one another are not friends.

"Note. In property my will takes the shape of a person. Now a person is something in particular; therefore the property is the personification of this will. As I give my will existence by means of property, property in its turn must have the attribute of being this in particular, *i.e.* mine. This is the important doctrine of the necessity of private property. If exceptions are made by the State, it is it alone that can make them; and often in our own days it has *restored* private property. So, for example, many nations have rightly abolished the monasteries, because in the last resort a collective institution has no such right to property as the person has."

Now if it is maintained that the reasonable necessity which

in Hegel's view demanded the existence of private property can now be met by a modification of the private ownership system, or even by some different system, that might fairly be urged without breaking your line of descent from idealistic or organic philosophy which is one with moral Socialism. But if you say that private ownership is, and always has been, simply the expression of individual greed, and the desire to be indolent and incompetent, then, by a phenomenon very common in controversy, you arouse a well-grounded suspicion that you are ascribing this foundation – the foundation of Moral Individualism – to the normal life of humanity, simply because it is the foundation on which your own views ultimately rest, and you are aware of no other. It appears to me that Economic Socialism wavers between these two attitudes, and that the latter, the polemic against private ownership, altogether and as such, betrays, as Hegel implies, an entire blindness to the essential elements of the social organism, which can only exist as a structure of free individual wills, each entertaining the social purpose in an individual form appropriate to its structural position and organic functions. It is perhaps a platitude, but one which we all of us are perpetually failing to apply, that throughout life the attempt to realise an abstraction as an abstraction is self-contradictory and a ruinous failure. To aim directly at pleasure for pleasure's sake means failure in happiness; to aim at duty for duty's sake means failure in morality; to aim at beauty for beauty's sake means failure in fine art; to aim at truth for truth's sake (the net result) means failure in science; to aim at the general purpose for the sake of the purpose as general means failure in social reform. I confess that I believe modern Economic Socialism to rest *in part* on this ineradicable confusion. "We want a general good life; let us make a law that there shall be a general good life." But, precisely as other-worldliness arises from the religious impulse when embodied in a mechanical form, so, and for identically the same reasons, does Moral Individualism arise automatically from the impulse of Moral Socialism when embodied in a mechanical form. You must let the individual make his will a reality in the conduct of his life, in order that it may be possible for him consciously to entertain the social purpose as a constituent of his will. Without these conditions there is no social organism and no Moral Socialism. This is the meaning of the doctrines of Aristotle and Hegel, and this it is which the ethical left wing of the Socialists, alluded to by Mr. Kirkup, appears to me wholly to ignore.

2. But the question is not one merely of the history of opinion or of ethical formulas. If it were, it would be too purely academic for even a philosophical discussion before the Fabian Society. It is one also of practical tendency – a difficult thing to grasp and bring home in detail; but I propose to indicate by one or two instances what I mean.

α. I have spoken of the theory of private property. Now, theoretical attitude communicates a bias, as everyone knows, to particular perceptions. I do not think I ever noticed a Socialist alluding, except with derision, to the duties of property. Of course you may maintain that you are right in fact – that these duties are a negligible quantity, or a ridiculous pretence. Time forbids me to argue upon the proper interpretation of this state of things, which indisputably exists in great measure. But, however this attitude may be justified, I want to point out what it amounts to. The long and short of it is that those who speak in this way do not really believe in Moral Socialism. To those who believe in Moral Socialism the source of a payment makes no difference to the duty it involves. So long as one can live, the duty of working for Society is imperative; if one has more than enough to live on, that is a charge – something to work with, to organise, to direct. Property is mediate payment with responsibility; salary is immediate payment. I never saw it recognised by a Socialist that property could be a burden. I wish to avoid overstraining, and I will admit against myself that my own class is probably the most selfish of all; that is, the class which has enough to tempt it into a little luxury, but not enough to constitute a notable responsibility and public charge. But this defect of a limited class does not justify a want of faith which misconstrues a fundamental factor of human morality. And this defect of faith is radical, and is connected directly with Economic Socialism. It means that the reason for equalising opportunity is not merely that you want to give nine-tenths of the people a better chance than they have now – to level up to the highest standard to which you may in practice be able to level up – but that you do not believe anyone will work unless his livelihood depends upon it. Now I cannot fight the battle of all human nature in five minutes; but I will lay down one principle as tolerably certain, and it is this: a man who will not work if his livelihood is secure without it will be an uncommonly bad workman if his livelihood depends upon it. Practically speaking, this whole view is to my observation false; and, technically speaking, it unquestionably is Moral Individualism. Here I am glad to have on my side the concluding pages of the Essay on "Industry under Socialism," which represents the ethical right wing, and, as I hope, the future of Socialistic ideas.

β. I have said that many Socialists speak as if they did not *believe in* the socialisation of the will. It is a corollary from this that they should not care about the socialisation of the will.

There are indications that the natural connection of Economic Socialism with Moral Individualism tends to realise itself in this respect also. I will adduce some instances which may at least explain my meaning.

(i.) I admit that I have not found in the Fabian Essays the direct disparagement of *thrift* which I anticipated that I should find. The only allusion to the subject which I have observed is the remark that thrift is preached by extravagant people, which doubtless is true. Otherwise, I think, the subject is somewhat severely let alone. I believe that I am not mistaken in saying that the inculcation of thrift is looked upon with coldness, if not with aversion, by modern Economic Socialism. It is said, and I do not know that Socialists would desire to deny it, that the introduction of Post Office Savings Banks into Prussia was prevented by the influence of Lassalle's movement upon the Government, the then Director of the Post Office being anxious to introduce them.

Now I am well aware of two things: first, that there are different kinds of thrift – speaking roughly, the selfish kind and the unselfish kind; and secondly, I am aware that there is no greater deterrent against saving than the impossibility of saving enough to be of any use. This is an every-day experience among the less wealthy class of professional men. But yet I appeal with confidence to anyone who has practical familiarity with the character and distresses of the working class, to say whether experience does not show that thrift among them goes with unselfishness and a sense of duty, and unthrift with selfishness and self-indulgence. I would rather, I think, have on my soul the sin which has been committed by Englishmen in high places, of speaking lightly of intemperance, than the sin of having let fall a word of discouragement for that foresight and self-control which is, and always must be, the ground and medium of all Moral Socialism. I see no ultimate discrepancy between the purposes of Economic Socialism and this elementary factor of morality. I do see a *primâ facie* antagonism between the two, in so far as Economic Socialism rests upon the individualistic fallacy of thinking that you can maintain a moral structure without maintaining the morality which is the cohesion of its units. It should be clearly understood that thrift, in the shape of a resolution to bear at least your own burdens, is not a selfish but an unselfish quality, and is the first foundation and the well-known symptom of a tendency, not to Moral Individualism, but to Moral Socialism. This point is not met by saying that it is hard to save on 19*s*. a week. We are speaking of a quality in moral character, which determines the happiness or misery of those who possess or do not possess it, in a way that goes far deeper into life than by mere success or failure in laying by a sum of money. The man who looks ahead and tries to provide for bearing his own burden is the man who can appreciate a social purpose, and who cares for the happiness of those dependent on him. Him, if he fails in part, you may safely help for a time; if he fails altogether, by exceptional misfortune, you should, I incline to think, distinguish him in your Poor Law treatment from the man who shows no signs of such a disposition. But to try and take away from him the one thing on which his manliness and his chance of happiness depend, by speaking lightly of the duty of carrying at least one's own burden, betrays a standpoint which is not that of Moral Socialism.

(ii.) I turn from a question of feeling and mode of speech to a question more directly practical. In speaking of the present Poor Law system, a chief fault to which a Socialist calls attention is harshness of administration and desire to save the rates. Now, that there was great brutality in Poor Law administration not very long ago, that signs of such brutality appear to crop up still from time to time, that defects arising from foolish economy are alleged against some Poor Law schools, and that the system of large district schools may require reconsideration, – all this appears to me to be true. And it is plain that sensible kindliness, the greatest possible care for education, and a differential treatment of those whose misfortunes are special and unavoidable, should be principles pervading the administration of the Poor Law.

Nevertheless, after all these allowances are made in justification of the Socialist criticism, I should say that it points in precisely the wrong direction. These matters, indeed, cannot really be discussed on a quantitative basis; nothing in actual life can be so treated. In all these social problems it is not really either a less or a more that is wanted; it is something *different*; something which would be more in some cases, and less in others. But if I must use roughly approximate terms of quantity, to which popular treatment always inclines, I should say that what is wanted is to lessen the amount of Poor Law assistance; to make the administration not more lax, but more strict; not more lenient, but more harsh. I observe that in the Essay on "Industry under Socialism" it is contemplated without a shudder that those who, in a reformed social system, and with a fair chance of work before them, deliberately refuse to support themselves, might without injustice be left to starve. Now the complication of deserved and undeserved calamity represented by our pauperism to-day cannot be thus regarded as meriting strictly penal treatment. On the other hand, the moral requirement suggested by the passage seems to me too low. We require more of a man than the willingness to work as an alternative to bare starvation. We require that in laying his plan of life, and not simply with a view to his own possible disaster, he should be guided by the principle that he will never become a burden to others like himself. Therefore you must judge these cases not merely by their present misery, but by their past selfish folly. And therefore we must treat the failure in self-support as something which, though we dare not now bring it, as the more socialistic Athenians did, within the compass of the penal law, yet demands not only the pity but also the reprobation of society. I look upon the exceptional case of destitution by pure misfortune in a manner analogous to that in which I regard a legal offender who is free, by some accident, from moral culpability. These cases there partly is, and more completely might be, a mode of hindering or of alleviating. Here is the sphere of individual kindliness and skill.

What do I want, then, to bring the thing to an issue? I

want all ordinary cases of destitution to be treated in the workhouse, with gentleness and human care, but under strict regulation and not on a high scale of comfort. I want all cases of exceptional misfortune which has finally frustrated foresight and persistent effort to be treated by individual skill and judgment, with pensions or in alms-houses, as suggested for *all* destitute cases in a Socialist publication. I want the State supplementation of the resources of those who are poor but not destitute, known as out-relief, to cease altogether. Here I must add a word to show the special bearing of this on my philosophical contention. You cannot restore a broken life by mechanical support. This deep and subtle relation between the character and circumstances shows itself not in one form but in many forms of evil which arise from the attempt. There is physical evil – this supplementation of resources, owing to the constant fear of deception, is never adequate, and actually causes the partial or entire starvation which it is intended to avert. There is economical evil – the rate in aid of wages; I need not enlarge on this. There is moral evil – the confusion of responsibility between the individual and Society as a whole. "I have paid rates for many years," a labourer out of work once said to me – "why should I not have my relief simply by asking for it?" The Economic Socialism of out-relief had driven this poor man into Moral Individualism; seeing the fund to which he contributed used to tide over the difficulties of the improvident, he thought that the State intended, in part at least, to take the duty of providence off his shoulders; his will was confused, and his life very probably ruined. No money will make up to a man for a broken mainspring in his social will.

There is one fundamental objection – or, rather, one incisive retort, for I cannot admit that it is an objection – which a Socialist may make to all this argument. He may say, "Is not, at least, inherited or unearned property an equally pernicious subvention to the rich as out-relief to the poor?"

I point out one distinction, and then give my general answer. Property is within the owner's control and is a permission to him to choose his work – of course an enormous indulgence. But Poor Law relief is not in the recipient's control, is a payment for idleness, and is not sufficient to set the life free to choose work. A large pension or gift of property to a man not yet demoralised would probably do no harm. This is the paradox about doles already known to Aristotle, and recognised by expert philanthropists to-day. Great expenditure which "sets a man up" does not as a rule demoralise; it is the little chronic subventions, which give no freedom and are actually consequent upon the failure of the social will, that cause demoralisation.

I do not think it can be denied that property *may* have a similar effect. Wherever it distracts from one social vocation, without forming the basis of another, there it operates as out-relief pure and simple, and there the strictures of the Fabian Essays have full application. With this concession, I pass from the distinction which I had to draw between property and out-relief, to the general answer which I make to the retort which consists in comparing them.

The answer is simply this: that two blacks do not make a white, and that the identification of property with out-relief, if established, might be a good argument for abolishing property, but could not possibly be a plea in favour of out-relief.

(iii.) And with out-relief I class all inadequate treatment of the symptom of social evil which is known as poverty. I mention especially large-scale organisations for free dinners at popular schools, and large-scale arrangements for giving employment to the casual unemployed.

In all these matters the same tendency is traceable – the tendency to adapt machinery to dealing with a large effect, superficially apparent, without distinguishing the very different classes of cause, demanding different means for their neutralisation, which concur in producing this large apparent effect. Especially in the problem of feeding the children who attend school every case needs special and separate investigation. It is certainly sometimes possible to persuade parents to pay for food supplied to their children, who before permitted it to be given to them for nothing. I have seen this done, on a very small scale indeed, and in this case there has been not only a physical gain to the child, but also a moral gain to the parents. I cannot strongly enough protest that to us who believe in the socialisation of the will, the treatment of these questions by large-scale machinery assumes the aspect, not of sympathy and charity, but of negligence and cruelty. Discrimination, if guided merely by the test of the child's immediate need, means on the whole that the wrong people are helped and the right people are not helped. To this I should prefer, if it were the only alternative, that all children should be given a free meal without discrimination; in which case there would not be the peculiar extra aggravation that just precisely in proportion as people fail to do their duty, the public does it for them. I may add, that under the present social system these advantages probably send up the rents in the neighbourhoods where they are provided, so that the happy landlord pockets the weekly value of the child's dinner. This, however, is not an argument that can ultimately carry weight with Socialists. It should weigh with everybody for the present, I think.

(iv.) It is plain, moreover, that Economic Socialism is anything but warmly disposed towards productive co-operation, the existence of which, as distinct from joint-stock shopkeeping, would hardly be gathered from the reference to the subject in the Fabian Essay on The Industrial Basis of Socialism. Although Dr. Ingram's opinion[8] is evidently, like the Fabian Essayist's, that no great importance belongs even to productive co-operation, yet it is worth observing that in the passage to which the Fabian Essay alludes he is discussing Cairnes' view to the contrary, and the modern economists whom he quotes against Cairnes are not quite spoken of as "modern economists in general." This is a matter of no real importance, except as an indication of a well-known Socialistic attitude of mind – of what almost amounts to a dread of all processes that chiefly depend on the socialisation of the will; because, I suppose, the primary antagonism between Economic and Moral Socialism is instinctively felt, without being theoretically demonstrated. The success of productive co-operation, I take it, in view of the modern successful management of joint-stock companies, is simply and solely an affair of the workman's industrial and moral education.

(v.) The word education brings me to my last set of illustrations, which are on ground more familiar to me. The Economic Socialist is willing, as I rejoice to see, to spend money on the children, but I do not see that, since the time of Robert Owen, his eyes have been very sharp to detect the real needs of education. Owen proposed that there should be national training colleges for teachers – a truly statesmanlike proposal, which I wish was included in the platform of some

---

[8] Encyclopaedia Britannica, Article "Political Economy."

party to-day. Probably, in his sympathy with Lancaster, Owen may have been careless about the size of the division entrusted to a single teacher, on which both Bell and Lancaster had absurd ideas. On this question experience has taught us much, and to double the present staff of teachers, at least in our infant schools, is a very moderate proposal. It would be much more important to give a piano to every Board School than to give "free dinners" to the children.[9] It is heart-breaking to see the children marching to the mere clapping of hands.

And one thing more is necessary to sound education. You must carry the parents along with you. There is nothing in this contrary to Economic Socialism; it seems to be successfully attempted in Godin's Familistère at Guise. But, like the other matters I have referred to, you can only do it by real enthusiasm for the socialisation of the individual will. No machinery can effect it. You must make it your duty, and inspire your manager with the zeal for this duty, to get the parents interested, until at last they come to know and care and act effectively in controlling the education of their children. The thing can be done. I have seen a beginning made – a very trifling one.

(vi.) And as a final instance, I would say one word upon the idea, often connected with Economic Socialism, of beautiful surroundings of life and the interchangeability of labour. Here again, I believe, we find, mingled with much sound insight, a theoretical confusion, the pursuit of an abstraction. Socialists always say, and quite rightly, that you cannot go back. Well, for that reason I think that you can never again be free from the intellectuality of modern life; and therefore I think that material beauty and splendour will never again have their old importance in our lives. We shall have, I trust, a devotion to beauty – probably a deeper beauty than before – and shall learn to avoid the sordid and hideous; but when a lad can buy Shakespeare for a shilling and read him in a garret, it is impossible that we should ever again absolutely depend for our chief spiritual nutriment on the beauty of the

---

[9] I must insist that this sentence does *not* mean that pianos, which I rejoice to see are to be given, are more important than the proper care and nourishment of school children. If I said that to pay for making school life happier is better than to pay parents to neglect their children, the saying might seem less hard.

more sensuous arts and crafts. I do not underrate these great goods of life; I am often accused of valuing them too highly. I only want to point out that the whole basis of mind and society is now definitely intellectual and ideal, and in the historical idea we have explicitly what the artistic tradition used to represent implicitly. "Literature is dirt-cheap,"[10] and everyone can read it; and though I cannot doubt that the fine arts of sense-perception have a future, yet the modern mind is so deep and so strong that it can bear, and to some extent must bear, the divorce from sensuous beauty, which would have killed the ancient Greek or mediæval Italian.

This brings me to the question of the interchangeability of labour. Here, as elsewhere, I do not think that Economic Socialism appreciates the depth of individuality which is necessary in order to contain, in a moral form, the modern social purpose. Each unit of the social organism has to embody his relations with the whole in his own particular work and will; and in order to do this the individual must have a strength and depth in himself proportional to and consisting of the relations which he has to embody. Thus, if the individual in ancient Greece was like a centre to which a thousand threads of relation were attached, the individual in modern Europe might be compared to a centre on which there hang many, many millions. You cannot go back to a simple world, in which the same man can conquer all knowledge, or be versed in all practice. If all are, as we hope, to share in the gains achieved by each, it can only be through the gigantic and ever-increasing labour by which every worker takes account, in his work, of its import for all. There should not be castes of workers, if caste means a social division; there must be classes of workers, because the increasing material of human knowledge and endeavour will more and more consume the entire lives and thoughts of those upon whom its burden falls.

This argument is not directed against rational provisions for doing away with unskilled labour, or for imposing some public activity on every citizen in excess of his normal vocation. It is directed against the idea that work becomes useful by being popular in the sense of being unspecialised and superficial; whereas it is plain to all who know, that only

[10] Fabian Essays.

thoroughness can impart universal significance, and that the claim upon the student, and artist, and scientist will more and more take the form, "It is expedient that one man should die for the people." This is very far from being a selfish contention on the student's part. In an age of universal education, the student's services, more than those of anyone else, will be obtainable, should society so choose, at starvation wages.

I need not multiply these illustrations. I have said enough to make my meaning clear. Economic Individualism and Economic Socialism are both obviously on the move, each of them desiring to make good its differently-founded claims to harmonise with Moral Socialism, which is the only thing for which any healthy human being, at the bottom of his heart, cares a single straw. The Moral Socialist looks on, confident that the forces of human nature will make the reality prevail, but not, at all unwilling to co-operate with those forces wherever he can find a purchase. And such a purchase would be found if it were possible to convince the Economic Socialist that in dealing with the social organism he is dealing with a structure whose units are the characters of men and women; and that in so far as he neglects to base his arrangements on the essence of character – that is, on the social or moral will – so far he is not dealing with the social organism as an organism, but rather as a machine – that is to say, from the point of view, not of Moral Socialism, but of Moral Individualism.

FAVORABLE ASPECTS OF STATE SOCIALISM
Joseph Chamberlain

THE advance of democracy during recent years in all popular governed countries has brought what is called the social question into great prominence. The greatest happiness of the greatest number, which was formerly only the benevolent aspiration of a philosopher, has become a matter of urgent practical politics.

Under the general name of socialism, the redistribution of wealth, the relations between labor and capital, and the extension of the functions of the state in regard to the industrial and domestic life of the people, have assumed a real and pressing importance.

New theories have been developed, and their practical application is already becoming a dividing-line between political parties. Exaggerated fears have been excited, and not less exaggerated hopes. On the one hand, timorous people have conjured up a vision of a desperate proletariat combined for the purpose of extorting from wealth a compulsory division of property, with the result that capital will leave its present investments, industry will be disorganized, trade diverted to other channels, and general insecurity will prevail, to be followed in due course by national disaster and ruin. On the other hand are to be found enthusiasts who indulge the hope that the legislation of the future, banishing to Saturn all the laws of political economy, will be able, as by a magician's wand, to exorcise the evils of our political system, and to redress the inequalities which individual character and circumstances, more often than the action of the state, have created in the lives of men.

These antagonistic views are supported by very different estimates of the present position of the masses of the people. The opponents of further state intervention point with confidence to the present position of the working classes as a satisfactory result of the sturdy maintenance of individual liberty and of the absence of grandmotherly restriction and control. They assert that by the practice of reasonable industry and self-denial the ordinary workman may live and enjoy his life. He may find opportunities for recreation and intellectual improvement, and may hope to rise in the social scale, and to leave his children with prospects better even than his own. According to these optimists, this is the best of all possible worlds, in which only the knaves and the fools fail to secure some of its numerous prizes.

The socialists, on the contrary, see in the condition of the wage-earners the evidence of the terrible struggle for life in which the weakest go to the wall and only a few exceptional natures can survive and prosper. They allege that the great modern developments in science and invention have only benefited a handful of favored individuals, while the vast majority have gained nothing, and have even suffered by comparison; their misery seeming more profound in the shadow of the enormous prosperity of the successful minority. According to this view, the rich have grown richer and the poor poorer, so that the gulf between classes is wider than it ever was before.

If either of these views is accepted as absolute and complete, the logical conclusion would appear to be the same; and the statesman would be justified in both cases, although for different reasons, in abandoning the hope of improvement by ordinary legislative means. In the first case, the argument would be to let well alone, and not to disturb arangements which had produced so thoroughly satisfactory a result. In the second case, the proof that all the legislation of the last generation, much of it socialistic in its character, had failed to make any impression on the general mass of misery and discontent would justify the refusal to proceed further along lines which had led to no beneficial result.

It will, therefore, be a matter of interest to ascertain at the outset the true facts of the case, and to see whether the information at our disposal enables us to decide with confidence whether or no the condition of the people at large has improved during the last fifty years. Such a comparison is the more necessary because the present generation is always too apt to concentrate its attention on the times in which it is living, and, while appreciating keenly its own difficulties and distress, to forget the greater evils of the past, and thus to ignore the methods of improvement which have been tested by experience, and which may therefore be safely continued in the future.

I took occasion, at a recent jubilee of the greatest and oldest of the friendly societies of Birmingham, to make such a contrast, drawn from the history of our town as well as from the general history of the country; and, although the picture is necessarily imperfect, it is suggestive both of the character and extent of the changes which have been already effected, and also of the legislation which has been chiefly instrumental in bringing them about.

Fifty years ago Birmingham was a town of 180,000 inhabitants, or about 40 per cent. of the present population. The ratable value was between £500,000 and £600,000, or rather less than one-third of what it is at present. There were at that time hardly any public edifices of any magnitude or importance. There were no parks, there were no free libraries, there were no baths, there was no art gallery or museum, there were no board schools, there was no school of art, and no technical institute or college. The era of street improvement had hardly begun. A large area in the centre of the town, which is now traversed by magnificent streets and occupied by some of the finest shops and warehouses, was one of the worst districts in the city, both from a social and a sanitary point of view. The streets themselves were badly paved, imperfectly lighted, and only partially drained. The foot-walks were worse than the streets. The gas and the water belonged to private monopolies. Gas, which is now sold at an average of two shillings and fourpence, cost then about five shillings per thousand cubic feet. Water was supplied by the company on three days in the week; on the other days those of the inhabitants who had no wells were obliged to purchase this necessary of life from carts which perambulated the town and supplied water from polluted sources at ten shillings the thousand gallons. It is not surprising that under these circumstances the annual mortality reached thirty in the thousand; now it is twenty in the thousand, and sometimes less. The only wonder is that it was not much greater, for there were whole streets from which typhus and scarlet fever, diphtheria, and diarrhœa in its worst forms were never absent. There were thousands of close, unventilated courts which were not paved, which were not drained, which were covered with pools of stagnant filth, and in which the ashpits and middens were in a state of indescribable nastiness. The sewage of the town was so partial that it only extended over about one-third of the area. In fact, to sum up this description, it may truly be said that fifty years ago Birmingham, although it was no worse than any other of the great cities in the United Kingdom, was a town in which scarcely anything had been done either for the instruction, for the health, for the recreation, for the comfort, or for the convenience of the artisan population.

Now, let us measure the change which has taken place in these conditions within the memory of living men, and we shall see that nothing less than a revolution has been peacefully accomplished. It is hardly too much to say that the Birmingham of to-day is everything that old Birmingham was not. The sewerage has been completed, a system of sanitary inspection is strictly carried out, the private monopolies have been acquired by the corporation, their supply has been improved and cheapened, and the surplus profits have been carried to the credit of the rates. The town is well paved with wood in the principal streets, and with stone where there is the heaviest traffic. The footpaths have everywhere been put in order. The courts have been paved and drained. An infectious-hospital has been established, to which all contagious diseases are at once removed. In every district of the city there have been provided baths and wash-houses, parks and recreation-grounds, and free libraries which count their readers by hundreds of thousands. A magnificent art gallery and museum has been erected, the visitors to which number nearly a million in a single year. Schoolhouses, under the management of the School Board, with large playgrounds attached, have sprung up everywhere, and now accommodate 40,000 children, the rest being provided for in the voluntary schools. Technical education is offered at the Midland Institute and the Mason College, and art education at the School of Art and its branches. The great local endowed school of King Edward's foundation has been reformed and placed under representative management, and by means of scholarships offers the opportunity of higher education to the poorest of our citizens. In fact, the ordinary artisan finds now within his reach the appliances of health, the means of refinement, and the opportunities of innocent recreation which formerly were at the disposal of only the more wealthy inhabitants.

This striking improvement has been brought about by the operation of what may be called municipal socialism. It is the result of a wise coöperation by which the community as a whole, working through its representatives for the benefit of all its members, and recognizing the solidarity of interest which makes the welfare of the poorest a matter of importance to the richest, has faced its obligations and done much to lessen the sum of human misery, and to make the lives of all its citizens somewhat better, somewhat nobler, and somewhat happier.

Popular representative local government is the powerful instrument by which these reforms have been effected. Unlike the imperial legislation, it is very near to the poor, and can deal with details and with special conditions. It is subject to the criticism and direct control both of those who find the money and of those who are chiefly interested in its expenditure. In Great Britain, at any rate, it has been free from the suspicion of personal corruption and it has always been able to secure the services of some of the ablest and most disinterested members of the community, who have been ready in this way to do the duty that lies nearest to them, and to do it with all their might.

It may, however, be supposed that this great work has been attended with enormous cost, and that property has been taxed unduly to provide for the wants and pleasures of those who contribute little or nothing to the necessary expenditure. There is no ground for such an opinion. The rates of Birmingham (if the charge due to the school rate and required to provide for a new service in the shape of elementary education be deducted) are less than they were thirty years ago, and the growth of the town and the increase in its wealth and ratable value have sufficed to meet these new developments of municipal functions. The present cost of all local work in the city, including poor-relief, education, and all the corporation expenditure, is about six shillings and sixpence in the pound on the assessed annual value of real property, which is probably 25 per cent. less than the actual value. Putting it in another way, the total charge is rather more than twenty shillings per head of the population, or about one-fifth of the charge of local administration in the city of Boston. Complaints of the burden of the rates are still heard from time to time, but they are less frequent and less forcible than in the past. It is more and more coming to be recognized that the expenditure is in the nature of an investment, and that dividends are to be found in the improved health and comfort and the increased contentment of the people.

An interesting evidence of popular appreciation was afforded some years ago when the corporation promoted a bill consolidating their acts and in many cases extending their powers. Among other provisions was one repealing the general law which limits expenditure on art and education to a rate of one penny in the pound, and substituting unlimited powers of taxation for the purpose. The bill was opposed, and a poll of the ratepayers was demanded. The promoters boldly admitted their intention to spend more money in this direction, and made it their chief claim to support; and the ratepayers of Birmingham came in great numbers to the poll and by a large majority approved the bill, which has since been passed into law.

We must now turn from the special case of Birmingham to a more general survey of the comparative state of the whole kingdom. In reading histories which deal with the first half of the century, and especially those which refer to the period between 1830 – before the first Reform Bill – and 1846, when the Corn Laws were repealed, one thing particularly strikes the observer, and that is the constant allusion to the turbulence of the times. Riots seem to have been of almost daily occurrence, and they were accompanied by long periods of exceptional distress. In the manufacturing districts there were serious disturbances, and it is significant both of the ignorance of the people and also of their destitution that these disturbances were generally attended by the destruction of machinery and the plunder of bakers' shops. In the agricultural districts the state of affairs was, if possible, still worse. There was not actual riot, but there were frequent outrages which took the form of incendiarism, so that on many occasions and during considerable periods the country districts were lighted up at night by burning ricks and flaming barns. The shopkeepers, especially the small shopkeepers who supplied the poor, were almost ruined by excessive taxation and by bad debts. The workingmen in the towns toiled for long hours and for an insufficient subsistence. In the country the agricultural laborers did not even secure the barest livelihood, but were compelled, not by way of exception, but as a matter of rule, to eke out their wages by the assistance which they derived from the Poor Law.

In his history of the time Mr. Spencer Walpole thus speaks of the state of the laboring poor:

"For many years the condition of the laboring classes in Britain had been growing more and more intolerable. The old conditions of labor had been changed, and the laborer had suffered from the change. Before the latter half of the eighteenth century the great mass of the laboring poor had been scattered throughout the country, owing to an almost feudal allegiance to, and deriving some corresponding advantages from, the neighboring landlord. But the discoveries of the eighteenth century terminated these conditions. The manufacturing industries of the country were collected into a few great centres, and the persons employed in these manufactures necessarily accompanied them. In one sense they had their reward: the manufacturers gave them better wages than the farmer, and better wages were of no slight advantage to the laborer. In another sense their change of occupation brought them nothing but evil. Forced to dwell in a crowded alley, occupying at night-time a house constructed in neglect of every known sanitary law, employed in the daytime in an unhealthy atmosphere, and frequently on a dangerous occupation, with no education available for his children, with no reasonable recreation to cheer his leisure, with the blue sky of heaven shrouded from his view by the smoke of an adjoining factory, with the rich face of Nature hidden from him by a brick wall, neglected by an overworked clergyman, regarded as a mere machine by an avaricious employer, the factory operative naturally turned to the only places where relaxation was possible, and sought in the public-house, the prize-ring, or the cock-pit the degrading amusements which were the business of his leisure.

"It so happened that, while the condition of the town operative was gradually becoming more and more wretched, the position of the country laborer was also changing for the worse. The old feudal ties which had hitherto connected the squire with his peasantry were being gradually loosened by the teachings of political economy. Improved agriculture and the introduction of machinery into farming were also altering the economy of rural districts. In the eighteenth century there were few large farms, there were comparatively few large fields; the corn was reaped by hand; the winters were passed in threshing it out by the flail; and the farmers had consequently work for their laborers at every season of the year. Threshing-machines altered this condition. They deprived the laborers of the demand which had previously existed for their work in the winter; and the farmers, in consequence, altered their system of hiring, and engaged the men, whom they had previously taken for a year, by the week. It so happened, too, that the vast reclamations of waste land which were made during the war pressed severely on the laboring poor. The common, on which every cottager had kept his cow, was annexed to the huge estate of the adjoining landlord, and the laborer found himself compelled to give up the beast which he had no longer the means to support. In many cases enclosures deprived the rural laborers of much more than their cow. They had been permitted, when the land was supposed to be worthless, to erect a little building on one side of the common, and to convert the patch of ground around it into a garden. In the eye of the law these men were squatters: they had no title to the cottage which they had erected or to the ground which they had reclaimed. The good of the country required the reclamation of wastes, and the little garden in the middle of the common came within the new fence-line of the rich squire. The cottage was demolished, the garden was ploughed up, and the cottager sank, at one blow, from the position of a small farmer, with a little house of his own, into that of a lodger at another cottage, whose sole source of livelihood was the wage which he received for his labor.

"The enclosures had been the indirect means of occasioning a considerable injury to the poor. But the Legislature, when it sanctioned them, had not foreseen the injury; on the contrary, it was universally imagined that the additional land which was brought into cultivation would increase the demand for labor, and so produce a permanent benefit to the laboring classes. The result, however, did not justify these expectations. The better wages which the laboring classes in a few instances received for a time were a poor compensation for the cow, the pig, and the goose which they were no longer able to keep. "Before the enclosures," said a laborer to Arthur Young, "I had a good garden, kept two cows, and was getting on. Now I cannot keep so much as a goose, and am poor and wretched." In a short time, moreover, the miserable laborers were deprived of the solitary advantage which increased wages had given them. The prospect of additional work led to early marriages, and to a consequent multiplication of their numbers. The peace, and the lower prices which succeeded it, did away with the new work and added to the number of laborers. Arable land was thrown into pasture; paid-off soldiers and sailors returned to their parishes; and the rate of wages fell and fell continually. Dazzled by the prospect of increasing the food of the people, the Legislature had enabled the landowners to plough up the common, and to throw down the humble enclosure of the cottager. The common was again turned into pasture; but it was supporting the squire's beasts, and not the peasant's. The peasant had seen his garden seized, his cottage demolished, his cow sold, his family impoverished, but the land growing no more corn, and receiving no more culture than before. The cry which Isaiah had raised 2,000 years before came home to the miserable laborer, and was repeated by the most eloquent, though not the wisest, of his advocates in Parliament: 'Woe unto them that join house to house, that lay field to field, till there be no place, that they may be placed alone in the midst of the earth.'"

This wretched condition of things was aggravated by the state of the Poor Law. Pauperism had reached perfectly frightful dimensions. At one time in 1833 the poor rate amounted to twelve shillings per head of the whole population, and it was estimated that one in seven, counting every man, woman, and child, was in receipt of Poor-Law relief. Crime rose in the same proportion as pauperism. In spite of an atrocious criminal code, which, at the beginning of the century inflicted capital punishment for no less than 200 offences, and which was not materially changed till twenty years later, the number of criminals continued to increase. Even the ameliorations which were made in the code produced at first no diminution in the number of criminals, which reached its highest level in 1842, when there were 31,000 committals for trial in a single year. In fact, it is probable that the stringency of the law in the earlier period led to laxity in its administration, and many persons escaped altogether because the penalty prescribed was altogether disproportionate to the offence. It has been reserved for modern times to reap the full advantage both of the alteration of the laws and the improvement in the character of the population. Last year, with a population which has nearly doubled, the total number of committals was only 13,000, while the nature of the crimes committed was certainly less serious than in former periods. In a single year – in 1834–480 human beings were sentenced to death, and the great majority were executed. Last year the capital sentence was pronounced in thirty-five cases, in twenty-one of which the full penalty was exacted.

It is no wonder that crime was rife when all the conditions were unfavorable to civilized existence. The working classes were expected to toil from early morning till late at night in buildings unprovided with the most ordinary sanitary arrangements. Wages were sometimes paid in truck, and often at the public-house, where a large part of the weekly earnings was spent before they were actually received. There was no leisure for any kind of mental improvement; there was no opportunity for innocent recreation. Brutal punishments and brutal amusements offered the chance of excitement to wearied bodies and jaded minds. Thrift was an unknown virtue, and when the wages were more than enough to keep body and soul together they were spent in coarse dissipation or cruel pastimes. There were no Factory Acts; there was no Mines Act; and there was no Truck Act. Women and children were forced to work as long as, or longer than, the men, and they were brutalized and degraded by the conditions of their labor. In the mines it was worse than it was above ground. We read of women almost without clothing laboring for sixteen hours a day, and of little children, with chains round their waists, dragging heavy weights along passages worse than the ordinary common sewer. Not only the health of the living was destroyed, but the health of future generations was seriously threatened.

I have spoken of the sanitary condition of Birmingham; but this was certainly no worse than the rest of the country. Typhus, which is the consequence of overcrowding and insufficient food, was prevalent in all the large towns and in many country places. In Liverpool alone 30,000 people were living in 8,000 underground cellars; while in Manchester one-eighth of the people were housed, if housing it can be called, in the same fashion. It was in these circumstances that an intelligent foreign observer – a German economist who visited England between forty and fifty years ago – wrote that he found by personal observation that the state of the working classes of Great Britain was deplorable and intolerable, and he predicted an inevitable and imminent revolution. English witnesses no less impartial and intelligent were equally gloomy in their predictions of approaching evil, and they seemed to be justified by the fact that the state of the laboring poor was getting worse instead of better. Mr. McCulloch, the economist, writing in 1845, expressed the belief that the condition of the laboring classes had deteriorated in the previous twenty-five years; while Lord John Russell in 1844 said: "If we compare the condition of the working classes with what it was a century ago, – say 1740, – it is impossible not to see that, while the higher and middle classes have improved, and increased their means of obtaining comforts, of obtaining foreign articles of luxury and facilities of travelling from place to place, the laboring classes – the men who either till the soil or work in factories – have retrograded, and cannot now get for their service the quantity of the necessaries of life they could a century ago."

Happily, things were at their worst. The tide turned, and it has flowed in the direction of improvement ever since. Legislation has done much, philanthropy has done something, and the intelligent efforts of the working classes themselves have done more. All these things combined have helped to make our country a healthier and happier and a better place than it was half a century ago. The burden of national taxation has been reduced, especially the proportion paid by the poorer classes. At the present time, if a workingman does not smoke or drink, he can hardly be said to be subject to any taxation at all beyond the four pence per pound which he pays on his tea and the small contribution which he makes indirectly through the post-office. Pauperism has greatly diminished, and the poor rate is certainly less than half of what it was before the new Poor Law. Crime has diminished in quantity, and has, on the whole, been mitigated in its character. Education has been brought within the reach of every workingman's child and within the means of every parent. Protection has been afforded against excessive toil and overwork; and the observance of proper sanitary conditions for labor has been universally enforced. The laws against combinations have been repealed, trades-unions have been legalized, and the workmen are able to meet the employers on more equal terms in the settlement of the rate of wages. The care of the public health has been recognized as a public duty and enforced both upon individuals and the local authorities. The trammels have been removed from industry; the taxes on food and on all the great necessaries of life have been repealed; facilities of travel and of inter-communication have been largely extended and developed; opportunities of self-improvement and recreation have been afforded to all at the cost of the community; and last, but not least, – since this is perhaps the indirect cause of many of the other results named, – the suffrage has been widened, until now every householder, however poor and however humble, has a voice in the government of his country and his full share of influence in the making of its laws.

It is not easy to measure the change which has taken place by statistics, but it may be illustrated by the following figures: Mr. Giffen, our most eminent living statistician, made a careful inquiry some time ago into the rate of wages at different periods, and he found that in the last fifty years they had advanced from 50 to 100 per cent. In the same time the hours of labor have been reduced on an average by 20 per cent. In very few trades do they now ever exceed ten hours, while in the majority they average nine hours, and in many they have been reduced to eight. The means for an innocent and profitable use of the leisure which has thus been afforded have been supplied by the action of the municipal and local authorities. Not only have the wages improved, but the cost of living has diminished. Bread is 20 per cent, cheaper on the average; sugar is 60 to 70 per cent, cheaper; tea, 75 per cent, cheaper; clothing, 50 per cent, cheaper. The cost of fuel, as represented by coal, has been diminished by one-half. Light, in the shape of gas or petroleum, is infinitely better and very much cheaper than in the time when tallow rush-lights were the only illumination within the reach of the poor. Locomotion has become easy and is placed within the reach of all; while the postage of letters, which averaged a shilling apiece, is now reduced to a uniform penny, or in the case of postcards, to one halfpenny for each communication. Only one article of commerce of great importance has increased in price, and that is meat in the shape of mutton and beef. Fifty years ago, however, mutton and beef did not enter into the ordinary consumption of the working classes; and if they tasted meat at all it was only in the shape of bacon. House rent has also risen, and in the course of the time of which we are speaking it has probably doubled. But house rent is a test of prosperity; and it is just because the working classes can afford to give themselves better accommodation that we find this great increase in the rate of house rent.

On the whole, it may truly be said that not only have the working classes more to spend, but that they are able to get more for the money which they do spend. This is confirmed by the extraordinary increase which has taken place in the consumption of the chief articles of food. Thus, for instance, the consumption of sugar is four times per head as much as it was fifty years ago; tea, three and a half times as much; rice, sixteen times; eggs, six times; and tobacco, twice as much. And lastly, in consequence, perhaps, of the better food and living and of the better house accommodation, as well as on account of the improved sanitary conditions, the death-rate has diminished, the health of the country has improved, and the expectation of life at the different age-periods is now from two to four years better than it was.

In the same fifty years the habit of thrift has been considerably developed. The working classes have had more money, and they have found it possible and advantageous to reserve a portion of their income as a provision against sickness and old age. During the half-century the depositors in the savings-bank have multiplied tenfold, and the amount of funds which have been placed there for security has increased from thirteen millions sterling to considerably over a hundred millions. In addition, there are cooperative societies with a million of members and fourteen millions of capital; building societies with fifty millions of liabilities; and friendly societies almost innumerable. With regard to the last, it is difficult to obtain exact returns, but in 1880 the Registrar reported that he had received returns from 12,687 societies, with 4,800,000 members and £13,000,000 invested funds. It is probable that the total figures are at least double those shown by these imperfect returns.

An impartial consideration of the facts and figures here set forth must lead to the conclusion that there has been a very great improvement in the condition of the people during the period under review, and that this improvement has been largely due to the intervention of the state and to what is called socialistic legislation. The acts for the regulation of mines and the inspection of factories and workshops, the Truck Act (preventing the payment of wages in kind), the acts regulating merchants' shipping, the Artisans'-Dwellings Act, the Allotments Act (enabling local authorities to take land and to provide allotments for laborers), the Education Act, the Poor Law, and the Irish Land Acts are all of them measures which more or less limit or control individual action. The pedantic adherence to supposed fixed principles of political economy has been so frequently invaded by this legislation that few people would think it worth while to appeal to them as conclusive against further action, and it is recognized that each case must be decided on its merits, and cannot be determined on purely abstract grounds. The late Professor Stanley Jevons, in his essay on "The State in Relation to Labor," lays down the modern doctrine in these words: "The state is justified in passing any law, or even in doing any single act, which, without ulterior consequences, adds to the sum total of happiness. . . . The liberty of the subject is only the means towards an end. Hence when it fails to produce the desired result, it may be set aside and other means employed."

It appears, then, that experience has shown that in many instances great advantages have followed the extension of the functions of government, and that no sufficient objection exists to their further application when good cause can be shown. It must not be supposed that such cause does not still exist, or that the reforms already accomplished have exhausted the possibilities of statesmanship. Unfortunately it still remains true that in the richest country of the world the most abject misery exists side by side with luxurious profusion and extravagance. There are still nearly a million persons in the United Kingdom who are in receipt of parish relief, and as many more who are always on the verge of poverty. In our great cities there are rookeries of ignorance, intemperance, and vice, where civilized conditions of life are impossible, and morality and religion are only empty names. In certain trades unrestricted competition and the constant immigration of paupers from foreign countries have reduced wages to a starvation level, while there are other industries – as, for instance, shipping and railway traffic – where the loss of life is terrible, and the annual butcher's bill is as great as in a serious war. In the agricultural districts the divorce between the laborer and the soil he tills is still the fruitful source of distress to the poor and danger to the state. The Corn-Law rhymer, Ebenezer Elliott, represents the laborers of his time as

"Landless, joyless, restless, hopeless,
Gasping still for bread and breath,
To their graves by trouble hunted,
  Albion's Helots toil till death;

and it will not be asserted that any marked or general improvement has yet taken place in the conditions of their labor.

These are the facts with which we have yet to deal; and the hope of the future lies in the awakening of the public conscience, and in its recognition of the duty of the community to its poorest and weakest members. We may be encouraged by the success of past efforts to persevere on similar lines, and to continue a policy which has been shown to afford practical results.

There is no need to abase the rich in order to raise the poor, and it is neither possible nor expedient to drag everything down to one dead level. We cannot, if we would, equalize the conditions and the capacities of men. The idler, the drunkard, the criminal, and the fool must bear the brunt of their defects. The strong, the prudent, the temperate, and the wise will always be first in the race. But it is desirable that the government, which no longer represents a clique or a privileged class, but which is the organized expression of the wants and wishes of the whole nation, should rise to a true conception of its duties, and should use the resources, the experience, and the talent at its disposal to promote the greater happiness of the masses of the people.

Section 4

The Herbert/Hobson Debate

A VOLUNTARYIST APPEAL
Auberon Herbert

"The widest possible liberty, only limited by the like liberty of all others." – HERBERT SPENCER.

"Progress is difference." – HERBERT SPENCER.

"Over his own body and mind, the individual is sovereign." – J. S. MILL.

Why believe in force, or compulsion of each other, instead of believing in liberty?

WE ask you to renounce force, or compulsion of each other, as a wrong instrument for securing political advantages for yourselves, or for advancing your own opinions and interests. We ask you resolutely to condemn force [except when employed simply and directly for defence] as an instrument unworthy and unfit to take any part in the work of true civilisation.

We ask you not to allow any governing body to pass laws which restrict and regulate the actions of those, who live honestly and at peace with their fellow-men – laws, which interfere with their social habits, or take any side in the disputes between employers and employed, or impose either compulsory services or compulsory payments of any kind upon the people.

We ask you not to allow Parliaments or Governments to use force for any purpose except to restrain force – that is, to "keep the peace" between us all, and to insure for all, rich and poor alike, perfect security of person and property – whether such property be public or private.[1]

We ask you to look both upon yourselves and upon all

---

[1] Where property belongs to the public, rules of course must exist as regards its use, and force must be employed – however sparingly – to ensure observance of such rules.

your fellow men as free men, free in mind and body by natural right, free to choose your own manner of life, to exercise your faculties in your own fashion, to reap the full reward of your labour, without paying a compulsory share to the State, and in return for this full perfect freedom to be ready to bear the burdens and responsibilities of your own life, whatever they may be, without asking Parliaments and Governments to grant favours and privileges for yourselves, or to place restrictions and burdens of any kind upon others.

We ask you to choose this full perfect freedom, as the highest and best gift that all persons, whether poor or rich, can possess; and to look upon all your fellow-men and women [so long as they live honestly and peacefully, and respect these same rights of freedom in all others], as SELF-OWNERS – that is to say, owners of their own minds and bodies, and of all property honestly and peacefully acquired.

*The self-owner, who owns his own faculties, owns
also property, since property is won by means of
faculties.*

We ask you not to fall into the slavish way of looking upon either Parliament or Government as the owner of property, that is won by individuals for themselves. We ask you to treat the earnings of men as sacred; to look upon all property, honestly and peacefully acquired, as belonging by right to those who have acquired it, and not as belonging to Governments and Parliaments, which – except so far as they keep the peace – have not shared even with a little finger in the toil of those who have won it. It is absurd to look for the ownership of John Smith's property in any person but in John Smith himself. All honest and peaceful men are the only true owners of their own property, just because they are the only true owners of those faculties of mind and body, by means of which property is created or won. In what way, we ask, would it profit a man if he were told that he owned his own body and mind, and if at the same time he were debarred, as some politicians and socialists propose, from the full and perfect possession, as an individual, of any of the good things of the earth – either from the possession of land, or of the products of land, for the sake of which the labours of his body and mind have been expended?[2]

The rights of self-ownership are supreme rights, and rest on the hard rock.
We ask you to place these rights of Self-ownership – these rights of free men over their own minds, bodies, and property – above all Parliaments, Governments, laws, institutions, all edicts of emperors, and all votes of majorities; and to believe that there is no edict of an emperor, no vote of a majority, which can take from the individual what he possesses as a moral right. We ask you to believe in these rights of Self-ownership, because they are, so to speak, founded on the hard rock, and can scarcely be disputed by those who take the trouble to think clearly. The truth of these rights rests on the evidence: (1) of natural facts; (2) of critical reason; (3) of morality, which itself depends for its own existence on the existence of these rights; (4) of human experience.

(1) On the evidence of natural facts: – First, because every individual possesses a separate and distinct mind and body – separate by itself, and not mixed up with other minds and bodies; and nature thereby affirms for us that the mind and body of John Smith belong to John Smith, and not to anybody else; secondly, because Nature is, so to speak, a thorough-going Free-trader. All improvement, whether of plant, animal, or man, only comes through the improvement of the individuals, and as the result of free competition in excellence – the individuals, which acquire new and superior qualities, gradually taking the place of the unimproved individuals, and in this way raising and improving the race. Thus difference, competition between the individuals, and the constant emergence of the improved individual, are the conditions of progress; whilst uniformity and artificial protection of any kind (which restrains this emergence of the improved type) are the conditions of failure and ultimate

---

[2] As regards inherited property, clearly the owner is the one person who can rightfully pass it on to whom he wills at death. It is absurd to place the claims or any non-owners and outsiders in competition with the rights of the owner. At the same time the dead owner should not be given the privilege of attaching conditions. Such privilege, implying the rights of the dead man to regulate a world he has left and property which has ceased to belong to him, must be held to be unreasonable.

extinction. It is owing to this law in nature that the plants and animals, which for a time have escaped competition [because they were secluded by a barrier of sea or mountain] are destroyed by the races which have undergone competition and selection, when the two races – so to speak, the free-trade race and the protected race – once come into contact.

(2) On the evidence of reason: – Because if John Smith is not the owner of himself, where shall we look for his owner? The idea of men owning each other is an altogether confused and contradictory and impossible idea; for if men own themselves, then they cannot own each other; and yet if they do not own themselves, they are just as incapable of owning each other, for how shall a man, who has no ownership in himself, be capable of owning his fellow-men?

(3) On the evidence of morality: – Becuase all our ideas of right and wrong are inseparably bound up with and depend upon this ownership of our own minds and bodies. How can we say what is right and wrong for John Smith, until we know if he belongs to himself or to others? If he belongs to himself, his right and wrong will be of one kind; if he belongs to others, then his right and wrong will be of another kind. Until you have settled to whom the ownership of human beings belongs, there can be no certain and definite morality, no certain and definite relations of men to men. Until you have decided once for all that John Smith is the owner of John Smith, there can only be a reckless and continual strife over the ownership of John Smith, in which in the end the strongest – the most brutal or the most cunning – must win. Remember also, whenever you are tempted to restrict your fellow-men, that Freedom and Morality are inseparable from each other for another reason. Where Freedom is not, morality is not. Only the free act is the moral act; only the free man is the moral being. He whose hands are tied by others, and who acts under constraint and fear of punishment, is hardly removed from the animal, that is bitted and bridled. A man only becomes a moral being – that is one who acts from a sense of right – when he possesses freedom. Morality and Liberty exist together, and cease together.

(4) On the evidence of human experience: – Because the history of progress has been the history of Liberty. Only as, one by one, the chains, binding the individual, have been broken, peace, industrial effort, and security, have become

possible, knowledge and reason have founded their empire, brutality has lost ground, and men have shed a large part of their old savage nature. Everywhere the free man has gained in vigour, intelligence, and conscience, over the restricted man.

All liberty carries with it conditions or limits.
From the principle of universal liberty follows another principle. There is one condition, or limit, which arises out of and goes with these rights of Self-ownership. If A.B. may act in a certain manner, it follows that C.D. must *not* act in a certain way – that is, in a way that would prevent A.B.'s action. Those who claim the rights of Self-ownership for themselves, those who claim to be the owners of their own bodies, minds, and property, are bound by that very claim not to encroach upon the same rights of Self-ownership in others. Our liberty or Self-ownership is therefore limited by the condition that we must not take away any part of the liberty or any of the rights of Self-ownership of others; in other words, that we must not injure by force or fraud the person or the property of others – for this is the plain and practical meaning of Self-ownership: – That the person, the faculties, the property, of each individual belong to that individual, and not to others – whether those others are private individuals, or a collection of persons, such as we call a Government; and therefore that we may not use force or fraud [which mean compelling or deceiving those who should be free agents] in our dealings with each other.

We must provide for the due observance of these conditions or limits.
From this principle of the limit of liberty there follows again another principle. We must take the necessary steps to insure the due observance of the limit. Every honest and peaceful individual, rich or poor, should be protected in his rights of Self-ownership. No individual should suffer a loss of these self-owning rights through the force or fraud of others. Whilst therefore we would not allow any Government to use force to take away the least part of the rights of Self-ownership from honest and peaceful citizens, whilst we would not allow such Government to use force to impose any compulsory payment or compulsory service, to use force to favour

any interest or any opinion, to use force to carry on any moral crusade, or to interfere with any action that is not in itself an attack upon the person or property of others, we would allow Government – in the phrase already employed – to USE FORCE TO RESTRAIN FORCE. We would employ the force-machine of Government to ensure that the limits of Self-ownership were not over-stepped, – in other words, to provide that no man, such as the thief, murderer, violent man, swindler, or foreign enemy, should be allowed to injure the person or property of others. If you ask us why force should be used to defend the rights of Self-ownership, and not for any other purpose, we reply by reminding you that the rights of Self-ownership are – as we have explained – supreme moral rights, of higher rank than all other human interests or institutions; and therefore force may be employed on behalf of these rights, but not in opposition to them. All social and political arrangements, all employments of force, are subordinate to these universal rights, and must receive just such character and form as are required in the interest of these rights. Force, which is at best a brutish thing, may be employed – when necessary – in the service of Self-ownership, but it can never be put on an equality with Self-ownership, can never be allowed to enter into conflict with it. Whenever this happens, whenever force escapes from the drudge's hole, which is its one fit dwelling place, and lays claim to universal direction, it should be treated as men treat the presuming pretender, who seeks to lay base hands upon a great empire. Indeed, to thrust aside the rights of Self-ownership in order to set up a system of force, can only be compared to placing an ape upon the throne and bidding him rule over human beings. It is the inversion of the true moral order.

As has just been said, we may rightly use the force-machine of Government to check force and fraud, in other words, to protect person and property (or again, in other words, to defend the rights of Self-ownership), but in order to understand this right of using force, it is necessary to perceive clearly what Government is, and what it is not. Government has no sacred, no super-human element in it. It is simply a machine created by the individuals of a nation for their own use and convenience. It is their servant and instrument; it can never, except by usurpation, become their master and owner. Whatever rights a Government possesses of using force, are rights derived solely from the individuals who have created it, for there is no other human source of any kind from which they can be derived. The Government is made by John Smith. It is true then that a Government may reasonably possess certain limited and definite rights; for if John Smith may defend himself, or his house, or his purse, with (defensive) force against (aggressive) force, then also he may transfer to the Government, which he and others like him have created, this office of using defensive force on his behalf; but if John Smith has no right, because he happens to be stronger than his neighbour to walk into that neighbour's house, and use force to compel him to educate his children, or to prevent his working more than eight hours, or to prevent his drinking spirits or beer, or to compel him to serve as a soldier, or to compel him to contribute to various under-takings to which he does not wish to contribute, then it is equally plain that no Government, created by John Smith, or any number of John Smiths, can have the right to do any of these things, which John Smith himself has no right to do. It is quite impossible for John Smith and those like him to create an institution in their own image, and then to give rights of using force to that institution – rights, which neither John Smith himself nor any of John Smith's fellows and equals possess in themselves. It is quite impossible to give to others what you do not possess yourself; just as it is equally imposs-ible for the created thing to possess greater authority than those who created it. Exactly the same truth holds good as regards majorities. Majorities are only collections of indi-viduals, and can never possess larger rights of using force than the individuals – of whom they are composed – possess. It is plain, therefore, that no majority can possess power over the person and property of John Smith – so long as he respects the rights of others – unless John Smith of his own free choice consents to make himself subject to the decisions of such majority. Remember always – numbers cannot affect rights. Numbers cannot create them; numbers cannot take them away. You may pile as many stones together as you like, but it will not alter their nature. Stones they were; stones they will remain. So it is with men. A million of men can have only the same moral rights [to employ force, for example] as one man.

At the same time, whilst we, the individuals (having in ourselves the right to protect ourselves against aggressive force), may commission the Government to use defensive force on our behalf – that is, to use force against those who, like the robber and murderer, are themselves users of force – we must never allow the Government to use force to compel any peaceable person to become subject to it against his own consent; or allow the Government to impose upon such person compulsory services, or compulsory payments, even for the sake of providing those systems of defence, which are necessary to us all. Freedom must always come first; and all services, however important, must come second. All men must join the State as free men, *with their own consent*; all men must serve it and contribute to it as free men and with their own consent. Otherwise men would cease to be Self-owners, and the disposal of their minds, bodies, and property would no longer rest with themselves, but with others – with those who claimed to be the Government. We ask you, therefore, to help us to change the present Compulsory State, with its usurped ownership of the minds, bodies, and property of men, into the Voluntary State, in which men would co-operate together for all their needs, as free men and Self-owners, not as those who have sold themselves into a bondage, from which, when once they have entered it, it is so hard to escape.

Summing up the voluntaryist principles

Let us sum up the great principles in a few words: –

The rights of Self-ownership, or Liberty – in other words, the rights of free unrestricted faculties – are supreme.

All political institutions must exist simply for the sake of Self-ownership. Self-ownership must never be sacrificed to any political institutions.

All force, which is not employed simply for defence, is an evil and a wrong, because it violates the rights of Self-ownership. We may only use force for one purpose – force to restrain force; we may only use it against one class of persons – the users of force.

All rights are universal. We, therefore, who claim the rights of Self-ownership for ourselves, must concede exactly the same rights to all others. All Liberty necessarily has limits.

These limits are drawn by force or fraud.[3] Our task, therefore, is to make a free world, everywhere, in everything, and for everybody, only barring force and fraud – whether it be the force and fraud of Governments or of private persons.

Government is nothing but an instrument, a creature, called into existence by the individuals, and employed by them for their service. It may receive from the individuals such moral rights as they possess in themselves of using force, but it can never receive from them larger rights of using force than they themselves possess; nor can numbers create rights.

The voluntaryist watchwords.
Now take as your watchwords: – Establish Free Trade in everything; face all competition fearlessly – don't try to escape from it by Chinese walls, or dodges, privileges, and artificial restrictions; let all peaceful faculties be unrestricted and unregulated; make liberty the universal basis of your thoughts and actions; remember always that laws are force, that the passing of laws means the use and the sanction of this evil thing – force; say resolutely to yourselves: – "force is destructive of moral rights; force is no true remedy for existing evils"; refuse to use force to advantage yourselves; refuse to use force to attack vices, or to fight moral crusades, or to carry out any sanitary reforms, which pass beyond the restraint of actions, that directly injure person or property; hate and despise force in all its forms; trust resolutely to moral weapons; fight with voice and pen the peaceful battle of persuasion; reason with and teach men – don't compel them; remember that a convinced man is worth everything, a compelled man is worth nothing; don't build up great governing machines with any powers, however slight, of compulsion lodged in the body of them – they will not remain your servants, they will always tend to become your masters; avoid all systems that make for uniformity, and that put all men, the good and bad alike, under the same regulations; favour difference – "progress is difference"; avoid all war – war between nations, war between classes, war between rich and poor, war between employers and employed; seek peaceful

---

[3] Fraud, from a moral point of view, is the equivalent of force. It cunningly eludes the consent of the person concerned, just as force violently overpowers it. *Consent* is the distinguishing mark of the Self-owner.

solutions by allowing every individual concerned to act after his own fashion; for the sake both of peace and of liberty, don't seek to mass men together in great fighting organisations; follow after peace with a whole heart, remembering that peace is the blessed child of liberty, and apart from liberty is only a dream; don't be a politician, for a politician too often lives by stirring up prejudice and passion and by persuading the people to use compulsion as their easiest and cheapest instrument; take no share in any action that divides the nation into two great factions, always fighting and quarrelling with each other; don't help the majority to force their opinions or interests upon the minority; don't be content to belong either to the party of those who compel or of those who are compelled; don't attack property in any form, even of the richest men – to attack any form of property, honestly acquired, is to weaken all forms of it; let there be no uncertainty for any living man about the reward of his labours, but keep the possession and enjoyment of property – this great basis of all human effort – perfectly steady and assured; get rid of all existing public debt; submit to severe voluntary taxation for a time so as to be rid of this curse for ever; let no penny ever be raised again on compulsory conditions; don't believe in the common compulsory fund, which is the devil's favourite instrument for teaching us all to quarrel with and hate and fear each other; never mortgage the faculties of your fellow-man for services, which he may not perhaps desire to have rendered to him; never deal with the faculties of any single man, living or unborn, as if they belonged to you and not to him, or place compulsory burdens on those who should exercise their own choice; above all never allow any man to be used compulsorily, in purse or person, for war purposes; work heartily in the cause of voluntary taxation, since voluntary taxation means not only the escape from State bondage and the victory of free faculties but means the ending of a long series of oppressions of each other – oppressions sometimes petty, sometimes almost destructive of energy and life – means the beginning of a long series of friendly services, joyfully exchanged, means the spirit of peace instead of the spirit of war, means a far truer and higher recognition of our common fellowship; train and fit yourselves to serve the Voluntary State generously; do all in your power to make it a good and efficient national instrument; whilst you employ it as a force instrument – strictly limited to force purposes – with great moderation and scrupulousness, employ it, as a Voluntary instrument and dependent upon Voluntary contributions, freely and without grudging, wherever it can perform useful public services or assist in our common civilisation; do not be persuaded for a moment that you cannot learn to contribute by gift or service under persuasion instead of compulsion; organize great national holidays for the collection of public revenue; but on no plea whatsoever give any man forcible control over the smallest part of your property, faithfully remembering that your property is the outcome of your faculties, that it has been won in the sweat of your brow, that it is a very part of you, and that he who rules your property also rules you.

Why force-methods are not only morally wrong but fail practically

(1) They are very costly, requiring complicated machinery, and hosts of officials to supervise officials. (2) They are too easily applied, without sufficient discussion, and therefore lead to grave mistakes. (3) A series of great departments with complicated machinery can never be controlled by the public, who have not leisure enough to understand the details. (4) Such departments, being uncontrolled, are liable to be expensively, and even corruptly administered. (5) When these administrative machines are created, they provoke bitter quarrels as to which party shall own and direct them; and thus divert the valuable energies of good workers from their own work. (6) The use of force discredits and weakens the moral weapons of reason and persuasion, turning moral reformers into mere politicians and force-men. (7) It makes those, who compel, brutal, and those, who are compelled, stupid. (8) Where force-methods prevail, there is only a short-lived toleration for the competition of voluntary methods. (9) Force-methods create a wrong moral atmosphere, encouraging men to believe that they may suppress anyone who differs with them, and anything that offends them. (10) They always tend to grow indefinitely – one measure of force making other measures of force necessary. (11) They give the first place to organisation and discipline, and the second or last place to conscience and sense of right. (12) They favour uniformity, mechanical arrangement and showy pretentious system, dis-

couraging difference, which is the first condition of progress. (13) They cannot discriminate, but put good and bad under the same conditions. (14) They cannot remedy human evils, but only produce a change of form in such evils. (15) They make the reform of all moral evils more difficult by driving such evils under the surface. (16) They prevent the improvement of men by shielding them *for a time* from the consequences of their actions.   (17) They always lead to persecution, involving mankind in a wretched perpetual war of punishment on the one side and evasion on the other side.

Land nationalisation, illogical in theory, and mischievous in practice.
When Land Nationalisers assert the right of everybody to possess the soil of a country, and deny the right of individuals to possess it, they overlook the many intellectual contradictions and fallacies in which they are involved by their creed. (A) If the individual has no moral right to possess the soil, then a multitude of individuals can have no moral right to possess it, since this multitude is simply composed of individuals, and neither the physical nor the moral nature of the individuals is in any way changed by their being brought together and placed side by side in one lot.   As already pointed out, a stone remains a stone, whether it is left by itself or made one of a heap.   All the stones in the world placed in the same company will not make them like potatoes, or in any way different from themselves.   (B) If it were true that the land of the country belonged to all the people, and could not belong to individuals, then the only form of tenure, which would be right, would be pure communism in its most extreme form – that is to say, that every person would have an equal right to use every acre or indeed every yard of land. Nobody would be morally entitled to place a building upon the land, or to cultivate it to his own use, for no person could take even temporarily from the Nation what belonged to it. If it is true that the land belongs to "everybody," then whatever the cost or inconvenience, we must give to "everybody" what belongs to "everybody." We cannot offer the Nation something in the place of its rights – for example, a share in the tax, levied on the owner, as the Land Nationalisers propose. That is mere playing with a great principle. If the land really belongs to "everybody," then give it to "everybody," if

it does not, why pillage the unlucky owners by taxing them? The truth is, that until the Land Nationalisers become pure Communists of the most extreme type, dealing with land as belonging to everybody, and therefore practically belonging to nobody – their position must remain quite illogical and contradictory, since in one breath they assert the existence of a certain right in the whole Nation, and then in their proposed arrangements they immediately and completely disregard it. (C) If it is true that the soil of a country belongs to everybody, then it is "everybody," and only "everybody," that can deal with it. No majority can deal with it. A majority is not "everybody"; a majority is only a conventional and artificial arrangement, not resting on any moral basis. It is only a part of "everybody" [sometimes indeed not really representing even the half of "everybody,"] and therefore without any true authority to deal with what belongs to "everybody," unless "everybody" first sanctions such an arrangement. (D) If the soil belongs to "everybody," then we must discover who is "everybody." The boundaries of nations consist of very artificial lines, often indistinct at present, and perhaps destined in the future to disappear altogether. If "everybody" is the true heir, then does not the soil of the world belong to all the races taken collectively, and not to the particular nations which happen at any given moment to possess particular bits? If this principle, "the soil belongs to everybody," were true, it must be interpreted in its widest and most logical sense; and in this case the Russian peasant or Chinaman may rightly claim a re-distribution of the world's soil in his favour. The Land Nationaliser denies that possession, or purchase, or inheritance, gives any rights to the present land holder as against the moral claims of "everybody," it is therefore impossible for him to put forward any such plea as possession, and to maintain that it confers a good title in the case of particular nations as against the claim of the whole human race. If the claim of "everybody" in a nation is better than the claim of the possessing individuals, then the claim of the whole human race must be better than the claim of the possessing nations. The whole soil of the world therefore must go into hotch-pot. (E) If the soil belongs to "everybody," then it is clear that the products of the soil must belong to "everybody." It is a very halting logic which asserts that what lies in the field belongs to "everybody," and what is taken out of the field in the form of hay, corn, roots, or wool (which are actually in part the converted soil of the field) can belong to particular persons. Whoever is the owner of the whole, is the owner of a part. The Land Nationaliser, therefore, if he wishes to make his creed logical, must join himself on to the State Socialists, and preach their doctrine, that not only the soil belongs to "everybody," but the soil products belong to "everybody." (F) At another point the Land Nationalisation logic equally fails. Nobody has made the land – it is asserted; but they have made hedges, roads, drains; they have dug, ploughed, manured and reclaimed land; so that it is truer to speak of land, in Mr. F. Harrison's phrase, as "a manufactured article," than as a raw natural article. But independently of the difficulty of separating what is artificial from what is natural, in the soil, if it were true that what is produced by nature cannot be owned by the individual, then there is another reason why the crop cannot be owned by the individual – for the solid part of the crop draws a larger part of its bulk from the air than it does from the soil, and therefore it is plain that if the soil cannot belong to the individual, because it is a natural product, neither can the crop belong to the individual, seeing that the larger part of it (the carbon element) is purely a natural product.

Now take the practical evil of Land Nationalisation. (1) When land had been made State-property, it would become one more of the incessant battle grounds of party. New theories, as regards the best way of dividing it amongst its owners, would be continually appearing; and as a consequence there would be a state of uncertainty and strife, paralysing effort and industry, by the constant settlements of the conditions of tenure. (2) The resulting complications would cause infinite annoyance. Every sort of perplexing and practically insoluble question would arise: – Should men hold only for a few years, or for life? Should the children succeed to the property held by the parents? If buildings and improvements could not at a given moment find a purchaser – should the State keep the land unlet, or force a sale of the improvements at a price that would represent but a small part of their value? Might a State tenant do what he liked with the land; or must he obtain State permission for all his dealings with it? What quantities of land might be sold to a tenant? Should it be by public auction? Or is every man who claims land, to be entitled to an equal share? Should this destructive taxation be placed on the land in the form of a perpetual settlement? If so, then the district that became prosperous would bear a light share of the general burden; and the backward district would bear a heavy share; if, on the contrary, this settlement (*i.e.*, the land taxation) might be altered the increasing of the tax would not only penalise and hinder enterprise, but it would encourage much political jobbery. (3) Nationalised land would mean an enormous increase of officialism, and probably of jobbery. The valuations, revaluations, questions of improvements, the appeals, the central machinery necessary to control local officials, would so increase official influences as to greatly depress the free action of the people. It is quite idle for the Nationalisers to cry out against officialism and to profess to favour Liberty, when they propose to add so immensely to the dominance of the State. (4) A fixed yearly rent from which there is no escape possible is a great discouragement to the most industrious men. Land (under a system of real ownership) is "the bank" in which they invest their labour during the years of their best strength. (5) In a progressive country it is of the first importance to have no fixed and uniform system. One of the great virtues of free trade – we mean free purchase and free sale – is that it lends itself so readily to the new wants of men as they arise. (6) The State as the one owner, would be almost certain to use its power despotically and unfairly. It must be remembered that what we call the State can never be the State in reality. What we call the State is only certain managing persons in a party. It is not the nation; it is not even the majority; but it is a small number of politicians in whose hands the majority place their guidance. What we call the State is therefore almost bound by its nature to act with a partiality that often amounts to corruption. (7) Any sudden wave of feeling at a general election, or any rash proposal passed by a House of Commons, might suddenly destroy half the value of the property that consisted of houses and buildings. (8) The countries such as India and Egypt, in which land is nationalised, are not the prosperous and progressive countries. They show that there is no magic in paying rent to the State, as the Nationalists so strangely contend, but rather a dull depressing effect, stereotpying existing conditions, and restraining the changes and developments that must prepare the ground for a higher civilisation. (9) The land of a country could only be nationalised by a great act of spoliation. It could not be paid for; and if it could be, we have no right to force those who don't wish to have it to incur this huge debt. The act would be simply an act of violent taking. But no such violent acts ever lead to prosperity. They destroy all fixed landmarks of conduct, they banish the idea of friendly co-operation, they unloose passions, and plunge a nation into a sea of unlimited strife, in which it is likely enough to be wrecked and lost. No violence ever stands alone; it is always succeeded by new acts of violence. (12) Lastly, the Nationalisers would destroy one of the greatest sources of human enjoyment. The attachment of the small owner to his plot of ground sinks very deep into his nature; and but for the mischievous effect of compulsory taxation, by which in many countries, the politicians have done their best to destroy the value of the land, the small owner's life might be very peaceful, and happy, and prosperous. What can the Nationaliser offer in return for this sense of security and happy attachment that millions of men feel throughout Europe for the land that they have bought, or their fathers have bought before them, in the sweat of their brow?

One last consideration should be borne in mind. During the past years many of the great organisations of the workmen have been fighting organisations. They will not remain much longer in that dangerous and unprofitable phase. Our workmen – so full of capacity for organisation – can do much better, as they themselves will find out, with their energies and their resources, than to spend their lives fighting the employers. In a near future, as some of us believe, the Trade Unions will re-organise themselves on a peaceful and progressive basis. They will become some of the largest owners of property in the country. The shillings that now go so uselessly into the war chest will be employed in amassing property of all kind, especially land. Every great Trade Union (and so also with the Co-operative Societies and the Benefit Societies) will not only have its hall and library and lodging-houses, but its farms in the country – its landed estate, combining use and pleasure, and offering employment when work is slack, and at all times a most healthful rest and change. It is difficult to realise how much more enjoyable life will become for the workmen of the cities, through the possession of land, held in good fee simple to deal with as they like. This is the next phase of development lying just in front of our great trade organisations; but in order that this great change may come easily, it is of the highest importance that all claims of the State to establish a monopoly in land should be resolutely resisted, and Free trade in land defended and enlarged.

Why state socialism, or the ownership by the state of all land, railways, houses, factories, mills, and machinery, would produce misery and not happiness.
(1) Because it would strip the individual of all rights of self-direction, placing him as regards the employment of his faculties and the conduct of his life, as regards his labour, his food, his clothing, his house, all his daily wants, his amusements, his home and family life, his education and therefore, as an eventual consequence, his religion, under State direction – in a word, changing the free individual into a bit of State property.   Only a little careful thought is needed in order to understand clearly the complete powerlessness of the individual in presence of the one employer and one owner of everything. (2) Because home life and family life, as we know them at present, would cease to exist – the State, when once it became the food supplier and the employer of everybody, refusing to allow children to be born except under its own conditions, and probably transferring the children at an early age to its own barracks. (3) Because, as the State would be responsible from hour to hour for the food, clothing, housing and employment of millions of men and women, it would be obliged to employ compulsion of a very strict kind, in order to prevent any disarrangement of so vast a system.   (4) Because, it would divide the nation into two bitterly opposed classes – those who rule, and those who are ruled; and in endeavouring to remove by violent methods the inequalities of wealth, that exist between rich and poor, it would introduce into every part of life the worst form of inequality – the inequality that exists between those who force their own opinions and interests upon others and those upon whom such opinions and interests are forced – the inequality that exists between the compellers and the compelled.   While every year under a perfectly free system would gradually and

peacefully lessen the difference between rich and poor, no time could ever lessen the differences between those who compel and those who are compelled. (5) Because no human skill or knowledge would be sufficient to direct successfully and without great failures the immense machinery by which a nation would be fed, clothed, and employed. The system would be a huge example of Protection, and, like all systems of Protection, would go rotten at the core, in the absence of that competition, which alone checks the growth of the evils which fasten on to every system that is made to depend on force. (6) Because a nation, divided in itself by its many differences of thought, and possessing no real unity, could not undertake the direction of such machinery, but would be obliged to place such direction in the hands of a few persons, holding absolute power. (7) Because it would lead to the most bitter struggles between opposed parties for the possession of this universal machinery – each party dreading to leave in the hands of its rival the possession of power, when such power was employed to direct all concerns of life. (8) Because, to sum up, State Socialism succeeds in combining in itself all the elements that are most opposed to real progress – the restriction and regulation of the individual; the confiscation of his faculties, whether he wills it or no, for the use of the State; an unlimited use of violence and spoliation to establish itself as a system; an unlimited use of force to carry itself on when once established as a system; a complete disregard of all the rights of minorities; and a belief – exaggerated to the point of superstition – in the rights of majorities, as if three men were something higher and two men something lower than their fellow-men; a belief in machinery and external appliances and great uniform systems, as if men lived by bread alone, and as if any gifts of the State could make up for the imprisonment of the spiritual or moral part of their nature within the prison-house of universal regulation. Add to these moral failures of Socialism, the practical evils that would arise – the huge army of officials; the imperfect direction and organisation of labour, and the constantly recurring mistakes in such direction of labour; the employment of spies and detectives to prevent abuses of every kind; the sharp military discipline; the oppressions resulting from personal power; the constant war between the officials and the people, – war of evasions on one side and of restrictions on the other;

the destruction of home life, and the bitter unending conflict for the possession of that power which would regulate everything.

Anarchy, a contradiction.

So also we reject the Anarchist creed. Well aware that there is a reasonable and peaceful group of Anarchists, quite distinct from the violent and half-insane groups, we believe that Anarchy is a contradiction in thought, – except indeed as taught by Tolstoi – the only consistent Anarchist – who refuses to use force even for self-defence. Those, who on principle bear injuries without resistance, are the only persons who have no need of a Government. In all other cases Anarchy (or no-Government) is a misleading term. So long as men intend to resist force and to protect person or property in any form, there must be government; and Anarchy would only mean the establishment by many groups of many forms of government, with very imperfect guarantees for the administering of justice, and great uncertainty as to what was or was not forbidden. The thing, government, would still exist, though broken up into innumerable fragments. The word would be changed, but not the institution. We Voluntaryists reject all such illusions as regards Government. We believe in a national Government, voluntarily supported, always kept subject to the rights of Self-owners, and only entrusted with force for the protection of person and property.

RICH MAN'S ANARCHISM
A REPLY TO MR. AUBERON HERBERT
J. A. Hobson

GIVEN a mind keenly logical but driven by the unconscious bias of "great possessions," it inevitably spins out a social philosophy like that of Mr. Auberon Herbert. If logic were a commoner gift of the "upper and undistressed middle classes," as Mr. Ruskin calls them, Mr. Herbert would have plenty of followers. There are a good many persons, Mr. Mallock, the Duke of Argyll, Lord Wemyss, to name prominent instances, who go a certain way with Mr. Herbert, but they have a well-founded instinctive fear of the policy of "thorough" in reasoning on social matters, which keeps them from "giving themselves away," as the more rigorous logician commonly does. Not that Mr. Herbert is absolutely "thorough," for it is the one step in logic which he refuses to take that undoes him. The Tolstoic position of complete anarchism, with its absolute reliance upon moral forces, is an ultimately temperamental attitude which it is not easy to controvert, retiring, as it ever does, when assailed, into hidden recesses of the spiritual nature of man. But Mr. Herbert's "voluntary state," with its coercion derived from the individual rights of its co-operative members, is nothing else than a timid form of rich man's anarchism which exploits the philosophic doctrines of monadism for the defence of unsound forms of property.

This, however, is but assertion. Let me proceed to proof. Mr. Herbert's position may, I think, be thus fairly summarised in his own terms. Every one, by natural and moral right, owns himself, his body and mind; with the faculties of this body and mind he creates property, which thus becomes his own by right; no one else has a right to interfere with this ownership of body, mind, and property; if they do so interfere, he has a right to resist by force, and by agreement with other similar self-owners to establish a Government and a State which shall act as his delegate in preventing attacks on his self-ownership. No State is justified in acting that does not act by the consent of all its members, and State action must be strictly confined to preventing attacks upon the individual rights of these members.

Now the terms "self-ownership," "property," "State," as used by Mr. Herbert, contain three sets of distinct, though related, fallacies.

Those related to his conception of State are fundamental, and may conveniently be treated first. To Mr. Herbert there is no such thing as Society, he does not even use the term. Therefore, the common idea of a State as the instrument of the self-government of a Society never presents itself to his mind. The thing called a Society is to him merely an aggregation of individuals, it has no corporate existence, no "self" which can be governed. Such terms as social or national life, will, conscience, conduct, are to him either unmeaning or incorrect. This being so, a State, if sound, is nothing else than an improvised and delegated activity of individuals, if unsound, a power, not ourselves, which makes for tyranny. Of this latter order is the rule of the majority, which has no right whatever to dictate to the minority, to tax them or otherwise to interfere with them in the alleged interest of the majority or of the nation as a whole. For a nation is not a whole, and it is a pernicious falsehood to regard it as such. What right has Society, or the State, to take away some of the property which I have made? Clearly none whatever, if Society or State is what Mr. Herbert assumes it to be. Once grant with him that a Society is nothing but a number of "self-owners" living in proximity, who are at liberty to cover with the ægis of self-ownership any material upon which they can impress their power, and his position is well-nigh impregnable. But what is the evidence for this being a real state of things? Mr. Herbert first appeals to "natural" facts, to attest the right of self-ownership. But "nature" attests no such thing. To Aristotle, and to many thinkers in all ages, the inferiority of some bodies and minds to others attests the "right" of slavery. Moreover, the mental separation is not a "natural" fact: nature not only shows everywhere direct contact of one mind with another in domination or subjection, but all the mental phenomena of social life are an express denial of the isolation of minds. The modern science of psychology brings a cloud of witnesses to prove the direct organic inter-action of mind and mind: the familiar experience of everyone exhibits thoughts, emotions, character, as elaborate social products. Mr. Herbert's "monadism" is merely a crude materialism which regards the mind as a secret core within the body, occupying place there and really a secretion of the brain. Only when one looks to the body and finds the mind in the brain, can one even plausibly sustain this doctrine of separate life and self-ownership. It is not merely that minds breathe a common atmosphere and habitually influence one another by constant interferences. An individual mind so dignified and so touchy about its self-ownership as to keep strictly to itself would not be a mind at all: self-consciousness could not exist except by such identification with, and at the same time differentiation from, other minds, as posits society. The so-called "individual mind" is distinctly a social product, made, maintained, and constantly influenced by other minds. Only when we confine our attention to bodies is Mr. Herbert's view of self-ownership even plausible.

"If John Smith is not the owner of himself, where shall we look for his owner?" seems to Mr. Herbert a convincing argument. But there is no reason why John Smith should "own" himself or any other person be his "owner" in Mr. Herbert's sense. The use of "self-ownership" begs the entire question. Just as there exists no separate self in his sense, so there is no own-ing.

"Morality" is pressed into the service of this individualism. It is quite true that "A man only becomes a moral being – when he possesses freedom." But the freedom required for moral conduct is not what Mr. Herbert means by freedom; it consists not in the absence of interference, but in the presence of opportunity. The history of progress is not, as Mr. Herbert conceives it, merely the growth of freedom from restraint, it is also the growth of social restraint. The State and the individual are not really opposed, so that the strength of the one implies the weakness of the other. The organised action of Society through the State is one of the most important instruments of the growth of positive freedom of the individual life. There is no individual in Mr. Herbert's sense except as a body: the mind, the conscious person does not exist apart from his relations to other persons: to suppose these relations absent is to make a false abstraction. For an individual it is doubtful whether such a thing as moral action can be imagined to exist, one's duty to oneself can hardly form the basis of any morality; the sense of obligation to others, of social conduct, is essential.

But all this, which is the commonplace of most social philosophies, implies the conception of a society which is not the mere addition of its individual members but an organic system of the relations between individuals. Without pressing the metaphysics of the question, an appeal to plain facts is possible. Is public opinion the mere mathematical resultant of individual opinions, are the feelings and the conduct of a crowd, the simplest form of social organism, merely the large-scale copies of the feelings and conduct of its constituent parts? Do we not know how the contagion of emotion will give a moral life, a character, even to a casual throng of citizens, inspiring beliefs and impelling actions which do not reflect the mere activity of the separate minds? If anyone doubts this, let him read M. Le Bon's interesting study of "The Crowd," or watch the living creations of a great dramatist, such as Shakespeare, or Victor Hugo. But these are the feeblest and least definite forms of social union. The social bond in a nation or a city is far more powerful. Can a national enthusiasm for war be resolved into the desire of individual American citizens to fight individual Spaniards, or *vice versâ*? To a materialist it is difficult, if not impossible, to prove the existence or reality of any non-material entity. Though common speech, thought, and experience attests everywhere the acceptance of the organic conception of social life in a city or a nation, Mr. Herbert has the effrontery to deny it. To him a society is nothing more than "numbers." "You may pile as many stones together as you like, but it will not alter their nature. Stones they were: stones they will remain. So it is with men." Mr. Herbert's statement even as to stones is incorrect. The nature of the stones which compose an arch is not ascertained by a separate investigation of the separate stones: the relative position which the several stones occupy is part of their "nature," and that position is imposed or determined by the nature of the arch as a unity or organization of individual stones. Even were Society merely an organization of persons in this sense, as perhaps an army or a factory may be held to be, it is an unity that is essentially different from the mere addition of its parts. But when we pass from a mechanical organization to a living organism, containing within itself a capacity of growth, Mr. Herbert's conception is still more false. Society is not, perhaps, an organism in the physical sense, though the material interdependence of man and man in a society, as that of trees in a forest, makes even this conception tenable: but the concession of physical independence is no bar to the unity of a moral organism for anyone whose thought has passed beyond the crude materialism which conceives mind as a physical function of brain. The "self-ownership" of mind, by means of which Mr. Herbert denies the moral unity of Society and posits all "rights" as individual possessions, is a fiction, not a "natural" fact. What Mr. Herbert's doctrine really aims to establish is, not so much the self-ownership of body and mind, which, so far as everyone is capable of it, is practically conceded in a "free" country like England, but the security of all existing rights of property which he seeks to deduce from self-ownership. Now the fallaciousness of this attempt to extend the ownership of self to outside material property can be demonstrated without positing Society as a moral organism. Admission of the rights of self-ownership, it is urged, implies the admission of the rights of "free, unrestricted faculties," and therefore the unfettered ownership of property created or won by these faculties, the land or products of land which constitute material property. Now, in the first place, Mr. Herbert makes a bold but illicit jump from self-ownership to something which is not even in his sense self-ownership. His principle, though it may justify him in retaining property in the labour or personal energy bestowed upon land and its products, by no means justifies him in claiming ownership of the materials furnished by nature. It may be, perhaps generally is, socially expedient to allow some such property, but it cannot be fairly deduced from any "right" of self-ownership. The doctrine of individual rights may give property in labour-power, but not in the material in which it is invested. This is not in the least involved in the rights of "free, unrestricted faculties." Mr. Herbert here leaps from a negative freedom to a very positive freedom which, as easily appears, involves a freedom to interfere with the opportunity of others to use their faculties. Mr. Herbert claims the right for favoured individuals to ear-mark particular pieces of earth (which their faculties have not created) and to hold them against others who need them as means of maintaining their rights of self-ownership in the narrower sense of the right of physical existence. Mr. Herbert elsewhere insists that "We – who claim the rights of self-ownership for ourselves, must concede exactly the same rights to all others." But his interpretation of property denies this. If unlimited amounts of "best" land and other material conditions were available, no difficulty would arise. But Mr. Herbert, by allowing first-comers to monopolise without restriction the best natural supplies, enables them to thwart and restrict the similar freedom of those who come after. Upon one who professes rigid logic we are justified in pressing the familiar, extreme instance of an island, the whole of which is annexed by a few individuals, who use the rights of exclusive property and transmission which Mr. Herbert assigns to them, to establish primogeniture. It is evident that the bulk of their descendants, and other outsiders who come there, have not the "perfect security of person and property," or "the right to exercise their faculties in their own fashion," or "to reap the full reward of their labour" which are stated to be prime inalienable rights of all. It is thus that the "freedom" of a few (in Mr. Herbert's sense) involves the "slavery" of many. The case of the land is, of course, merely the crucial instance of familiar economic phenomena, wherever absolute private ownership of land or of other essentials of life is permitted. On a given piece of land every one is to be free to increase and multiply without restriction and to claim for his own any land or product into which he puts his labour. You have thus an unlimited demand for a limited supply, and yet Mr. Herbert's "freedom" requires that every one should be satisfied, and no one should interfere with the property of anyone else. The dilemma requires no fuller setting.

No possible adjustment of these conflicts between individuals which of necessity arise from the "niggardliness" of nature, is possible by reference to individual rights. If, as Mr. Herbert has admitted, self-ownership involves material opportunities for the use of faculties, this can only be secured equally for all, as he demands, by social arrangement, that is to say, by the State guided by considerations of social right or expediency. The falsehood of Mr. Herbert's antithesis of individual and State is here proved, for the motive and the result of such State interference will be to create or arrange the largest aggregate of freedom or "self-ownership" in the very sense he accords to the term. In order that all or the greatest number may have the fullest freedom to use their faculties and reap the reward of their labour, Society must act for the good of itself, considered as a whole.

Mr. Herbert posits as a first principle of property, that all property is by right individual. I have first shown that his own doctrine, for its application, requires the admission that land and all natural opportunities are "social," and that only by treating them as such can the "rights" of individuals be conserved.

In the second place, the means by which property is acquired is not, as is alleged, by the use of individual faculties alone. Even in the most primitive form of human life, property is really the creation of the organic co-operation of the family or tribal group: this most primitive division of labour strictly disables us from imputing any single product to the activity of the individual who was alone directly engaged in producing it. The hunter and his industrial squaw, by their mutual support, enable one another to produce whatever is produced in food, or clothes, or shelter. By a nice and almost infinite series of gradations, we pass from the simple co-operation to the highly complex co-operation of a modern society. Mr. Herbert still supposes an individual can, by himself, produce a piece of property. Now firstly, there is, as we have seen, no such individual; the modern man, in mind at any rate, is himself a highly social product; his thoughts, feelings, the skill with which he works, the tools he employs, all essential to his effective labour, are made by society. Upon material got from nature, and administered by society, he bestows this socially educated skill under the organized protection of society, without which protection, as all history teaches, individual industry is impotent. Nor is that all. The property which Mr. Herbert seeks to conserve, is not really the ownership of a material thing, that is generally useless to the individual, it is the "value" of the property which he really prizes: that value is a strictly social product dependent upon the needs, the appreciation, and the purchasing power of other persons working with the same social protection and aid which he himself enjoys, and having developed, by slow process of social civilization, an elaborate system of markets and mechanism of exchange. This is what is meant by saying that property is social in origin and nature. No one can make anything by himself that is worth making: is it a cobbler making a pair of shoes, he cannot get the leather without social help, his tools and the knowledge of his craft are elaborate social products, the security with which he works is given by society, the price he gets for the shoes (which is the property he seeks) is determined by social habits. All these facts the gospel of self-ownership ignores.

Again, not only the origin and the value but the use of property involves social considerations. We cannot live for ourselves alone, *i.e.*, as Herbertian individuals, dwelling in proximity and in physical as well as moral relations to others; no single act is purely self-regarding, though for convenience we may, with J. S. Mill and others, make this distinction. Certainly the use of property is not purely self-regarding. Not merely does the contagion of example assign a social meaning to every use of property which is known to others; there is not even that physical separation which the rights of self-ownership require; the effect of a public-house upon neighbouring property and its value, the directly physical influence of insanitary property of any kind, involve the right of social interference, upon the ground that the existence and use of such property is essentially social. An almost incredible perversity or obtuseness of vision prevents individualists from facing these facts when they frame their indictment against the unjust encroachments of public authorities upon the rights of property.

Property, then, being social as well as individual in origin, value and use, must be limited by due regard to the social good. As an institution it cannot be defended upon individualist grounds: the so-called "rights of property" must be delegated from or sanctioned by Society, on the ground that they are socially needed to encourage the activity of individuals or definite groups of individuals by allowing them to exercise, within limits of use or time, an exclusive control over certain portions of the material world.

The objection to any State action, in which every member of the State does not acquiesce, has been shown to rest upon a false denial of the organic unity of a State: where some object, it is not the case of a majority coercing a minority, for that is a mere return to the false conception of Society as "numbers," but of a weaker or less decisive action of the social will. But while it is right to admit that Mr. Herbert's Voluntary State is a just, logical consequence of his denial of organic society, it is also right to recognise that it does not release him from the practical difficulties of oppressive and coercive conduct imputed to tyrannous Governments. Take the case of Oldham, already the most co-operative town. Suppose its co-operative faculties developed to the utmost, so that all the inhabitants of the town were members of a Voluntary Co-operative Society which owned and administered all the property and industry of the place. What would be the actual position of a child born in Oldham and grown up to manhood? He would have to do whatever work he was ordered to do by an elected Board, at whatever wages they appointed, to live in the locality and kind of house they chose to sanction, to use his "liberty" and spend his time and money subject to restrictions from this coercive Authority. If he objected to such restricted freedom, he could leave Oldham. Thus in a "Voluntary State" would arise the same practical coercion which Mr. Herbert and his friends denounce in a modern State, and they have the same alternative open to them. If they don't like it they can leave it, and pass away from a state of positive freedom, socially made and socially supported, to the state of negative freedom which alone they can even plausibly derive from individual rights, and which would in the modern state of the world, signify freedom to starve. Anyone who seriously considers the different coercive manifestations of the human will through law, customs or public opinion, will recognise that the only "voluntary state" in Mr. Auberon Herbert's sense, is the one-man state.

SALVATION BY FORCE
Auberon Herbert

My criticism upon Mr. Hobson's recent paper in defence of Socialism[1] must be that he takes much trouble to prove that which is not in dispute, that which almost all of us, I presume, are ready to admit, and which, when admitted, can be of no use as regards the defence of the Socialist position, whilst he altogether passes by the real point at issue – the crux of the whole question – by which Socialism has to stand or fall.

Now let us get to business and see how the matter stands. Mr. Hobson justifies Socialism – or the compulsory organisation of all human beings – by the fact of our social interdependence. In many forms of words he returns again and again to the same point of view. Psychology brings, he tells us, "a cloud of witnesses to prove the direct organic interaction of mind upon mind;" Society is "an organic system of the relations between individuals;" "the familiar experience of every one exhibits thoughts, emotions, character as elaborate social products;" "minds breathe a common atmosphere, and habitually influence one another by constant interferences." We are not, as he says, to look at "numbers," but rather at "the action of the social will." Without examining critically these metaphors, that he employs, we need not so far have any quarrel. We are all agreed probably that we are subject to innumerable influences, that we all act and re-act upon each other in the great social whole, that the environment constantly affects and modifies the individual. Marvellous indeed is the great subtle web of relations in which we are all bound together – man and nature, man and man, body and mind, nation and nation, each for ever interacting on the other. But what in the name of good logic and plain common sense have this universal interaction and interdependence to do with the fundamental dogmas of Socialism? Socialism rests upon the assumed right of some men to constrain other men.

[1] "Rich Man's Anarchism," by J. A. Hobson. – HUMANITARIAN, June, 1898.

It naturally exhibits several varieties; but all the thorough-going forms of it are so far alike that they depend upon universal compulsory organisation. It must be always borne in mind that Socialism differs from other systems in this essential, that it recognises, and, so to speak, sanctifies compulsion as a universally true and proper method; and the compulsion, which it sanctifies, must for practical reasons, as well as for the assumed virtues in compulsion itself, be left undefined and unlimited in extent. It represents the belief that prosperity, happiness, and morality are to be conferred upon the world by force – the force of some men applied to other men.

That may be, or may not be. Force may be the greatest and most far-reaching thing in the world; or it may be the weakest and most contemptible. But before we discuss the strength or the weakness of force as a reforming instrument, before we decide what force can or cannot do on our behalf, we have to consider, first of all, if we have a moral right to employ force. The Socialist assumes – he is obliged to assume for the sake of his system – that men have a right to use force for any purpose and to any extent that he desires, in order that he may be enabled to restrain men from using their faculties for their own individual advantage. If you ask which men are to be the depositories of force, he can only answer, the biggest number of men; or if not the biggest number, then such a number of men as by efficient organisation can succeed in obtaining possession of power and in retaining it.

I need not spend time in proving this point. Every thorough-going Socialist, who is willing to deal frankly in the matter, will admit that Socialism rests on the corner-stone of force. Private property is by force to be turned into common property; and when that has taken place, no individual will be allowed to acquire private property or to employ it for his own purposes, except to a very small extent, and under strict regulations. John Smith could not be allowed to work for Richard Parker, as this would be a return to the system of free labour, and must necessarily endanger the system of State labour. Richard Parker could not be allowed to open a shop and sell his wares to John Smith, for this would be to allow free enterprise and the individual acquisition of wealth once more to re-appear in the world. The whole meaning of

Socialism is force, applied in restraint of faculties. For good or for evil, it is the attempt to place all men and all human affairs under a compulsory system; and to allow no free system to exist by the side of its own system, which would be necessarily endangered by such rivalry. It differs from every free system in this essential particular: that under liberty, you may give away your own liberty, if you think good, and be Socialist, or anything else you like; under Socialism, you must be Socialist, and may not make a place for yourself in any free system.

Now we can all see that any writer, with the literary abilities and instincts possessed by Mr. Hobson, who under these circumstances proposes to plead the cause of Socialism, finds himself involved in considerable difficulties. He has to apologise for and to defend a system of universal force, and he instinctively dislikes the task. Of course he might openly take force under his protection, declare that it was the reformer's true weapon, and glorify the whole business of compelling all dissidents. But the systematic glorification of force is an awkward piece of work; for as it is generally conceded for good and for evil that we are all to be free and equal in forming our opinions, so as a necessary consequence it must be conceded that we are to be free and equal as regards the methods of advancing our opinions. A method that is good for one must be good for all; and in accepting the method, we must expect to find that, here too as in every other human matter, considerable differences will exist as regards the application of the method. *Tot homines, tot sententiæ*. Tastes must vary. Some men will prefer the confused mixture of force and liberty that usually prevails under the system of party government; some men will prefer the stronger article of compulsory Socialism; some men will prefer military despotism; and some the force of the Anarchist, who employs dynamite as a social corrective. On what ground can the believers in force quarrel with or even very seriously criticise each other? They are all fellow-worshippers in the same temple, and at the shrine of the same principle. Once admit that force is right in itself, and then you cannot pick out any special sect or party, confer special privileges upon them, and declare that they alone, and nobody else, are entitled to use force. That would be a mere arbitrary and fanciful selection, as arbitrary and fanciful as picking out

certain opinions, and declaring that these opinions are orthodox, and that all other opinions are heterodox. If force is
good in the hands of some men, it is good in the hands of
other men; if it is a good instrument to serve some causes, it
is good to serve other causes. You can't have a monopoly in
the use of so valuable "a resource of civilisation." If the
Socialist with his compulsory system can succeed in justifying
his use of force so also can the ordinary politician, or the
military despot, or the dynamiting Anarchist, with his newly-
awakened perceptions that force can be applied in very
uncomfortable fashions, without any machinery of government, or policemen, or soldiers. Having once arrived, after
much searching of heart, at the belief that we must concede
to all men the right to think as they like, and having got rid
of the old-world idea that we can authoritatively pronounce
some opinions to be good and some to be bad, we must take
the further step, and admit that every holder of opinions has
an equal right to use the same methods of advancing his
opinions. In a word, we must concede equality as regards
the method of advancing opinions, just as we have conceded
equality as regards the holding of opinions. We must therefore choose between either altogether rejecting force as an
instrument for advancing our opinions and our interests, or
recognising equality in the use of method – accepting, so to
speak, free trade in force, even if this last alternative is not
altogether reassuring as regards the peaceful and friendly
relations of men to each other. This difficulty therefore con-
fronts the Socialist. If he is resolved to employ a frank and
consistent logic, he must admit that force is a good instrument
in the hands of all who can possess themselves of it; or
employing the defective and halting logic that all his predecessors in power have employed, he must try to persuade us
that force is good for him, but not for the rest of his fellow-
men, and claim, in common with the other worshippers of
force, that there exists a mysterious dispensation given from
some unknown quarter in his own special favour.

But the literary difficulties of those who plead for the compulsory organisation of all men, under the name of Socialism,
do not end here. I will not touch now upon the difficulties
of conceiving that you can organise society upon the principle of dividing every five men in the nation into two groups
– a group of three men, who have all rights, and a group of

two men, who have no rights, of turning the three men into those who own others, and the two men into those who are owned by others. Apart from the verdict, which reason and morality if fairly questioned, must pass upon every system which splits the nation into a crowd that owns, and a crowd that is owned, into a conquering and a conquered faction, the Socialist, who plainly and frankly invites men to banish freedom of action from the world, will find himself opposed by a large number of persons who, as the result of living in a fairly free country, and who, guided by their feelings and daily experience, have a strong moral and intellectual dislike to force. It is only a few persons as yet amongst us who consciously submit themselves in this matter to the discipline of first principles; but there is a large number of persons whose general habit of thought and whose instinct tell them that force is the wrong method, and that discussion, persuasion, the light of reason and the attraction of example, are the right method. They see that force is at best a clumsy and brutal argument. They remember the wise saying: "Any fool can govern with bayonets." They see that those who use force most freely are as a one-eyed race, with very limited perceptions, able to perceive dimly the immediate consequences, but not the more remote consequences of what they do. And just as these disbelievers in force see that those who accustom themselves to the use of force grow stupid, and not only stupid but brutal, so they see that those, who are subject to force, also grow stupid in their own way, indifferent, apathetic, and generally revolutionary in temper. They see that mistakes made under force-systems are apt to persist, that they are not easy to discover or remedy, when you have discouraged the growth of all other systems by their side. They see that every force-system requires a great complicated machinery, and that this machinery always eludes popular control, and falls under the management of some not very intelligent or disinterested clique. They see not only that every act of force requires continual new extensions of force, but also that force breeds many forms of intrigue and deception. Even when you have force in your hands, it is not an easy task to compel a great number of persons to do what they don't want to do – it is much like the labour of making water flow up-hill; and force, therefore, naturally allies itself to trick and to management. The moral transition is always an easy one.

Those persons who have taken the one short cut readily persuade themselves to take the other short cut. No believer in force truly respects his fellow-men. He always slightly despises them, even whilst he serves them. They tend to become to him mere material for carrying out his views. His views may be honestly and sincerely held; they may be excellent in themselves; but when he uses force on their behalf he commits the capital mistake of exalting himself and his views into the first place, and of degrading his fellow-men, with an intelligence and conscience like and equal to his own, into the second place. Thus it comes about that the user of force loses all hold on moral principles; he becomes a law, and a very defective law, to himself; and thus it comes about also that politics – which are simply the method of force – are in every country not only the battlefield of opposed fighters, but the hot-bed of intrigue and corruption. The career of a politician mainly consists in making one part of the nation do what it does not want to do, in order to please and satisfy the other part of the nation. It is the prolonged sacrifice of the rights of some persons at the bidding and for the satisfaction of other persons. The ruling idea of the politician – stated rather bluntly – is that those who are opposed to him exist for the purpose of being made to serve his ends, if he can get power enough in his hands to force these ends upon them. Is it wonderful then, if trick and intrigue grow rank and fast in the garden of politics; or that amongst the many things which you may find there, you will rarely find flowers that are fragrant, and fruits that are clean and wholesome?

And again, men see another evil, which arises where the use of force is admitted. So long as we remain in the region of discussion and persuasion, so long there is a sure guarantee that the truest view will gradually prevail. The truest view necessarily commands the best arguments, just as it gradually attracts to its side the higher class of minds; and therefore having the best arguments and the best fighters on its side must win in the free open field, sooner or later. But when we abandon the free open field, in which reason and persuasion, the appeal to reason and the appeal to conscience, are the only admitted weapons, and allow force to be recognised as an equally righteous method, then this certainty of ultimate victory for the truest view entirely disappears. Why? Because force enlarges and degrades the issues. It adds inducements of an effective, if of a very coarse kind, in order to win men over to its side. As long as we are only seeking to persuade, we can only offer the fruits of persuasion. We can promise men that they shall be better, happier, more prosperous, by certain changes in their conduct, but we cannot promise that they shall find to-morrow or the next day five shillings or five pounds, magically placed in their pocket, without any effort of their own. But this is exactly the kind of promise that force can make; indeed, not only can make, but must make. From the nature of things, force cannot fight a pure battle, or appeal simply to pure motives. There is nobody amongst us who can become possessed of force, unless he can first of all induce a very large number of persons to fight on his side. To be the possessor of force you must possess a force-army; and your force-army must be larger than the force-army of any of your rivals. How are you to collect together and keep together such a force-army? You cannot do it by appeals to reason and conscience, for that is a slow affair, which wins its way by influencing individuals, and these individuals, who are influenced, are influenced by the same appeal in very different degree and fashion. To obtain a force-army, capable of defeating another highly organised force-army, you must bring in the recruits in shoals and masses, you must bring them in on a given day, at a given spot, you must bring them in in such a state of discipline, that they will all keep step together and follow their leader like one man. But if appeals to reason and conscience, being, as I have said, essentially individualistic in their action, cannot produce disciplined masses on the given spot and at the given moment, force has a store of arguments exactly suited for the purpose. Give me force enough, and I can promise you almost any material prize for which your heart lusts. If you are a poor man, I can promise you three acres and a cow, gratuitous education, State pensions, and State insurance, novels provided at the public expense, and taxes thrown upon your richer fellow-citizen; or better still, all private wealth converted at a touch of my wand into public wealth; if you are a rich man, I can promise you bigger armies and fleets, more territory, more glory, and many noble opportunities of making a splash before the eyes of the world;

and if you are nervous about the safety of your possessions in these Socialistic days, I can turn the nation into an army for your convenience, and submit it to military discipline – an excellent way, as some persons think, of conjuring away, at all events for some twenty-four hours, all Socialistic dangers.   Give me force enough, and I can offer every kind of glittering ware for every class of customer.   In this way, if I am only a skilful buyer of men, I can recruit my force-army; and when I have recruited them, I can pay them out of the prize-money which I employ them to win.

From certain practical points of view the system is excellent, as the politicians have discovered, only you must not ask from it, what it cannot pretend to offer – any test as regards the moral and intellectual value of conflicting views; or, if does offer you such a test, it can only offer it by the rule of contraries.   If we wished to be ingenious, we might perhaps say that the moral and intellectual value of the views, which are backed by force, is generally in inverse proportion to their momentary attractiveness.   The more any particular kind of political prize-money attracts, the less clean, and sound, and wholesome, and really desirable in itself, it will probably be discovered to be under searching criticism.   I do not know if the philosophers will some day be able to extract a more definite moral canon for our guidance as regards the attractions of force, but meanwhile, we may content ourselves with certain homely but useful truths.   You cannot possess force, without first recruiting a force-army; you cannot recruit a force-army, without the free use of prize-money; and you cannot offer prize-money without putting the prize-money in the first place, and the appeal to conscience and reason in the second place, with a very large interval disclosing itself between the two classes of inducements.[2]

I have dwelt at some length on this question of force, because it is *the test-question*, by which Socialism has to be

---

[2] A qualification ought to be made here.   Where force has inflicted much suffering on a people, in such cases, as crushing taxation, protection, restriction of faculties, military despotism, etc., the sense of wrong may be quite sufficient *without prize-money* to make a nation remove the cause of its suffering, and to undo what force has done.   But apart from such cases, the present race of politicians cannot reasonably hope for place and power except by the generous use of prize-money.   Force-armies, like all other fighters, must be paid.

tried. Socialism under-takes to save the world from all its sorrows by a greatly extended use of force, a use of force, far exceeding the force which even emperors and despotic Governments employ; and what the philosophical and literary defenders of Socialism – I do not mean the mere promisers of prize-money – have to do is to convince us first of all that force is a right weapon in itself – that we are morally justified in using it against each other; and secondly, that it is likely – as far as we can judge by past experience – when applied in this new universal fashion, to make men better and happier. Socialism intends to found itself upon force; and therefore we stand upon the threshold, and call upon it, before it goes any further, to justify force. Does Mr. Hobson do this? Does he lay any moral foundations for the use of force? Does he satisfy us that three men may rightly do whatever they please with the minds, bodies and property of two men? Does he satisfy us that the three men can produce any lawful commission for saying to the two men: "Henceforth your faculties belong to us and not to you; henceforth you are forbidden to employ those faculties for your own advantage, and in such fashion as you choose; henceforth they are to be employed for what we are pleased to call the public good." In another paper, I hope to follow Mr. Hobson's argument, and see how far it is suited to remove the hesitations and scruples of those who believe that every man and woman are the true owners of their own faculties, and that every forcible annexation of these faculties by others has prevented the world from discovering the ways of true happiness.

LOST IN THE REGION OF PHRASES
Auberon Herbert

I OWE many apologies both to the Editress and to Mr. Hobson for the long delay which has taken place as regards this discussion. I can only hope that they may both be willing to forgive me. And now to our business in hand. I tried in my last paper to show, that whilst Mr. Hobson had written with much literary skill an interesting paper about Socialism, he had left the great fortress untaken, even unbeseiged, which stands in the way of the advance of Socialism. He made a delightful excursus into the region of metaphor and literary imagination, but he never troubled himself to convince us that force was a weapon which the larger number are morally justified in using against the smaller number, or that, when used, is likely to produce the happiness which we all desire. But if Mr. Hobson did not raise this all-important question, but passed it by, as skilful leaders sometimes pass by strong positions, which threaten heavy loss for those who attack them, he tried to open out a new road towards his end with no little literary ingenuity. By the way of metaphor and abstract conception he sought to steal our senses from us, inspiring us with the Socialistic temperament, and leading us along pleasant and flowery paths towards that new form of Catholic Church, in which he invites us to find our rest. Some of his readers probably felt much the same influence gently stealing over them as they have felt in listening to some of the great Jesuit teachers. In both cases the real issues are passed by, and side issues, sentimentally and artistically tricked out, are skilfully put in their place. It is only natural it should be so. Our Socialist friends and the Jesuits plead for their own causes in much the same spirit. They both believe absolutely in great external organisations; they each put their own external organisation above and before everything else; conscience, judgment, and will are, on a fixed system, bent and bowed before it; and reason and individual judgment, who always demand to stand at the gate with erect head, become to both of them as the voice of the Evil One moving man to his ruin. If I remember rightly, even Luther spoke of reason as "the harlot" – I presume because reason requires that every claim put forward by authority should first pass before its own tribunal.

Now let us examine Mr. Hobson's apology for Socialism, and see how far it carries us. I think I am right in describing his paper as an attempt to reduce the individual to nothingness, and on the ruins of the individual to exalt and glorify "the social organism." The individual deserves no thought or consideration at our hands; he is the product of the Social Entity; all that he is and all that he has are borrowed from the Social Entity; not only his material possessions, but his very qualities and thoughts – just as a flower, we might say, contributes nothing of its own, but borrows all its beauty and fragrance from the air and the soil on which it feeds. To which little parable – which I freely offer to Mr. Hobson for his acceptance and use – I must however attach the Individualist's comment – that it is the skilful chemistry of which the flower is master that turns these contributions of a lower order to its own profit; and that it is just on account of this marvellous vital power that the flower is far higher in rank than the elements which it transmutes into colour and fragrance.

Now let me ask, is there any solid reality in this view of the Social Entity, or must we treat it as a mere literary creation? When we oppose the Social Entity to the individual, are we not tricking ourselves with words; are we not simply opposing some individuals to other individuals? If the individual is moulded and formed by the Social Entity, it can only mean that he is moulded and formed by other individuals. If John Smith's thoughts are formed for him, it is as the result of what other John Smiths have spoken or written. If you like to christen all these other John Smiths by the rather fine name of "Social Entity," there is no great objection, perhaps, provided only you keep the simple truth in view that it is the individuals who act on each other; and (setting aside the action of the forces of nature and the existence of higher beings than man) that in no conceivable way can we think of influence as passing except from individuals to individuals. So also with our material debt to each other. If in an expanding community A.X. grows rich, because, as a doctor, he has more patients to look after, or as a tradesman, because he has more customers to serve, or as a landowner, because he has more persons to whom to sell his land, it is in every such case the result of the actions of some definite individuals affecting other definite individuals. If the individuals who come to reside in a place increase the prosperity of A. the lawyer, B. the doctor, C. the tradesman, and D. the landowner, so in return do these four persons increase the prosperity of those for whose wants they provide in their different ways. It is the exchange of services and useful commodities by which each benefits the other, and each in turn is benefited. The increase of prosperity simply results from the interaction of the individuals amongst themselves. It seems cruel to break butterflies on logical wheels and to deal harshly with Mr. Hobson's poetical creation, but outside and beyond this action of the individuals there is no place left of any kind for the action of the Social Entity. Like so many other things of imposing pretensions, it fades into nothingness at the touch of simple analysis. Again, even if Mr. Hobson could make good the existence of his Social Entity, as distinct from the action of individuals, would he be any nearer the object that he has in view – the investment of the Social Entity with supreme importance, and the reduction of the individual to insignificance? If the Social Entity – supposing that such a thing existed apart from the individuals – acts upon the individual, so beyond dispute must the individual in his turn, as regards the work that he does and the thoughts that he thinks, act upon the Social Entity. What therefore might be claimed for the one must also be claimed for the other. The two factors, being placed in opposition to each other, would then simply cancel each other – would "go out," as school-boys say about opposed factors in a sum of arithmetic. What then is left of the supremacy of the one, and the insignificance of the other? The truth is that the contrast that it is attempted to draw between the individual and the Social Entity is a wholly unreal one. You might as usefully contrast pence and pounds. The Social Entity really means: some individuals; nothing less and nothing more.

And here it may be useful to follow Mr. Hobson a little further in his adventurous attempt to get rid of the individual. Many things have been dared and attempted by philosophers in their day; but the elimination of the individual out of the social system is an undertaking that throws into the shade most other philosophical exploits. Mr. Hobson writes: "The modern man, at any rate, is a highly social product; his thoughts, feelings, the skill with which he works, the tools he employs, all essential to his effective labour, are made by society." Again: "The so-called individual mind is distinctly a social product, made, maintained, and constantly influenced by other minds." "Other minds," I think, must be a slip of the pen, for that is simply to make the plain and matter-of-fact statement that individuals influence each other. Mr. Hobson should have written "influenced by the Social Entity." Again he writes: " . . . the conception of a society which is not the mere addition of its individual members, but an organic system of the relations between individuals." So, we poor mortals are evidently greater than we know. John Smith, like most of us addicted to the prose of every-day life, has probably looked on himself hitherto as an individual, possessing a distinct separate body and mind of his own, not in any way to be confused with the body and mind of his neighbour Thomas Robinson. At the same time John Smith is quite aware that he shares, in common with Thomas Robinson and his other neighbours, a certain number of thoughts, feelings, and interests; he knows that he agrees with them on some points, whilst he disagrees with them on other points. But no amount of such agreement has hitherto affected John Smith's conviction that his individuality is one thing, and the individuality of Thomas Robinson is another thing. At last, however, better days are coming for good John Smith. The new knowledge and the new gospel have abolished his old status. Henceforth he is invited to exchange his prose for poetry, and to look upon himself, not as an individual, but as part of the Social Entity, as a something included in "an organic system of the relations between individuals." It sounds grand, even if it is a little difficult to understand. Let us piously hope that John Smith will not only understand, but will also profit by his newly-acquired dignity, if not mentally or morally, at least by finding more bread and cheese in his cupboard.

Then Mr. Hobson illustrates his idea of the individual who is lost in the crowd (I am afraid that this is a very homely presentment of the fact, which Mr. Hobson himself would express by speaking of a man's inclusion in the "organic system of the relations between individuals") by appealing to the state of a nation at war. "Can a national enthusiasm for war," he asks, "be resolved into the desire of individual American citizens to fight individual Spaniards, or *vice versâ*?" Even a crowd, "the simplest form of social organism," is something more than a large scale copy "of the feelings and conduct of its constituent parts." Now, how much of this will bear analysis? Is it not all conceived in the dangerous region of metaphor and abstraction, and, I must add, of exaggeration? If a crowd, a town, a nation, is not in each case a collection of individuals – more or less acted upon, it is true, by certain common feelings, more or less possessing certain common interests – what can it be? That when you bring men together for any purpose, either for the purpose of listening to speeches or for some common undertaking, such men act upon each other in a very marked manner, both for good and for evil, sometimes heightening the good that is in their nature, and sometimes heightening the evil, is what we all daily know and experience; but I cannot see how this heightening of emotion can in any way affect the fact that those who thus influence and are influenced are individuals, each with his own set of feelings, each with his own separate body and mind, and each with his own responsibility (to which Mr. Hobson must very much object) for what he does with that mind and body. Because John Smith and Richard Parker are under the influence of the same class of feelings, or are engaged in seeking the same ends, that does not in any way get rid of the individuals John Smith and Richard Parker, or put in their place a new sort of being made up half of Smith and half of Parker, or – to state the case of the Social Entity even more exactly – made up of some twenty or thirty millions of Smiths and Parkers. But why should we create this monster, simply because men under certain states of feeling act powerfully on each other? A man, I presume, still remains a man, and a woman a woman, even when their feelings are so heightened by the words and actions of others, that they are, as a consequence, more ready to die for each other, or to cut each others' throats – as the case may be. There at the bottom of it all – whether it is a crowd shouting for war, a political party rejoicing over an election victory, a body of school-boys triumphant over the victory of their eleven or their eight, a professional body clamouring for some professional interest, a clerical meeting denouncing some heresy, a Socialist congress rejoicing in the onward march of universal coercion, a trades-unionist body denouncing non-unionists, or a gathering of capitalists drawing tighter the bonds of their organisation – there in every case are the individuals sharing in some common aim, and therefore sharing in the same feelings – the John Smiths and the Thomas Robinsons, exciting both themselves and their fellows by the old love of strife, or the old craving for Utopia, and borrowing what is both good and bad – sometimes ugly passions, and sometimes splendid devotion, from each other.

This, then, is the first point to notice – that no literary phrases about social organisms are potent enough to evaporate the individual. He is the prime, the indispensable, the irreducible element in the whole business. The individual has a far too solid and matter-of-fact existence to be eliminated by any arts of literary conjuring. Now take the second point. Is there a resemblance, on the one side, between the individual and certain social wholes, in which he is included, and on the other side, between an organism and its component parts? The answer must be: yes. All parts included in wholes have a generic likeness to each other of a certain kind. A brick in a house, a muscle in a body, have each of them relations to their own whole (the house and the body) which may be compared to the relations existing between an individual and the various social bodies in which he is included. But if there is a certain resemblance, there are also striking differences. The life of the muscle exists simply for the sake of the organism. Taken out of the organism it dies, and has no further use. So with a brick. Like the muscle, it does not exist (excluding, perhaps, the case of a certain town in the Midlands on election days in the old times) for its own sake. It has no use or purpose apart from the building in which it is to form part. It is not an end in itself. In these cases the organism is greater than the part; but with the individual it is not so. He is included in many wholes – his school, his college, his club, his profession, his town or county, his church, his political party, his nation; he forms part of many organisms, but he is always greater than them all. They exist for him; not he for them. The child does not exist for his family, the boy does not exist for his school, the undergraduate for his college, the member of a church or club, or trades union, or co-operative society, or joint stock company, for his church, club, society, trades union, co-operative society, or joint stock company, the member of a village or town does not exist for his village or town, or the member of a nation for his nation. All these various wholes, without any exception, in which an individual is included – these so-called organisms of which he forms part – exist for the sake of the individual. They exist to do his service; they exist for his profit and use. If they did not minister to his use, if they did not profit him, they would have no plea to exist. The doom of any one of them would be spoken, if it were found to injure, not to benefit, the individual. He, the individual, joins himself to them for the sake of the good they bring him, not in order that he may be used by them, and be lost to himself, as the brick is lost in the house, or the muscle in the organism. The individual is king, and all these other things exist for the service of the king. It is a mere superstition to worship any institution, as an institution, and not to judge it by its effects upon the character and the interests of men. It is here that Socialist and Catholic make the same grand mistake. They exalt the organisation, which is in truth as mere dust under our feet; they debase the man, for whose sake the organisation and all other earthly things exist. They posit *à priori* the claims of the external organisation as supreme and transcending all profit and loss account, and they call upon men to sacrifice a large part of their higher nature for the sake of this organisation. They both of them sacrifice man, the king, to the mere dead instrument that exists for man's service. But why is a man to be sacrificed to any organisation? How can any organisation stand in front of, stand higher than, man? Test the matter by mere common sense. Could we go to a man and say: "You will be so much worse off materially, mentally, morally, by joining such and such an association, but for the sake of the association itself I entreat you to join it." Does not every person, who pleads for an association, take pains to show that in some way, materially or morally, the individual will be profited by joining it; and in so speaking he bears evidence to the simple truth that the association – whatever it be, church, nation, or penny club – exists for the individual, and not the individual for the association.

There is another striking example of this tendency to put

phrases in the place of realities in Mr. Hobson's paper. We all of us depend, says Mr. Hobson, upon services rendered by and to each other; we are all of us influenced by the thoughts and actions of each other; therefore – so the argument seems to run – we can have no individuality of our own, we can have no private possession of our own faculties (still less, of course, of the property won by faculties); no rights over ourselves; being parts of the social whole, and not in reality separate individuals, we cannot own ourselves, we can only be possessed in common; we can only share in owning all our fellow-men, whilst at the same time we ourselves are owned by our fellow-men. Humanity, in the Socialist view, cannot be divided up into such valueless and insignificant fractions, as individuals; it must be treated in a more dignified manner – wholesale, in the lump.

Now let us put these curious abstractions into more concrete form. My baker and I every day exchange services. He leaves me so many loaves, and I put into his hand so many bits of money. We are both of us quite content with this arrangement; but because I depend (in part) upon his bread, and he depends (in part) upon my shillings, given in payment, therefore for the sake of this common dependence we are both to be bound up together, whether we wish it or not, in Mr. Hobson's universal compulsory organisation. How little, during our simple and innocent transactions, did either of us realise the yoke, which we were silently and unconsciously forging for our own necks and for the necks of the rest of the world. Because quite voluntarily and for our mutual convenience one of us bought, and the other sold, therefore henceforward all our relations are to be regulated by an all-embracing compulsion. That may be literature, but it is not logic, and it is not reason. The syllogism, I presume, would run: We all depend upon the exchange of voluntary and mutually convenient services, arranged according to our own individual likings and requirements; *therefore* we are to be placed, as regards our material wants, under the system of universal compulsion, which has been amiably devised for us by Mr. Hobson's friends in their spare moments of abstract contemplation, and which may not in any way correspond to our own individual likings and requirements. Take, now, the case of the intellectual services which men perform for each other. I read the writings of certain authors and am influenced by them; and perhaps in my own turn try to influence others; therefore, as a penal consequence of this intellectual influence I am to be placed under a universal compulsory system which is to undertake the regulation of my mind, and of all other minds. This syllogism again, I presume, would run: We all influence each other by our words and our writings; *therefore* we are all to be yoked together under a system of intellectual compulsion, chosen for us by others." Literature apart, I think Mr. Hobson will admit that it is a bold transmutation of unlike things unto each other – voluntary service and the free exchange of influence, passing into the universal compulsion of each other, worked by the votes of a majority. If he has not as yet hit upon the alchemist's stone, he has at all events discovered the secret, that lies at the opposite pole, of degrading gold into lead.

   In all the annals of reasoning – and they are many and strange – was there ever such a perverse method followed of reaching a conclusion? And to what is it due? It is all due to the fact that the Socialist is under the unhappy destiny of having to plead for an impossible creed – a creed founded on old-world reactionary and superstitious ideas, that are only waiting half-alive to be decently buried for ever by the race that has suffered so much and so long for them. The Socialist, as an individual, is often infinitely better than his creed of power-worship. You can't read the papers of Mr. Hobson or of some other Socialistic writers without feeling that generous impulses and desires, and in a certain sense large ideas, run through them; but unfortunately all these generous impulses and large ideas turn, like fairy gold, to dust and ashes, because they are wedded to compulsion, which degrades all that it touches. What can be pettier, narrower, more reactionary, more superstitious and irrational, than the worship by the Socialist of majority rule – the crowning of every three men, because they are three, and the moral and material effacement of every two men, because they are two; or the building up of a gigantic fabric of unlimited power, with the arbitrary suspension and limitation of the faculties of the individual in every direction? What moral or intellectual redemption can possibly be found for such a system? It would be as narrow and stifling as a prison cell; as full of trick and intrigue as the inner council chamber of the College of the Jesuits; as timorous and despairing as the creed of the ascetics, who pronounced the world to be evil and the cloister to be the only safe place in it; as brutal as the politics of a Napoleon or a Bismarck. Is there any reason, then, to wonder that men, with the literary tact and ability of Mr. Hobson, seek, almost unconsciously to themselves, to cover up the dead bones of their system with metaphor and abstract conception, and to ask us to admire the something of their literary manufacture, which has as little to do with the real thing, as hothouse flowers have to do with the poor decomposing remains that lie inside the coffin on which the flowers are flung. The highest art in the world cannot gild Socialism. It is impossible to make beautiful the denial of liberty. To slightly alter a famous saying – Socialism is the negation of all personal rights, erected into a system; and literature, even in the hands of a master, is powerless to make us look with anything but scorn on that negation. The bones and the bare skull grin through all the false decorations that you hang about them, making them only more the ghastly, the more skill you expend in trying to adorn them. I would suggest to Mr. Hobson whether it would not have been truer art to have left on one side the plaster and stucco work of literature, and to have simply said: "Our creed is a brutal and stupid one – all compulsion is brutal and stupid – but the world is an evil one, and its evils must be pounded with cudgel and club, just in such fashion as we can most easily get at them."

And here, in conclusion, I am tempted to say a rather unkind thing. Is not our friend the Socialist the very one special person in the world who is unfit to preach the doctrine of his Social Entity? Granting its existence – where is the Social Entity to be found? Our answer must be that it can only be found in the whole mass of individuals – in the whole nation, with all its many differences, freely allowed to find their own expression; and not in that mock imitation of the nation, a majority worked by the politician's machinery. There is, as I believe, a something which we may rightly call the Social Entity, but Mr. Hobson and his friends skilfully contrive to turn a blind eye in its direction, to pass it by on one side, and thus conveniently to miss it altogether. They do not see that it is vain to look for it in any faction or part of a nation overriding other factions or parts of a nation; that it is vain to look for it in a handful of men sitting in a council chamber and fondly imagining themselves to be the nation; that it has nothing to do with laws and regulations, and the effacement of the individual by a system of huge and complicated State machinery; but that it can only be found where all bodies and minds are free, and each individual gives his contribution of bodily or mental labour voluntarily, after his own kind and his own fashion. Clearly the Social Entity must embrace the whole, no part excluded; otherwise the very idea of unity – of organic oneness – at once disappears. Freedom is the only one thing that offers a possibility of such unity, because under freedom no man can place another man in subjection to his views, and because unrestrained difference offers the nearest and truest approach to true unity which this world allows. The unity of unrestrained difference is a far truer unity than the unity of compulsory sameness. Let us take a simple example. Suppose a country, where education is free, in the true sense, free from all possibility of Government compulsion and authoritative direction. Then, in every effort and every experiment made, in every joining together for practical purposes of those who are in sympathy with each other, in every formation of co-operating groups, in every discussion of the truer meanings of education, in every meeting called, in every book or letter written, you have the real expression of the Social Entity. Whatever force of conviction, whatever practical energy there is anywhere in the great mass of individuals, these find their outlet and their own method of working, and represent the Social Entity for exactly what it is in its reality. The Social Entity must be represented by free contributions of mental and bodily labour, for only in such a way is it possible for every individual, without exception, to take part in the expression of the common life and work. It cannot be represented where there is an effacement of minorities by majorities, where there is a cooked-up thing, called representation, which simply means the utterly false and artificial merging of thousands of persons into one person, and where one faction imposes its will on another faction, whilst the great mass of individuals simply look on, and a handful of self-seeking and self-glorifying persons act in their name. What is there of "entity" and what of "social" in such systems? The truth is, that the Socialist, unknown to himself, is the most anti-social of all human beings, and, if he had his way, would render all true social action impossible. His creed of universal compulsion and wholesale effacement of the individual is the very essence of anti-socialism. The true social life is the sum of all individual differences and energies; and if these component elements are to be suppressed, the resulting whole, the Entity, necessarily disappears. Mr. Hobson – will he forgive me? – is the deadliest enemy conceivable to his own creation, his well-beloved Social Entity, just because he makes war upon the individual. In slaying the unit he slays the whole, that is compounded from the units. In truth, under his system the individual, who is the living active element of the Social Entity, and apart from whom the Social Entity is a mere phrase and nothing more, is not simply to be suppressed, but is sentenced to an even harsher and more ignominious fate. Hitherto, most of the tyrants and autocrats, who have tried the experiment of fashioning the world in their own image, have been content, like the present German Emperor, with planting their Imperial feet upon the individual, and so suppressing him; but it has been left for Mr. Hobson and his friends to discover a more subtle and deadly way of abolishing him. They have buried him alive in the Social Entity, and explained him away. Even the modest luxury of a theoretical existence is denied him at their hands. And what "ploughing of the sands"; what good literary labour thrown away! For, as we have just seen, the more you suppress the individual, the further the possibility of the Social Entity, in its true sense, recedes. There is only one result you can get out of the suppression of the individual, and that is the organised dominant faction, triumphing over the defeated faction. Every form of Socialism only represents the dominant faction – that and nothing more; and if Socialists wish to bring names and things into a true correspondence with each other, they should change their name and call themselves the Anti-Socialists. But that is to ask for much. For they are at present lost in the region of phrases, and have yet to learn the simple truth, that there is no real social life conceivable, apart from the free movement of the individual and conscience.